FINDING THE OASIS

Unveiling the Intersection of
Mind, Body and Spirit

SANDEEP MALL

www.popularprakashan.com

Published by
Asmita Mohite for
POPULAR PRAKASHAN PVT. LTD.
301, Mahalaxmi Chambers
22, Bhulabhai Desai Road
Mumbai - 400 026
info@popularprakashan.com

© 2024 Sandeep Mall
First Published 2024

(4553)
ISBN: 978-81-966313-6-9

WORLD RIGHTS RESERVED. The contents are original and copyrighted. No portion of this book shall be reproduced, stored in a retrieval system or transmitted by any means, electronic, mechanical, photocopying, recording or otherwise, without the written permission of the author and the publisher.

Disclaimer: The views and opinions expressed in this work are the author's own and the facts are as reported by the author, and the publisher is in no way liable for the same.

Cover design: Abhilash RS, Narrative
Layout: Anjali Sawant

PRINTED IN INDIA
by Saurabh Printers (P) Ltd.
Plot No. 67 A-68, Ecotech, Ext. I
Kasna, Greater Noida-201306 (U.P)

"This book is ambitious in its scope, but Sandeep pulls it off. He has kept it credible, by citing several scientific studies, and relatable, by sharing his own life experiences. The narrative style is brisk and easy too. A practical guidebook for wellness and healthy living, I'm sure readers will find themselves referring to it repeatedly for different situations and phases of their life."

— **Parminder Singh**
Chief Commercial & Digital Officer, Mediacorp

"I found it incredibly comprehensive, simple yet touching upon all multidimensional aspects of living a good life. For most of us, including me, the definition of a healthy life is limited to nutrition, work out, good habits and so on and so forth. The chapters touch upon physical, mental, emotional and social well-being as wheels of a clock, the gear train, all working together in a synchronised beat. The questions at the end of each chapter allows one to internalise and your personal anecdotes show authenticity and doable. The chapter "Confronting death and celebrating existence" brought tears to my eyes. The book has my heart."

— **Priti Rathi Gupta**
Founder, LXME

"With its clear language and genuine commitment to change, it resonates with readers at every stage of life. For those at crossroads or facing obstacles, this work stands as an essential guide, making profound insights accessible to all."

— **Shantanu Moitra**
Music Composer

"Sandeep's book is one of the most authentic, credible and insightful journeys I have read in recent times. MUST READ for everyone. Because by the end of the book a change will trigger in you. And that's the right beginning."

— **Vivek Ranjan Agnihotri**
Film Producer & Director

Praise for the book

"The conversation around deep health though — across physical, mental, emotional, spiritual — is a much needed one. And I am glad Sandeep, through his own life experience, decided to initiate this conversation. Start one, with yourself. Today."

— **Ankur Warikoo**
Entrepreneur

"Drawing from personal experiences that showcase resilience, *Finding the Oasis* serves as a reminder that true transformation unfolds when we acknowledge our vulnerabilities and commit to daily growth. Seamlessly interweaving science, life teachings, family values, and spirituality, this narrative offers a credible and relatable journey. I am sure many individuals will gain invaluable insights and be motivated to integrate actionable recommendations from this enriching read in their lives."

— **Jhulan Goswami**
Former Captain, Indian Women's Cricket Team

"The narrative is captivating, and your personal experiences, coupled with the techniques for achieving 'deep health', have been enlightening. I'm grateful to have learned a new perspective."

— **Harsh Goenka**
Chairman, RPG Group

"This book offers practical advice and guides readers to discover their personal oasis amid the bustling desert of daily demands. A good read for those seeking balance, rejuvenation, and a harmonious existence."

— **Harsh Mariwala**
Chairman, Marico Ltd.

"In an age of fleeting health trends and quick solutions, Sandeep Mall describes his approach to well-being in this book beautifully. He champions the idea that genuine health stems from simple, daily choices. Whether it's a balanced meal or indulging in a sport, these modest shifts in behaviour can lead to profound health transformations in the long run. I am sure everyone reading the book will unearth lessons that they can implement in their path to wellness."

— **Nithin Kamath**
CEO & Founder, Zerodha & Rainmatter

This book is inspired by and for my Twitter (now X) community.

Contents

Foreword		9
Preface		11
Acknowledgments		15
From Mirage to Oasis – Embracing the Concept of Deep Health		17
Section 1	The Shortcomings of Conventional Health Practices	21
Section 2	Desert Sands to Lush Greens – Nurturing The Physical Body	27
	2.1 Demystifying Nutrition for Health	29
	2.2 Unlocking Health Through Exercise	47
	2.3 Sleep, the Silent Healer	67
Section 3	Soothing Spring – Cultivating Emotional Health	85
	3.1 The Positive Power of Stress	88
	3.2 From Isolation to Illumination	110
	3.3 From Mid-Life to My Life	122
	3.4 Confronting Death and Celebrating Existence	133
	3.5 From Fury to Freedom	143
	3.6 Dialogue Over Discord	153

Section 4	Crystal Clear Waters – Fostering Mental Clarity	167
	4.1 Inner Echoes	169
	4.2 Calm in Chaos	180
	4.3 Joyful Journey	195
	4.4 Beyond Work	206
Section 5	Deep Wells of Wisdom – Cultivating Spiritual Health	213
	5.1 Transcendent Trust	216
	5.2 Resurgence	223
Section 6	Gathering Grounds – Understanding Environment, Connections and Family	237
	6.1 Shaping Spaces, Shaping Self	239
	6.2 Network of Strength	255
	6.3 Together In Joy	267

Unveiling my Inner Oasis	283
References	290
About the Author	299

Foreword

I met Sandeep on Twitter. In this age where people craft their social media personas, I first thought Sandeep was a health-conscious executive in his 40s. To my surprise, I discovered he was nearing 60 and a grandfather. When I initially met him, he appeared not only as a physically fit, alert, and aware individual but also as someone exceptionally mature. Engaging with Sandeep was enlightening. Beyond his physique, he showed depth in various domains, including business. He became someone I could trust and who inspired my physical well-being aspirations. His influence, especially on Twitter, underscores the impact one individual can have.

Sandeep's journey started with a pivotal accident in New York, highlighting how our lives can shift suddenly. This brush with life's fragility set him on a transformative and introspective path. In moments of vulnerability, he mustered resilience, rebuilding his life around the principle of profound health. Sandeep's experience speaks to the power of transformation arising from challenges and emphasises the need to proactively care for our health.

In *Finding the Oasis*, Sandeep presents the idea of deep health, which goes further than merely being disease-free. It is about flourishing in life, acknowledging the intricate ties between our physical, mental, emotional, existential, relational, and environmental states. Sandeep's story captures the heart of deep health, and his insights can guide those desiring holistic well-being.

What distinguishes this book is its hands-on approach. Sandeep offers not only his story but also a plan for those aiming for deep health. He integrates personal stories with expertise, shedding light on diverse health facets, from diet and fitness to mental strength and spiritual well-being. This book serves as a comprehensive resource for anyone wanting to elevate their life.

Sandeep advocates for enduring lifestyle changes instead of fleeting remedies. He stresses the importance of consistent self-care as a pillar of long-term wellness. As an entrepreneur who understands the balance of well-being, this message strongly resonates with me. With life's myriad responsibilities, we often sideline our health. Sandeep's tale underscores that our health remains paramount, and overlooking it has significant implications. *Finding the Oasis* calls us to centre our health, placing it at the heart of success and contentment.

The book isn't merely instructive; it is a call to transformation. Thought-provoking questions at each chapter's end prompt self-reflection and personal exploration. Engaging with these queries can lead to meaningful growth.

To conclude, I salute Sandeep for bravely sharing his journey and crafting this essential guide. *Finding the Oasis* stands as a lighthouse for those wanting genuine well-being. I am confident it will motivate many to embrace the path of deep health.

Let Sandeep's narrative inspire you to prioritise your well-being. Remember, the most precious oasis often exists within us.

— **Vijay Sekhar Sharma**
Founder & CEO, Paytm

Preface

"Every new beginning comes from some other beginning's end."
— Seneca

November 20, 2009, Max Hospital, Saket, New Delhi

The hospital ward boys wheeled me inside the operation theatre, the wheels rolling quietly against the sterile floor. As I lay on the cold operation table, my body immobile and vulnerable, I found myself staring blankly at the blindingly bright light hanging above me. It seemed to encompass the room, its intensity causing my eyes to water slightly.

Amidst the anticipation and unease, a doctor, clad in the customary green scrubs, approached me. His face was covered by a surgical mask, but his eyes conveyed a sense of calm and expertise. I recognised him as the anaesthesiologist, responsible for ensuring my comfort and safety during the impending surgery. His voice cut through the tense silence, breaking the spell that the bright light had cast upon me.

"How did this accident happen?" he asked, his tone both professional and compassionate. The question jolted me out of the present, pulling me back to that fateful morning in New York.

On a sunlit May 24, 2009, in New York, the city was alive with Memorial Day weekend festivities. Wrapping up my two-week business trip, I ventured downtown, drawn by the sales and the city's attractions, from Central Park's jogging tracks to Fifth Avenue's iconic stores. Traditionally, I visited tech hubs like the

Apple store and B & H Photo store to indulge my gadget passion, taking a breather from my demanding job. My work had me constantly glued to my Palm Treo, addressing client needs across global time zones. These trips also meant shopping sprees, my way to compensate for time away from my teenage sons.

As I drove to New Jersey on the George Washington Bridge to meet my cousin, the rhythm of A R Rahman's "Jai Ho" uplifted me. Suddenly, an unexpected collision ahead turned my peaceful drive into chaos. My car was the last in a 20-car pile-up. The scene around me was one of confusion and panic. The sounds of screeching tires, honking horns and shattering glass reverberated through the air. Thankfully unharmed, I declined hospitalisation from the arriving paramedics, just wishing for a cab to take me to the airport to take my flight back home. In hindsight, I realised the gravity of the situation that I had initially underestimated. The collision had claimed the lives of two individuals, a sobering reminder of the fragility of life and the randomness of fate.

After returning to India, I carried on with my demanding work schedule, pushing through discomfort and pain that gradually escalated. It was only when persistent tingling and pain in my extremities, pushed me to seek medical attention, that the extent of my injuries was revealed. An MRI showed a partial tear in my spinal cord, a consequence of the accident's impact on my C4 and C5 vertebrae.

Surgery was required to address the damage and the subsequent recovery phase was long and challenging. The post-surgical phase marked the beginning of an arduous and protracted rehabilitation process. The recovery journey would be long and filled with challenges, and the pain that had initially plagued the left side of my body would likely persist for the rest of my life. Throughout this journey, I grappled with depression, the physical changes and the limitations imposed on my once-active lifestyle.

For nearly two years, physical activity remained limited as my body gradually healed from the trauma it had endured. During this period, I found myself succumbing to the effects of a sedentary lifestyle, gaining weight and growing older in appearance. One day, as I gazed in the mirror, I was confronted by a disheartening sight — the man staring back at me appeared worn out, tired and aged beyond his years. Overwhelmed by these physical changes and the emotional toll they had taken, I descended into a state of depression.

To compound matters, my medical reports painted a bleak picture. In 2010, my company recognised the pivotal role I held as the primary person understanding and managing the business. To address potential risks, they suggested a Keyman insurance policy with an ample coverage for me. However, a thorough health check was needed before finalising this insurance.

The health results and subsequent consultations with the doctor were shocking. My cholesterol was at 300 mg/dL, triglycerides at 380 mg/dL, uric acid at 8.3 mg/dL, fasting glucose was 120 mg/dL and my blood pressure was 160/100 mmHg. Beneath the success of an entrepreneur, I unknowingly represented a 'walking sick' profile. The highs of business success blinded me to the impact on my health.

My quest for success had affected my health. Stress, lack of sleep and self-neglect led to an imbalance eroding my vitality. I was unaware that my body and mind needed holistic nourishment. Even walking a mere 100 metres proved to be a strenuous task, leaving me with a feeling that life had lost its essence. **It was in this moment of despair that I realised something had to change, and it was up to me to initiate that change.**

Fuelled by a rejuvenated determination and longing to regain my health and joy, I commenced on a transformative journey. Recognising the challenges ahead, I was resolute in embracing lifestyle shifts. Leaning on the expertise of healthcare specialists, I adopted a holistic regimen blending physical activity, balanced nutrition and mental health awareness.

The journey was not swift or devoid of hurdles. It demanded consistent effort, tenacity and indomitable will. Over time, the benefits of my healthier lifestyle surfaced. I shed excess weight, regained vitality and the looming clouds of depression lifted.

Each day marked a stride towards holistic wellness. My persistent discomfort transitioned from a constant nemesis to a testament to my resilience. I realised the essence of self-nurturing, prioritising both my bodily health and inner serenity.

The accident that had initially plunged me into darkness ultimately became the catalyst in my profound personal growth. It taught me to cherish life's precious moments, to listen to my body's needs and to embrace the power of resilience in the face of adversity.

Did I really know after that day, my life would never be the same again?

It was an ending for a new beginning. My Second Innings of Life, as we know it.

On the day of that accident, I was 43 years old, weighed 78 kg, and was suffering from hypertension, high triglycerides and elevated cholesterol levels, high uric acid and insomnia due to my erratic work schedule and incorrect lifestyle. I was just a one-man army and had work commitments towering up till the Himalayas.

Acknowledgments

Writing *Finding the Oasis* has been a voyage of introspection and discovery, and like every significant journey, I was never truly alone.

First and foremost, my heartfelt gratitude goes to my parents, whose unwavering belief in me has been the foundation upon which I built my dreams. To my wife, Minoo, my anchor in every storm, thank you for your patience and support. To my sons, Sameep and Divyansh, your youthful perspective and zest for life kept me invigorated and inspired throughout this journey.

My sister, Sangeet, deserves special mention. From the very first day, she was the sounding board for all my ideas, providing invaluable feedback and encouragement at every step.

My deepest gratitude goes to Sangeeta Mall. A single tweet from me, and she graciously connected me to the publisher, Popular Prakashan, turning my dream into a journey. I'm immensely indebted to Rajesh Agarwal, Gayatri Manchanda, Mohit Chauhan, Sukumar Ranganathan, Chitra Narain, S. Sivakumar and Shubho Sengupta for their detailed and enriching feedback on each chapter, elevating the content significantly. Finally, a big shoutout to Rohit Varma and his brilliant team, who masterfully captured the soul of my book in its stunning cover design.

Sneha Arora, your eye for detail astounds me. Thank you for poring over the manuscript with more dedication than even I did, catching and correcting every oversight. I am also grateful from Kratika Singhal for the illustrations used in the book.

Additionally, I wish to extend my gratitude to all the individuals whose stories and names feature in this book. Your lives and experiences brought authenticity and depth to *Finding the Oasis*. To the respected authors and eminent personalities whose work I've quoted, your insights and wisdom have been the pillars that added depth and perspective to my narrative. I want to express gratitude, to Dr. Peter Attia for his teachings via podcasts, blogs, and his book *Outlive*, and to Precision Nutrition, where I obtained my certification in Nutrition, Sleep, and Stress Management. Your contributions, directly and indirectly, have been instrumental in shaping this book into the cohesive tapestry of knowledge and experiences that it is.

To Vijay Sekhar Sharma, for penning the heartfelt foreword, and to stalwarts like Harsh Mariwala, Jhulan Goswami, Harsh Goenka, Nithin Kamath, Vivek Ranjan Agnihotri, Parminder Singh, Ankur Warikoo, Priti Rathi Gupta and Shantanu Moitra, your graciousness in reading the manuscript and letting me associate your esteemed names with this book is something I cherish deeply.

Last but by no means least, to all my mentees: this book encapsulates many of the tools we have explored together. Your journeys have been my learning ground, and for that, I am eternally grateful.

Here is to all who've been a part of this oasis, making *Finding the Oasis* not just a book, but a tapestry of collective wisdom and experiences.

From Mirage to Oasis – Embracing the Concept of Deep Health

"Health is a state of complete harmony of the body, mind and spirit. When one is free from physical disabilities and mental distractions, the gates of the soul open."

— BKS Iyengar

Amid health myths, trendy diets, and quick fixes, we often overlook true well-being. *Finding the Oasis* shines as a guiding light in this chaos. This journey offers a deep, all-encompassing view of health beyond mere physical well-being.

Deep health[1], as detailed in this book, isn't merely the lack of disease. It's a vibrant state of physical, mental and social well-being. It emphasises the unity of body, mind, emotions, environment and spirit.

In *Finding the Oasis,* we examine our body's intricate mechanisms, our minds and their amazing connection. We study balanced diets, exercise, sleep and meaningful social interactions. We also venture into mental strength, emotional stability, spiritual wellness and environmental harmony.

This book's goal is to reshape your view of health. It prepares you with the knowledge and means to cultivate a truly healthy life, empowering you to make choices that uplift your well-being. It offers a fresh perspective on your body, celebrating its marvels rather than its flaws.

Finding the Oasis explores depths beyond the visible. It challenges you to be an engaged participant in your health journey. It inspires you to appreciate, nurture and cherish your body that supports you through life.

Deep Health Is About Flourishing, Not Just Existing!

Imagine yourself in your old age, whether it be 20, 30, or even 40 years from now. What do you envision? Perhaps you conjure up an image of an older, weaker version of yourself, with grey hair, relying on a walking stick and struggling to perform everyday tasks. It's a common portrayal, one that suggests a physical decline and limitations. However, let's challenge that narrative.

Envision a future where you are sharper, stronger and brimming with energy, surpassing even your current self. There might be a receding hairline and a few wrinkles here and there; but there are no wheelchairs in sight. You engage in activities independently, mentor others with invigorating energy and pursue your passions, whether it's running marathons or playing competitive tennis. In essence, you can lead a life filled with the same vigour and strength as those half your age. You may find it difficult to believe, dismissing it as fiction or an impossibility, but let me assure you that it is indeed possible.

What Is Deep Health?

Deep health is a whole-person, whole-life approach to health, including six primary dimensions: physical, mental, emotional, existential, relational — social and environmental.

Deep health does not come from a pill or surgery. It emerges from a balanced diet of fresh, whole foods, adequate exercise paired with genuine rest, fresh air, clean water, genuine human interactions, sincere emotional expression and a life filled with purpose and joy.

Deep health isn't a momentary fix or temporary solution. It represents a life-long dedication to nurturing ourselves in a comprehensive manner. It's an understanding that well-being is a continuous journey, not a final destination.

Embracing sustainable lifestyle habits and making conscious choices is crucial to nurture our enduring vitality.

In this book, you will uncover research-driven insights, valuable advice and actionable strategies. Delving into modern science, timeless wisdom and personal stories, this book offers a broad understanding of deep health. Instead of overwhelming you with medical terms or rigid guidelines, the aim is to enlighten you, imparting tools and knowledge to make decisions that bolster a more vibrant, fulfilling life.

How To Use This Book?

"Sow a thought and you reap an action; sow an act and you reap a habit; sow a habit and you reap a character; sow a character and you reap a destiny." — Ralph Waldo Emerson

Illness brings along challenges. Beyond physical discomfort, there are layers of emotional, mental and spiritual turmoil that you have to contend with.

Your health's responsibility lies with you, reflected in your daily habits. As a health coach, I have guided numerous successful entrepreneurs and professionals on their wellness path. This book puts together common health issues faced during mid-life, offering insights and advice for your journey.

This book aims to be a thoughtful workbook, not a swift read. Chapters are crafted to be read and contemplated weekly, letting you absorb and adapt their insights to your life.

At the end of each chapter, reflective questions encourage deep introspection. A blank page follows, inviting you to pen down your thoughts and feelings. Start from any chapter that resonates with you. Each chapter is self-contained yet connected, offering a flexible reading experience. It breaks down many factors influencing one's health.

Use *Finding the Oasis* as a guide and introspection tool. Answering the questions at the conclusion of each chapter is vital. Share the experience with a friend or family member, exploring its content and questions together for a communal understanding.

Revisit this book often. Its content remains timely and universal. When you return to it, your reflections will deepen your understanding. The journey to deep health is personal, but seeking support from your loved ones can be enriching.

I have two hopeful expectations from the readers of this book. First, that it encourages reflection on life situations. And second, that it motivates you to act, as action is pivotal to achieving health goals.

I hope *Finding the Oasis* supports you in making impactful decisions, by offering knowledge and confidence to pursue your deep health aspirations. May you find the courage to question, the insight to comprehend and the prudence to transform as you read. Let's start your journey to deep health! Let's get fitter together.

Section 1

The Shortcomings of Conventional Health Practices

"The doctor of the future will give no medicine but will instruct his patient in the care of the human frame, in diet and in the cause and prevention of disease."
— **Thomas Edison**

Sunil was like my brother. He was employed at a large enterprise, located near my factory, and we would frequently share meals together throughout the week. On Sundays, we would often gather at his house to play card games with his family. In October 2009, he underwent his routine health examination, and all his test results appeared normal. However, in November, he began experiencing difficulties in swallowing food. Upon investigation, it was revealed that he had reached an advanced stage of rapidly progressing cancer in his oesophagus. Tragically, we lost him within three months. He was merely 42 years old.

Medical science, despite its remarkable advancements, often finds itself grappling with a significant challenge: **intervening at a point in time when diseases have already firmly taken hold, sometimes rendering the intervention too late to yield optimal outcome.** The consequences of such delayed interventions can be devastating, both for individuals and their loved ones.

In our current healthcare landscape, the prevailing approach tends to prioritise reactive measures rather than proactive ones.

Individuals typically seek medical attention when symptoms become apparent, prompting a diagnosis that may reveal a disease already in advanced stages.

We have made great strides in the field of medicine; mending bones, eradicating infections, supporting damaged organs and addressing severe spinal or brain injuries. We have saved lives and rejuvenated bodies on the edge of collapse. Yet, for chronic diseases like cancer, heart issues, or neurological disorders, our achievements are limited. Resetting the clock for these conditions often seems out of reach, not for want of trying. Modern medicine has invested greatly in tackling these diseases, but progress, especially against fighting cancer, has been slow.

The declared "War on Cancer" and the allocation of impressive chunk of funds have yet to significantly lower cancer mortality rates in the past five decades. This is a concerning trend given the investment.

The consistent increase in Type 2 diabetes presents a major health concern. And with an ageing population, Alzheimer's and other neurodegenerative diseases become more daunting, especially with few effective treatments in sight.

Dr Malay Nandy is a prominent medical oncologist in Delhi NCR and is also a cherished friend. We embark on wildlife photography trips together. He shares his distress each time he must inform a cancer patient they have around six months to live, understanding the disease probably existed in their body long before detection. A disturbing fact is diseases like cancer and cardiovascular issues become more prevalent as we age, yet the onset of these diseases often remains hidden for a long time.

They infiltrate the body, progressing quietly before showing their lethal nature. For instance, someone might appear to succumb "suddenly" to a heart attack, but the ailment could have been progressing for close to two decades. This slow descent towards death is more gradual than most understand. Dr Peter Attia, in his book *Outlive*[2], underscores the need for early detection and intervention. There's a push to transition from merely reacting to diseases to proactively addressing them, emphasising screenings, risk assessments and prevention.

Treatments for advanced lung cancer have seen progress, but they do not rival the benefits of lifestyle changes, especially abstaining from smoking. Interestingly, the simple act of banning public smoking globally has saved more lives than many sophisticated medical treatments. Yet, traditional medicine still predominantly steps in only upon diagnosis.

A couple of years back my dad's blood HbA1c report came at 6.4 per cent, implying an average blood glucose of 137 mg/dL. He was 0.1 per cent away from being declared Type 2 diabetes. He was pre-diabetic and at that stage guidelines typically recommend incorporating mild exercise, making loosely defined dietary modifications, considering the use of a glucose control medication and implementing 'regular monitoring'.

Essentially, the approach seems to be a passive one, adopting a wait-and-see attitude to determine if the patient eventually progresses to full-blown diabetes before addressing the issue urgently. If his HbA1C report had come at 6.5 per cent which implies average blood glucose of 140 mg/dL, he would be Type 2 diabetic and given extensive treatment, including drugs that help the body produce more insulin, drugs that reduce the amount of glucose the body produces, and eventually the hormone insulin itself, to ram glucose into their highly insulin-resistant tissues.

With just 3 points lower mg/dL, he was off standard guidelines for the treatment of diabetes. Type 2 diabetes exists within a spectrum of metabolic dysfunction that extends far beyond the point at which a diagnostic threshold is crossed on a blood test. It is essential to recognise that Type 2 diabetes represents the final stage on this continuum.

Intervention is necessary well before the patient approaches that critical zone, as even the diagnosis of pre-diabetes is considered a late development in the progression of the disease. Treating Type 2 diabetes as a binary condition, akin to a common cold or a broken bone, is both absurd and detrimental. It fails to acknowledge the complex and gradual nature of the disease and the need for proactive and nuanced interventions at earlier stages.

I firmly believe that our primary objective should be early intervention to prevent the development of Type 2 diabetes or any other lifestyle diseases. It is imperative that we adopt a proactive approach rather than a reactive one. Shifting this mindset should be our initial stride in combating the progression towards slow death. Our aim should be to prolong and preserve a healthy life, free from disease, rather than enduring a prolonged period of illness. This necessitates intervening before things start to go out of hand, as I personally discovered in my own journey.

Back in 2010, I did not like what I saw in the mirror. I was sporting the stereotypical "dad bod" with sagging shoulders, a protruding belly and slender arms and legs. However, the issues I could observe externally paled in comparison to the alarming results revealed by my blood tests. To my astonishment, I discovered a host of serious problems, including a severely imbalanced lipid profile, elevated blood pressure, high levels of uric acid, decreased testosterone and elevated blood glucose. It became evident that I was akin to a ticking time bomb, poised to explode sooner rather than later.

The Shortcomings of Conventional Health Practices

The greatest shortcoming of medicine lies in attempting to address these conditions at a stage when they have already become deeply entrenched, rather than taking preventive action before they take root. Consequently, we overlook important warning signs and miss crucial opportunities for intervention when we still have the chance to effectively combat these diseases, enhance health and potentially extend lifespan.

Have you heard of Easter Island? It's the most remote inhabited place on earth. It has nearly 1,000 statues, some almost 30 feet tall and weighing as much as 80 tons. But the mystery about where the people, who have built these statues, have vanished is a great one. The leading theory is that the society collapsed centuries ago; after islanders over-harvested the island's palm trees.

The trees were used to move the massive monolith heads to higher ground. Overharvesting led to a proliferation of rats. The rats ate the seeds. Then trees went extinct. Without the palm trees, the islanders could not build canoes to fish. The islanders had to hunt birds. Birds went extinct and vegetation stopped getting pollinated. With their food source collapsed, the population eventually died. How could the islanders not see it? Because it was a slow-moving disaster. This is what the **Creeping Normality Effect** is, and it is affecting most of us.

Giving my own example, I can't tell a specific date when my health deteriorated and I was almost obese. I let my health decline day after day. I let it deteriorate slowly and I never realised it. Ninety-nine per cent of people would change if it happened overnight. Your metabolic bad health is a result of a slow-dripping poison. We slowly lower our standards. We continually increase our tolerance for misery. Our health does not become terrible overnight.

One of the most profound realisations I have come to is that modern medicine does not holistically address the chronic diseases linked with ageing. Yet, these diseases will probably top the list of mortality causes. This gap is partially attributed to the intricate nature of these conditions, acting more as continual disease processes than sudden afflictions like the flu. Yet, optimistically, there's a silver lining to this insight.

Lifestyle diseases accumulate effects over time due to various risk factors. However, many of these factors can be somewhat easily mitigated or eliminated. Importantly, these diseases have overlapping characteristics that make them responsive to similar intervention strategies and behavioural modifications, topics that we will delve into in this book. I am confident that we possess sufficient knowledge to change the trajectory.

My overarching goal is to meticulously craft a hands-on guide that elucidates longevity principles. Through this book, I ambitiously hope to help you extend not just your lifespan but also your quality of life, enabling you to operate at a vitality level akin to someone decades younger. It's pivotal to understand that I'm not advocating a strict action blueprint. Rather, I passionately aim to equip you with insights and tools for a holistic wellness mindset. For me, this odyssey has been relentlessly persistent, marked by a steadfast dedication to learning and refining the assimilated insights. By disseminating this knowledge, I ardently wish to steer you towards a parallel journey of introspection and personal evolution.

Section 2

Desert Sands to Lush Greens – Nurturing the Physical Body

"It's not what we do once in a while that shapes our lives. It's what we do consistently."
— **Anthony Robbins**

Our body is a miraculous machine, wonderfully complex and fantastically efficient. It propels us through the bustling rhythms of our day-to-day lives, respond with resilience to the various stressors we encounter and house the entirety of our being; mind, emotions and spirit. In recognition of these incredible feats, it becomes evident that nurturing our physical body should be one of our utmost priorities.

Demystifying Nutrition For Health

Just as a high-performance car requires premium fuel to run optimally, our bodies require high-quality nutrition to function at their best. Everything we consume, from our breakfast choices to our evening snacks, influences our energy levels, mood, cognitive function and overall well-being. But the world of nutrition can be overwhelming with its myriad diets and food trends.

The secret lies in simplicity and balance. Fill your plate with a rainbow of fruits and vegetables, lean protein, healthy fats and complex carbohydrates. Each of these food groups offers unique nutrients that our body needs to thrive. It's important to remember that there's 'no one-size-fits-all' approach to nutrition. Listen to your body, observe how different foods make you feel and tailor your diet to what makes you feel energetic, satiated and nourished.

Unlocking Health Through Exercise

Regular physical activity is another vital component of nurturing our body. Movement circulates oxygen and nutrients to our cells, helps us maintain a healthy weight, strengthens our cardiovascular system and even boosts our mood through the release of endorphins, our body's natural 'feel good' chemicals.

Whether you prefer a brisk walk in the park, an intense session at the gym, or a calming yoga routine, the most important thing is consistency. Try to incorporate some form of movement into your daily routine, your body will thank you for it.

Sleep, The Silent Healer

Finally, in this section we talk about sleep, an often under-appreciated aspect of health. Sleep is the time when our bodies recover, repair and rejuvenate. Quality sleep improves cognitive function, emotional well-being and even impacts our dietary choices.

To enhance your sleep quality, maintain a consistent sleep schedule, create a restful environment free from distractions and establish a relaxing pre-sleep routine that signals your bod'y it's time to wind down and rest. Avoid using screens close to bedtime, as the blue light emitted can interfere with your body's natural sleep-wake cycle.

Nurturing your physical body is not a short-term venture but a life-long commitment. It's about respecting and caring for the vessel that carries you through life's ups and downs. By prioritising nutrition, physical activity and sleep, you lay a solid foundation for a deeply healthy, vibrant and fulfilling life.

2.1 DEMYSTIFYING NUTRITION FOR HEALTH

"In this food, I see clearly the presence of the entire universe supporting my existence."
— **Thich Nhat Hanh**

If you are an active participant in the social media sphere, you may have noticed an increasing number of heated debates unfolding around the topics of diet and food. It seems that everyone has an opinion to share, regardless of the platform.

From Facebook groups to X (formerly Twitter) threads and Instagram comment sections, it's evident that diet and food have become polarising topics. These virtual discussions often spiral into ugly arguments, showcasing the passion the individuals harbour for their dietary beliefs and practices.

Whether it's discussions about the merits of veganism, the efficacy of low-carb diets, the health benefits of organic food, or the controversial aspects of fast food, it's clear that these conversations are driven by strong views and often conflicting opinions. There is a reason why nutrition and diet is the subject with the highest number of books by various authors on Amazon.

Nutrition, at its core, is surprisingly straightforward. It fundamentally adheres to a few key principles: moderate your calorie intake, neither too high nor too low; ensure ample consumption of protein and essential fats; acquire necessary vitamins and minerals; and steer clear of pathogens and toxins like mercury or lead. Beyond these guidelines, our understanding remains somewhat limited. We do not know as much as we think we do with absolute certainty.

In general terms, numerous age-old adages about diet probably hold some truth: for instance, if your great-grandmother would not recognise a food item, it might be best to avoid it. Similarly, ultra-processed foods should be avoided. Consuming a variety of plants is beneficial. Animal protein, while a point of debate for some, is fundamentally safe for consumption. Considering our evolution as omnivores, most of us can likely maintain optimal health on a balanced, omnivorous diet.

The root of this issue lies in the subpar quality of many nutritional studies. This inadequate research subsequently results in misleading media reporting, fuels aggressive debates on social media and creates widespread confusion among the public. This conundrum leaves us grappling with questions like, "What should we consume (and avoid)? What constitutes the right diet for an individual?" Misinformation and contrasting views only complicate these inquiries further, making it more challenging to find clear, reliable answers.

Metabolism – How We Turn Food Into Energy That Our Cells Can Use

We get energy from food. Have you ever thought about how fat loss happens? I mean, if you lose 5 kg weight, where does it go? Do you poop, pee, or sweat? Tiny bit of it, yes. Most of it you breathe out. Yes, with every breath you take out you lose some fat. Let's understand how we lose fat by breathing.

The very basic prescription for fat loss is diet and exercise. When we exercise, we start to breathe heavily. If you do it enough, consistently and if you are patient, you are going to lose fat.

Imagine you consume a meal with a mix of macronutrients – carbohydrates, proteins and fats. When the food leaves your gut and enters your bloodstream, it isn't in the same form as it was on your plate. Instead, it has been broken down into its component macronutrients. In your blood, you won't see visible bits of your meal, but you will find protein, fats and glucose – a by-product of carbohydrates. Our gut essentially breaks down the food into these individual macros, providing us with some energy in the process.

Carbohydrates are a chain of six carbon molecules. The process of glycolysis breaks down this six-carbon chain into two 3-carbon molecules, which are further broken down into two 2-carbon molecules. Through this simple process, we lose two carbon molecules from the original six-carbon chain.

When we inhale oxygen, it combines with the free-floating carbon to create carbon dioxide (CO2), which we exhale. The remaining carbon molecules are further broken down in a process called the Krebs cycle, leaving us with no carbon. If we have sufficient oxygen, we will breathe out all the carbon in the form of CO2. Thus, when we metabolise carbohydrates, we are left with energy, water and CO2.

The breakdown of fats operates slightly differently. Fats are converted into triglycerides and fatty acids. A triglyceride consists of three glycerides linked by a three-carbon glycerol backbone, with several fatty acid chains attached. These fatty acids are themselves chains of carbon molecules, and the length of the chain determines the type of fatty acid.

The three-carbon glycerol backbone undergoes the same process as carbohydrates, eventually turning into CO2, water and energy. The long-chain fatty acids are also ultimately broken down into two carbon molecules, which follow the same Krebs cycle process, resulting in energy, water and CO2. Fat metabolism is an aerobic process, requiring oxygen. Protein is broken down into amino acids, which are further broken down into three and two carbon chains. The by-product of this process is NH2, which we excrete through urine. Protein metabolism also requires oxygen.

When we use this information to optimise our exercise routines, we find that carbohydrates are used directly by the active muscles, while fats are used by the whole body. For instance, if you are running and feel a burn in your calf, that's the energy from the carbohydrates in your calf being used. Energy from fats does not work in the same localised way — it comes from the entire body. This is why spot reduction isn't possible, the energy from fats can come from anywhere in the body, not just the area you are exercising. This also explains why it takes time for energy from fats to reach the muscles where it's needed, while carbohydrates stored in your muscles are readily available. Understanding this can help you decide when to eat more carbohydrates or fats in relation to your exercise regimen.

What To Eat?
Modern industrial food is meticulously engineered for convenience, affordability, and extended shelf life, often prioritising taste and palatability over nutritional value. The design aims to cater to the fast-paced lifestyles prevalent in contemporary society, providing quick and easy options for individuals with hectic schedules. The accessibility and widespread availability of these processed foods contribute to their increased consumption. However, the disadvantages of relying on such foods are substantial. They are frequently high in refined sugars, unhealthy fats, and artificial additives, leading to concerns about obesity, cardiovascular diseases, and other health issues. Additionally, the lack of essential nutrients and fibre in many processed foods can contribute to deficiencies and digestive problems. The long-term consequences of a diet dominated by modern industrial food underscore the importance of balanced and nutrient-rich alternatives for overall well-being.

Just as tobacco manufacturers sought to profit immensely from an abundant agricultural commodity, resulting in a product — cigarettes — that slowly but surely harmed the consumer, the modern food industry has trodden a similar path with ultra-processed foods. The key ingredients that characterise these foods can be nearly as detrimental to people's health as tobacco when consumed in large quantities, as it often occurs in our current food culture.

These ingredients include added sugars, highly refined carbohydrates with minimal fibre, processed oils and other calorie-dense foods. These components may enhance taste and extend shelf life, but their excessive consumption can lead to an array of health complications, mirroring the damaging health consequences associated with long-term tobacco use.

For perhaps the first time in human history, a large segment of the global population has access to an abundance of calories. However, our evolutionary history has not prepared us for this scenario. Nature, unconcerned with our obesity rates or diabetes prevalence, has not equipped us with inherent controls for this abundance.

The low-quality, ultra-processed foods undermine our nutritional goals in two significant ways. Firstly, it promotes overeating, as these foods are typically designed to be hyper-palatable and easy to over-consume. Secondly, the ubiquity of these processed foods tends to displace more nutrient-dense options from our diet, such as protein, which are essential for maintaining optimal health. As a result, even while over-consuming calories, we may still be undernourished in vital nutrients, creating a paradox of plenty.

All the different types of diets that people argue over have one thing in common; they are designed around one of the three strategies for weight management, calorie restriction, dietary restriction (This method entails reducing or eliminating certain components within the diet, such as carbohydrate, meat, sugar or fats) or time restriction (Intermittent fasting or multi-day fasting).

In essence, if you are over-eating, a condition affecting approximately $2/3^{rd}$ of the population, you would need to implement at least one of these calorie reduction techniques. This could mean meticulously monitoring and reducing your overall food intake, eliminating specific food items, or narrowing the window of time during which you allow yourself to eat.

Carbohydrates

Carbohydrates, or "carbs", often spark a great deal of debate and confusion. However, it's important to note that they are not inherently "good" or "bad", though some types are more beneficial than others. It's crucial to match the quantity consumed with both tolerance and necessity; it's a process that has become significantly easier with advances in technology. We now have access to data that eliminates the need for guesswork.

Carbohydrates serve as our primary energy source. During digestion, most carbohydrates are transformed into glucose, which is used by all cells to produce energy in the form of ATP (Adenosine Triphosphate). Any excess glucose, beyond our immediate needs, can be stored in the liver or muscles as glycogen for short-term use or as fat in adipose tissue or elsewhere for long-term storage. This storage decision is influenced by the hormone insulin, which increases in response to the rise in blood glucose levels.

It's widely understood that consuming excessive calories isn't beneficial. When these surplus calories come from carbohydrates, they can lead to various health issues, including non-alcoholic fatty liver disease (NAFLD), insulin resistance and Type 2 diabetes. Individual responses to glucose intake can vary widely. What may seem like an excess of glucose or carbohydrates for one person might be just enough for another.

For instance, an athlete participating in high-level endurance events might be able to consume and efficiently burn 600 to 800 grams of carbohydrates daily. However, if an individual with a sedentary lifestyle consumed the same amount on a regular basis, they could potentially develop diabetes within a year. We have access to a tool nowadays that allows us to comprehend our personal carbohydrate tolerance and our responses to specific foods. This tool is referred to as Continuous Glucose Monitoring or CGM.

A CGM does not actually measure the glucose levels in the blood. But it measures the glucose levels in the interstitial fluid. It's able to impute what is the glucose level in the blood without having to sample the blood. Your CGM connects to your phone and at every scan, it provides a reading of your glucose levels. These levels are represented in a glucose graph on the phone app, providing you with a live understanding of how your body's blood glucose looks like at every scan.

I used the CGM for a year or so to understand what food types were working best for me and what were not. I found that some of the 'healthy' foods were not healthy for me like sweet potatoes. I noticed that Paneer purchased from the market spiked my glucose higher than Paneer made at home. I also found a way to manage my sweet tooth. If I ate my dessert along with food rich in high fibre, say, a plate of leafy salad and green veggies, the GI effect of the dessert would substantially reduce. Another way to blunt the sugar spike was to consume a glass of lemon water or include cinnamon in food.

Glucose monitoring is a useful tool not just for diabetic people but for non-diabetics and those who want to optimise their food to manage focused work and exercise. I also found that every time I did some intense work my glucose would spike and with few physiological signs, I could manage it better. It's a tool for anybody who is interested in improving their health because it gives you the best real-world insight into these three metrics:

- What's your average blood glucose?
- How much does it vary?
- How high are the peaks and how often do you have them?

With this knowledge, you can find ways to manage the spikes and your health better. There is no "correct" amount of carbohydrates that's best for everyone, all the time. Some people function better with more carbohydrates, and some function better with less. As you can now understand there is no definitive answer to how much carb or what type of carb is best. In other words, you do you!

However, when it comes to choosing the best quality carbohydrate sources, well, not all carbs are created equal. Complex carbohydrates that come from whole-food sources like vegetables, fruits, legumes and whole grains tend to keep us feeling full longer. They also travel with passengers: micronutrients, phytonutrients, fibre and water — perhaps even some protein and healthy fats. They keep our blood sugar and insulin levels stable, releasing their energy gradually. And the fibre they contain, which can be soluble or insoluble, has the added benefit of feeding our friendly gut bacteria, lowering cholesterol and keeping our bowels moving.

Simply said, highly processed carbohydrates digest quickly but tend to leave us unsatisfied. They have been stripped of nutrients. Their passengers are often high amounts of sodium along with industrial chemicals such as flavourings, trans fats or preservatives. They tend to stimulate our appetite and leave us wanting more. They can cause fluctuations in our blood sugar and insulin levels. That means we can finish a whole box of cookies and still crave more. And half an hour later, we are hungry. Maybe even "hangry".

In general, we should try to eat mostly complex carbohydrates from whole-food sources. However, simple, fast-digesting carbohydrates can be useful in a couple of situations, particularly with higher-level athletes who need rapid refuelling around training and competition, or people who are under-weight and have trouble eating enough.

Eat The Rainbow

Eating colourful vegetables is highly recommended. In fact, the advice is to consume vegetables of five different colours every single day. But why the emphasis on different colours? A key reason is that this variety is beneficial for the bacteria that reside in our gut, collectively referred to as our microbiome, along with their associated genes.

Research in this area is a relatively recent phenomenon, but the significance of a healthy microbiome for our mental and physical health is becoming increasingly clear. The human gut is teeming with microorganisms, ranging from 30 trillion to 400 trillion, compared to our body's own cells which number from 5 trillion to 724 trillion.[3] Hence, it's no exaggeration to say that we might have more microbial than human cells in our bodies.

Current understanding suggests that an ideal microbiome is the one that is diverse, adaptable and capable of sharing functions. These microbes have evolved with us over millions of years and help us process the food we eat. In return, they offer us numerous benefits. For instance, certain species of these microbes produce serotonin, a hormone linked with mood, while others manufacture vitamins. However, the composition of our gut microbiome has been drastically altered by modern industrial living, stress, food additives, overuse of antibiotics and more.

Improving our damaged microbiomes is possible through simple dietary changes. While we are constantly told that vegetables are good for us, the reason is not often explained. It turns out, our gut bugs thrive on plant-based fibre or pre-biotic fibre found in abundance in vegetables like broccoli. The fibre in such vegetables feeds these bugs and in turn, they produce by-products such as short-chain fatty acids (SCFAs), including butyrate, which have anti-inflammatory properties.

Furthermore, feeding the microbiome boosts other parts of our body, such as the immune system. Around 70 per cent of our immune system activity takes place in and around our gut. This underscores the importance of our gut in protecting us from the external world.

Our ancestors consumed between 50 and 150 grams of complex fibre or Microbiota Accessible Carbohydrates (MACs) per day, which is about 10 times the quantity most people eat today.[4] These MACs feed our gut bugs and are abundant in vegetables, fruits and legumes.

To enhance your microbiome, it's suggested to include five different vegetables in your daily diet. If possible, choose vegetables of different colours to foster the growth of beneficial bacteria and ensure maximum gut-bug diversity. Different coloured vegetables contain different phytonutrients that offer various health benefits. For example, red foods like tomatoes contain lycopene, which may reduce the risk of certain cancers and heart disease.

Orange foods like carrots are rich in beta-carotene, which bolsters our immune system and promotes healthy vision. Green vegetables like broccoli contain chlorophyll, which aids in controlling hunger, and the list goes on.

Protein
The significance of protein cannot be overstated; the term itself is derived from the Greek word *'proteios'*, meaning 'primary'. Protein, along with amino acids, are fundamental building blocks of life. They are essential for the construction and maintenance of lean muscle mass. As we age, the loss of muscle becomes an increasingly prominent issue, and rebuilding it becomes more challenging. Therefore, maintaining an adequate intake of protein is critical.

Unlike carbohydrates and fats, protein isn't primarily an energy source. We do not depend on it for ATP production, nor do we store it like we do with fats (in fat cells) or glucose (as glycogen). If your protein intake exceeds what your body can incorporate into lean mass, the surplus will simply be excreted in your urine as urea. Essentially, protein is all about structure.

The 20 amino acids that compose proteins serve as the construction materials for our muscles, enzymes and numerous vital hormones in our body. They contribute to everything from the growth and maintenance of our hair, skin and nails, to the formation of antibodies in our immune system. Furthermore, nine out of these 20 essential amino acids must be obtained through our diet as our bodies cannot synthesise them.

The first thing to understand about protein is that the standard dietary recommendations for daily consumption are woefully inadequate. The current recommended dietary allowance for protein is a mere 0.8 g/kg of body weight.[5] While this might be the bare minimum required to stay alive, it is far from the optimal amount needed to thrive. Numerous studies indicate that this level of protein intake leads to muscle loss in elderly individuals even over a short period of two weeks.

The exact amount of protein one requires can vary individually. With my mentees, I generally set a minimum baseline of 1.6 g/kg/day, which is double the current recommended dietary allowance. The optimal amount will differ depending on factors such as activity levels, overall health and individual metabolic needs. Just like there's no 'best diet', there's no single 'best protein'.

To meet our nutritional needs, we need to get protein from a variety of sources. This will give us a range of amino acids, such as –
- Non-essential amino acids, which we produce in our body.
- Essential amino acids, which we must get from our diet; and

- Conditionally essential amino acids, which we can make ourselves, but not always effectively, so it helps to get extra from the diet.

We may also need more protein if we are trying to lose weight, as protein can help keep us feeling full longer. **It's crucial not to overlook the importance of protein.** Unless you have a specific medical condition which requires low protein diet or you are eating protein without fat or carbohydrate, its impossible to eat too much protein. Protein is incredibly satiating. It's the one macronutrient that is absolutely critical to our health and wellness goals. There is technically no minimum requirement for carbohydrates or fats, but failing to consume enough protein can undoubtedly have negative consequences, especially as we age.

Fat

Carbohydrates are primarily a source of fuel and amino acids are primarily building blocks, but fats are both. They not only serve as an efficient source of fuel but also act as building blocks for numerous hormones (via cholesterol) and cellular membranes.

Consuming the right combination of fats can aid in preserving metabolic equilibrium and is crucial for brain health, given that it's largely composed of fatty acids. From a day-to-day perspective, dietary fat often provides a stronger sense of fullness compared to many types of carbohydrates, particularly when consumed alongside protein.

Fats are molecules that mainly consist of carbon and hydrogen atoms assembled into lengthy chains known as hydrocarbons. The fats present in our bodies and food are formed from fatty acids and glycerol, constituting triglycerides or other fat-based entities, such as cholesterol. The fat's structure will influence how it functions within our bodies, with saturation playing a significant role.

Saturation can be compared to cars occupying spaces in a parking lot; the extent to which the hydrocarbon chain is filled with hydrogen determines the level of saturation. A fully hydrogen-filled chain represents saturated fat, while partial hydrogen occupancy leads to unsaturated fat.

Unsaturated fats come in two varieties: monounsaturated fats with a single unsaturated carbon, and polyunsaturated fats with multiple unsaturated carbons. To digest fat, the body decomposes triglycerides into fatty acids and glycerol. Most sources of dietary fat comprise a blend of saturated, polyunsaturated and monounsaturated fatty acids. This diversity is beneficial since our health flourishes best with a mix of fat types. Consuming a broad selection of assorted, whole, less-processed foods ensures this balance naturally.

A balanced diet should include a range of fats – saturated, monounsaturated and omega-3. All of them contribute to our health by balancing hormones, supporting brain and nervous system function and regulating inflammation. This generally means increasing the intake of foods like olive oil, avocados and nuts, while moderating the consumption of items like butter and lard. It also suggests reducing the use of oils rich in omega-6, such as corn, soybean and sunflower oils. Additionally, it's beneficial to seek out ways to boost the intake of high-omega-3 polyunsaturated fatty acids (PUFAs) from marine sources, including salmon and anchovies.

Trans fats are the only type of fats that should be minimised or entirely eliminated from our diets. Predominantly stemming from industrial fat processing, trans fats involve the artificial addition of hydrogen ions to an unsaturated fat, making it solid at room temperature and remarkably shelf-stable. Over time, excessive trans-fat consumption can increase the risk of various chronic diseases.

How To Eat?

Do you recall the dining table instructions from your parents?

"Pay attention to your food! No running about while eating. Sit up straight. Chew your food thoroughly."

In some families, there was even a reminder to respect the food. Regardless of cultural, religious, socio-economic or national differences, most children have probably heard similar directives from their parents. I, for one, used to detest this counsel. Reading a comic book while eating seemed much more appealing than just sitting and eating. As I grew up, I came to understand that this advice was essentially promoting mindful eating, a skill that can be developed from a young age.

We have a 3 year old toddler at home, and I can attest to the challenges of feeding her. We are constantly brainstorming creative ideas to encourage her to eat, with at least two of us involved in the process. Often, I find myself performing silly dances to her nursery rhymes or imitating animal sounds. At other times, in desperation, we resort to showing her videos on YouTube just so we can coax a few mouthfuls of food into her. Witnessing her eating while engrossed in videos was like looking into a mirror. I was guilty of routinely picking up my phone, browsing YouTube, checking emails and WhatsApp, or watching Netflix during meals. The urge to fill the gap of free time while eating, rather than savouring the meal in front of me, was overwhelming.

Studies[6] now suggest that excessive screen time can hinder a child's development, causing them to become unresponsive and have difficulty falling asleep. It's crucial for parents to enforce a no-screen-time policy during meals. However, for this to be effective, parents need to set an example. Children do not learn from lectures; they learn from observing their parents' behaviour.

Mindful Eating

Mindfulness involves focusing on the present moment and calmly acknowledging and accepting your feelings, thoughts and bodily sensations. When applied to eating, mindfulness embodies more than just focusing on the individual but extends to the food you consume. It involves truly paying attention to the food you eat, which may lead to decreased consumption of less healthy foods. Essentially, mindful eating is about being entirely present for every aspect of your dining experience, from purchasing and preparing to serving and consuming your food. Making this a regular practice may involve changing how you approach meals and snacks.

The benefits of mindful eating include enhanced digestion, better hydration, more effortless weight loss or maintenance and greater satisfaction with meals. On the other hand, rapid eating can lead to poor digestion, increased weight gain and diminished meal satisfaction. **The takeaway is simple: slow down your eating and enjoy improved health and well-being.** Developing awareness can be beneficial not only at mealtimes but also during shopping and cooking. It helps us to make decisions that are influenced by the knowledge of our body's needs, rather than by external thoughts, emotions or impulses.

Our mind is powerful, and without proper training, it can be susceptible to both emotion and habit. We meditate to train our minds and to find the space to make healthier choices for our overall health, not just our body shape or weight. The starting point for this shift in perspective is to ask yourself one simple question: **What's your relationship with food? The "best diet" is one that is sustainable and manageable for you in the long run.** Studies indicate that the minutiae of diets[7] — such as the exact macronutrient ratio, particular food selections, or the specific type of carbohydrate consumed — are not as consequential as once thought. Essentially, various diets can aid in achieving diverse health goals, but their effectiveness relies on an individual's ability to adhere to them consistently.

'Good nutrition' should be founded on robust scientific data, which is constantly updated as more reliable information becomes available. Good nutrition should also accommodate an individual's personal preferences and fit seamlessly into their everyday lives.

Some basic rules that will work for most people, who are metabolically fit, revolve around a balanced and diverse diet, engage in regular physical activity and maintain a healthy weight. Here are some key points to consider:

- **Balanced diet:** Incorporate a variety of nutrient-dense foods from all the food groups including fruits, vegetables, whole grains, lean proteins and healthy fats. This provides a broad spectrum of essential vitamins, minerals, fibre and other nutrients.
- **Portion control:** Even healthy foods can lead to weight gain if you consume them in large quantities. Be mindful of portion sizes.
- **Hydration:** Water is essential for good health and supports every system in your body. Aim to drink enough water each day to keep your urine light yellow to clear in colour.
- **Limit Processed Foods:** Processed foods can be high in unhealthy fats, added sugars, and sodium. Opt for whole, unprocessed foods whenever possible.

Pause & Reflect
- How would you describe your current relationship with food? Is it a source of pleasure, fuel for your body, a means to control weight, or something else?
- In terms of nutrition and diet, what are your short and long-term goals? For instance, are you aiming to lose weight, gain muscle, improve performance in a sport, manage a health condition, or simply maintain your current health status?
- What does your typical daily diet look like? Does it include a variety of food groups, providing you with balanced macronutrients (carbohydrates, proteins and fats) and a wide range of vitamins and minerals?
- How often do you engage in physical activity? Do you tailor your nutrition to support your level of activity?
- Do you experience any health issues or symptoms (like fatigue, poor concentration, digestive problems, skin issues, etc.) that could potentially be diet-related?
- Have you ever tried to follow a specific diet plan (such as low-carb, vegan, paleo, etc.)? If yes, what was your experience? Did it improve your health, cause stress or create any eating disorders?
- How mindful are you during mealtimes? Do you take the time to appreciate your food, eat slowly and listen to your body's hunger and fullness cues?
- Are there any barriers that prevent you from improving your diet (e.g., lack of time, knowledge, cooking skills, financial constraints, etc.)? How might you overcome these barriers?
- Do you feel confident in your ability to make healthy food choices? Or do you find nutrition information confusing and overwhelming?

✎ PAUSE & REFLECT INSIGHTS

2.2 UNLOCKING HEALTH THROUGH EXERCISE

"The secret of getting ahead is getting started."
— **Mark Twain**

To most people, healthy movement = exercise. They associate it with activities like cardio, weightlifting at the gym, cycling, etc. However, moving your body encompasses a broader spectrum, including enhanced cognitive abilities, stronger social connections, and the expression of your life's purpose.

The term "healthy movement" for most people means exercise or fitness or looking better or weight loss and sometimes vanity. In my 10 plus years of exercising, here is the most important thing I have discovered: developing a body that moves well is the ticket to a place where you feel capable, confident and free.

Human life has become structured in a way that makes it very easy to avoid movement. We sit in cars on the way to work. At work, we sit at our desks for most of the day. Then we come home and sit down to relax. That's not what our bodies are built for; therefore creaky knees and stiff backs have become the norm. As humans, we move our bodies to express our wants, needs, emotions, thoughts and ideas. Ultimately, how well we move, and how much we move, determines how well we engage with the world and establish our larger purpose in life.

When we move well, we experience holistic benefits, positively impacting our physical, emotional and cognitive well-being. Healthy movement enables us to…

- Feel physically and emotionally sound.
- Function productively in our daily activities.
- Enhance our thinking, learning and memory capabilities.
- Interact effectively with the world around us.
- Communicate and express ourselves authentically.
- Foster connections and build meaningful relationships with others.

We do not require structured 'workouts' to move; our ancestors did not need them when they engaged in various activities for survival and enjoyment, like walking, climbing, running, swimming and playing. At the age of 93, my grandmother is remarkably healthy. All her blood markers are within the normal range, and she continues to be strong and independent, moving around the house without any assistance, not even requiring a walking stick. She never went to a gym. Instead, she stayed active and fit by diligently performing various household chores. From fetching water from the well to grinding grains and cleaning, she managed it all effortlessly. Her active lifestyle and dedication to manual tasks have contributed to her well-being and vitality. Along with that, she has never eaten any ultra-processed food or food sold in packets in supermarkets.

'Working out' has become a modern concept to encourage us to re-acquaint ourselves with the regular movements our bodies, have known and loved throughout human history, but may have lost and forgotten over time. Over the past 200 years, the Industrial Revolution has brought about significant changes in the society. While it has led to remarkable progress and advancements in civilisation, it has also brought along new challenges, including the emergence of diseases such as cancer, diabetes, dementia, heart ailments and others. These health issues have become more prevalent in modern times, possibly linked to the changes in lifestyle, environment and diet influenced by rapid industrialisation and urbanisation.

This does not imply that civilisation is inherently "bad" or that we should revert to a hunter-gatherer lifestyle. I, too, prefer living in our modern world with its conveniences and comforts rather than enduring the hardships of rampant disease, random violence, and lawlessness that existed in our ancestors' times. The advancements of modern life have undoubtedly extended our lifespans and enhanced our living standards.

However, it's essential to acknowledge that certain conditions in our modern existence can unintentionally hinder our longevity in various ways. The environment we have built has the potential to be toxic in several ways concerning our eating habits, our level of physical activity (or lack thereof), our quality of sleep (or lack of it), and its impact on our emotional well-being. The complexities and challenges of our contemporary society may require us to be mindful of our well-being and make conscious efforts to maintain a healthy and balanced lifestyle.

Our lifestyle has changed, but our movement remains crucial to our brains' programming and how we engage with the world. We must prioritise incorporating movement into our daily lives. Our bodies are naturally designed to be active, but the demands of modern life often force us to sit for extended periods during long commutes and desk-bound work for eight hours. Physical inactivity is a significant contributor to premature death,[8] accounting for five percent of all global deaths according to the World Health Organisation. Surprisingly, it's a greater health risk than being overweight or obese and can be as harmful as smoking.

Whether inactivity is truly as bad as smoking might be debatable, but the undeniable truth is that prolonged sitting poses substantial health risks, more than we typically realise. To improve our well-being and longevity, we need to find ways to incorporate more movement and break free from the constraints of our sedentary lifestyle.

Walk More
Walking is a simple activity that you already are aware of. Just place one foot in front of the other, and you can walk anywhere. Whether you step out of your front door, walk from your workplace, or go to places you frequently visit like the grocery store or a shopping centre, walking requires no special equipment. If you walk as a form of exercise, a comfortable pair of shoes, preferably sneakers, is best. Other clothing and gear are

not essential. The best part is that walking is gentle on your knees and the rest of your body since it's a low-impact, joint-friendly exercise, unlike running where both feet leave the ground.

Walking has been recognised as a healthful practice for over 2,400 years, with Hippocrates famously stating, *"Walking is a man's best medicine."* Modern research[9] supports this notion, showing that walking provides numerous health benefits.

The first intervention may seem deceptively simple, as it involves setting a goal of walking 10,000 steps a day, which is admittedly an arbitrary number. It's essential to recognise that walking alone cannot counterbalance a poor diet; unhealthy eating habits will still have negative effects on your health. Nevertheless, embracing this straightforward rule can guide us towards leading a more active lifestyle.

For many individuals, walking acts as a stepping stone towards greater physical activity, serving as the starting point of a journey from a sedentary state to optimal movement. Like breathing, walking is a fundamental process that our brain carries out without the need for conscious control, making it an integral part of our core activities.

Initially, 10,000 steps might seem like a significant number, but it's more achievable than we realise. Many people naturally accumulate a couple of thousand steps throughout the day without engaging in structured exercise. In fact, just 1,000 steps are approximately equal to 10 minutes of walking. Therefore, if you can walk without much discomfort, reaching the 10,000 steps goal is within your grasp.

Incorporating more movement into your daily routine and embracing simple activities like parking your car a bit further, taking the stairs instead of the lift, walking during telephone calls, going to the office printer for printouts, or walking to the water kiosk for hydration at home or the office can make a significant difference. By integrating these small habits, you can often achieve the 10,000 steps goal without the need to go out for a dedicated walk. It's all about making conscious choices to stay active throughout your day, making it an enjoyable and achievable part of your routine.

Your feet are essential assets for walking, so it's crucial to take good care of them. Starting with purchasing the right shoes and socks, you can ensure their well-being. However, caring for your feet should not be limited to exercise. Here are some simple ways to pamper them and prevent potential problems.

- **Limit heel time (for women):** High heels can lead to back, knee and foot problems. Whenever possible, opt for heels no higher than three-quarters of an inch to protect your overall foot health.
- **Put your feet up:** Taking a few minutes each day to lie back with your feet propped up can reduce swelling and enhance circulation, promoting foot health.
- **Go barefoot:** Allow your feet to breathe and stretch out by walking barefoot, which also engages foot muscles more effectively than wearing shoes. However, limit barefoot walking to safe indoor environments to avoid potential hazards.
- **Stretch your toes:** Counteract the effects of prolonged shoe confinement by lacing your fingers between your toes and holding for a minute on each foot. Aim to do this at least once a day to improve flexibility.
- **Massage your feet:** Revive tired feet by rolling each foot over a tennis ball or a cold/frozen water bottle. Self-foot massages or enlisting your partner's help can ease soreness and stiffness and enhance circulation.
- **Keep your toenails trimmed**: Keeping your toenails well-groomed prevents rubbing against the front of your shoes, reducing the risk of potential foot issues.

Build Your Aerobic Fitness – Zone 2 Training

Aerobic exercises lay the foundation of endurance for all aspects of life, whether it's running a marathon or playing with your kids or grandkids. These exercises are vital in preventing chronic diseases by enhancing the health and efficiency of your mitochondria. That's why training for aerobic endurance is essential for overall well-being.

Mitochondria, the tiny intracellular organelles, play a crucial role in producing our energy. These cellular 'engines' can burn both glucose and fat, making them essential for our metabolic health. Maintaining healthy mitochondria is vital for the well-being of our brain and for controlling harmful factors like oxidative stress and inflammation. I firmly believe that having healthy mitochondria is integral to overall health, which is why I prioritise long, steady endurance training in Zone 2 to support their well-being.

Zone 2 is a specific intensity level used by coaches and trainers in endurance sports to structure training programmes.

For most training models, Zone 2 remains consistent, involving a speed where you can still maintain a conversation, although it might be slightly strained. This translates to engaging in aerobic activity at a pace that falls somewhere between easy and moderate.

Zone 2 exercise primarily engages slow-twitch muscle fibers, also known as Type I fibers. These fibers are highly aerobic and fatigue-resistant, making them well-suited for sustained, lower-intensity activities such as those associated with Zone 2 training. Slow-twitch fibers rely on oxidative metabolism, utilising oxygen efficiently to generate energy, mainly from fats. Engaging these fibers helps improve endurance, promote fat metabolism, and enhance cardiovascular efficiency.

If we increase our intensity, we start involving more type 2, or 'fast-twitch', muscle fibres. These fibres are less efficient but more powerful and produce more lactate due to their ATP production process. Lactate itself is not harmful and can be recycled as fuel by trained athletes; but when it is combined with hydrogen ions, it turns into lactic acid, causing the acute burning sensation in our muscles during intense efforts.

The efficiency of our mitochondrial "engine" plays a crucial role in how rapidly we can clear lactate from our system, allowing us to sustain greater effort while remaining in Zone 2. If we feel excessive burning during this type of workout, it indicates that we might be pushing too hard, producing more lactate than our body can efficiently eliminate. Striking the right balance in Zone 2 helps optimise endurance training while avoiding unnecessary strain and fatigue.

How Can You Know Your Zone 2 Hr?

The easiest way to know your Zone 2 range is to calculate your maximum heart rate (MHR). MHR is approximately **220 - Your age (220 minus your age)**. This is a very crude way but works well with most of the population. Your Zone 2 will be between 65-75 per cent of that number.

To help individuals gauge their effort level when starting out, I ask my mentees to rely on their Rate of Perceived Exertion (RPE) or the 'talk test'. It's essential to assess how hard they are working and how easy it is for them to speak during exercise. At the top of Zone 2, they should be able to talk, but not particularly interested in holding a full conversation. If they cannot speak in complete sentences at all, they may be pushing into Zone 3, indicating they are going too hard. On the other hand, if they can comfortably converse, they may be in Zone 1, which means the effort is too easy.

The output in Zone 2 can vary significantly based on an individual's fitness level. Hence, using RPE or the talk test is a practical and adaptable approach to ensure the workout remains within the appropriate intensity range.

As we get older, the health of our mitochondria becomes crucial. The aging process often sees a decrease in the number and quality of mitochondria, a significant aspect of aging. The good news is that this decline isn't necessarily irreversible. Mitochondria show remarkable adaptability, especially in response to aerobic exercise, which triggers the creation of new and more efficient mitochondria, a process known as mitochondrial biogenesis. Moreover, exercise helps eliminate dysfunctional mitochondria through mitophagy, a recycling process. Regular engagement in aerobic exercises, particularly in Zone 2, consistently improves mitochondrial health. Remember, the more you use them through consistent exercise, the better you preserve and enhance mitochondrial function, offering substantial benefits as you age.

Zone 2 offers a significant advantage as it is easily accessible, even for individuals who have been sedentary. Depending on your fitness level, a brisk walk or walking uphill can get you into Zone 2. There are various activities to achieve this, such as riding a stationary bicycle at the gym, walking, jogging, running around a track, or swimming laps in the pool. The key is to find an activity that fits your lifestyle, brings enjoyment and allows you to maintain a steady pace that meets the Zone 2 criteria, where you can speak in full sentences, but just barely.

The amount of Zone 2 training you need depends on your individual circumstances. Even two 30-minute sessions per week can provide enormous benefits for those who are new to this type of training. For most people to experience improvements, about 150 minutes per week of Zone 2 exercise is typically the minimum required once you overcome the initial challenges of trying it for the first time. Recognising the exceptional benefits of

Zone 2, it has become a cornerstone of my training plan. Three times a week, I spend about an hour riding my stationary bike at my Zone 2 threshold.

Build Your Vo2 Max – Anaerobic Exercises

Peak aerobic cardiorespiratory fitness, quantified by VO2 max (maximal oxygen consumption), stands as one of the most powerful indicators of longevity. VO2 max represents the maximum rate at which a person can utilise oxygen and is measured during exercise when one reaches their upper limit of effort. The higher the amount of oxygen your body can efficiently use, the greater your VO2 max will be.

Imagine VO2 max as the 'gas mileage' of your body. Just like a car's fuel efficiency, VO2 max represents how well your body utilises oxygen during exercise. The higher your VO2 max, the more 'kilometres per litre' of oxygen your body can efficiently use, allowing you to go farther and perform better in physical activities. It's like having a powerful engine that enables you to keep going at your best for longer periods.

A higher VO2 max indicates that someone can efficiently consume more oxygen to produce ATP, which translates to better performance in activities like riding or running or even running to your gate at the airport with a heavy backpack. During my wildlife photography travels, I have experienced a significant difference, especially when carrying almost a 15 kg backpack filled with my camera equipment. At some point in life, you may cherish the opportunity to take your grandchild to the zoo. If they happen to tire, you will want to be able to carry them on your lap and continue exploring together.

In essence, a higher VO2 max allows you to do more, pushing your physical capabilities to greater levels.

High-Intensity Interval Training (HIIT) is a great way to increase your VO2 max. I would recommend beginners to start doing it once they have done three to four months of aerobic training.

HIIT is usually defined as exercise consisting of repeated bouts of high-intensity work performed above the lactate threshold (a perceived effort of "hard" or greater) or critical speed/power, interspersed by periods of low-intensity exercise or complete rest. There are many ways that definition can be achieved, however, the graph below provides a broad illustration of the concept. The general basis of high-intensity interval training can be described simply as follows –

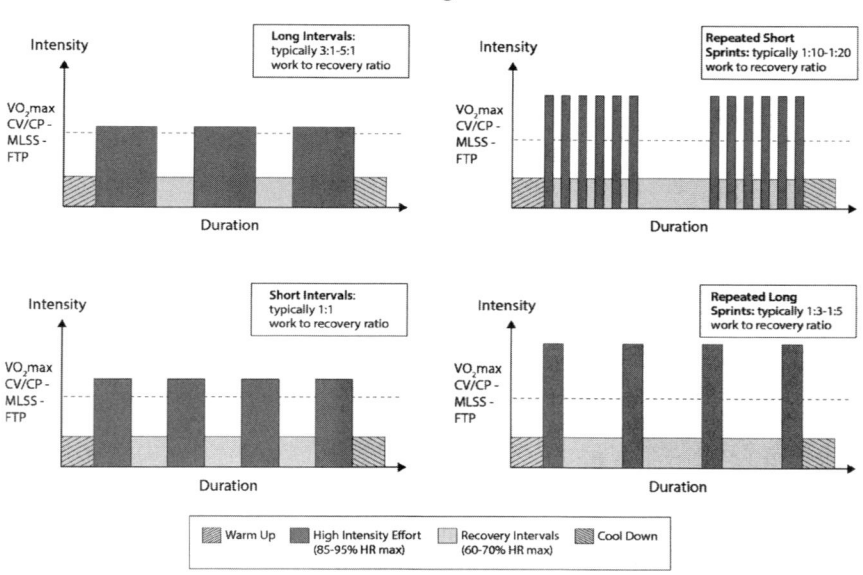

VO_2max - maximal oxygen uptake; CV/CP-critical velocity/critical power; MLSS-maximal lactate steady state; FTP-functional threshold power.

Imagine performing a bout of exercise at an intensity above your lactate threshold, or critical velocity/power. To be clear, this is an exercise intensity that is unsustainable and one at which your brain would eventually force you to lower your intensity, if you were to sustain it for as long as you could. It feels hard, and you know that fatigue would be inevitable at this pace if you were to hold on.

Higher levels of sugar-burning glycolysis are needed generally to sustain the energy demand and lactate accumulates to high levels typically at the point of fatigue. Now, if we took that same high-intensity effort and separate it with pauses that include periods of complete rest or lower levels of active recovery, that glycolytic energy rate is eased so that lactate production is more in check, whilst the cardiovascular strain remains high, and perceived effort, although still high, is reduced and manageable.

A few bodyweight jumps and burpees is not HIIT. In the context of HIIT and the science that underpins it, high intensity means "above 90% VO2 max". To qualify as an effective HIIT session, you need to accumulate around 10 minutes of work at VO2 max. That does not mean the workout needs to be only 10 minutes long, it's more like 20-30 seconds to accumulate 10 minutes of true 'red zone' VO2 maximum intensity work.

Bodyweight exercises, no matter how 'hard' they feel and how out of breath they may leave you, will not hit this intensity of effort. Not even close. The best way to do HIIT can be by running, spinning, rowing etc.

It's important to note that an anaerobic exercise places significant stress on the body, so it's crucial to ensure proper form and technique to minimise the risk of injury. If you are new to anaerobic training, it's advisable to work with a qualified fitness professional who can guide you and design a safe and effective programme tailored to your goals and fitness level.

Build Your Muscles – Strength Training

My initial exposure to the world of fitness began relatively late in life, in 2011 when I was 45. By then, I already bore the characteristics of a stereotypical "Dad bod," slender arms and legs, sagging shoulders and an excess of fat around my waist. The first few weeks at the gym were a humbling experience, filled with a sense of intimidation and embarrassment. The sight of muscular, seasoned gym-goers had me contemplating a hasty retreat. My saviour in this overwhelming situation was my first trainer and neighbour, Rajeev.

Without his guidance and encouragement, I might have succumbed to my insecurities and abandoned my gym journey on the very first day. But his support kept me grounded, providing the motivation I needed to persevere. And indeed, perseverance paid off. After a month of consistent effort, I began to notice a transformation. A change for the better, a glimmer of progress, making all the initial struggles worthwhile.

Strength training, a potent tool for health maintenance, has been consistently validated in numerous studies[10] as a formidable defence against various diseases and the ageing process. Research involving participants up to 98 years of age has demonstrated that strength training can significantly enhance longevity and independence among the elderly. Yet, astonishingly, this powerful health intervention is often overlooked in medical recommendations. Think back to your last doctor's visit. You likely received advice to improve your health; perhaps to cut back on sugar, limit salt intake, incorporate regular walks or lose weight. However, it's probable that strength training was not explicitly mentioned.

This oversight extends to the general public and even to the medical community, with muscles often relegated to the periphery of health discussions. However, the way you care for and strengthen your muscles can profoundly impact your overall health. By underscoring the importance of strength training, we can better equip individuals to improve their health and combat the challenges of disease and ageing.

Properly executed resistance training, resulting in muscle growth, offers a plethora of benefits, acting as a holistic healthcare approach. The realm of health benefits provided by muscular tissue is vast and includes efficient waste processing, blood oxygenation, insulin level regulation, bone-mineral density optimisation, metabolic rate increase, body fat reduction, aerobic capacity enhancement, flexibility improvement and a significant reduction in injury risk. Moreover, it assists in executing daily tasks with less physical stress, wear and tear.

Strength training not only enhances muscle size but also improves their strength, making daily life activities easier and expanding what one can do. It is also associated with improved gastro-intestinal transit time, linked with a reduced risk of colon cancer. Muscle mass is metabolically active, and any decrease with age lowers the resting metabolic rate. Strength training counteracts this, improving resting metabolism, glucose metabolism and insulin sensitivity. Importantly, it helps reverse harmful processes leading to fat storage by promoting glucose uptake into muscle cells and reduces circulating glucose and insulin levels.

Resistance training is also beneficial for body fat reduction, improved lipid profile, reduced resting blood pressure, increased bone mineral density, relief from arthritis and lower back pain alleviation. Moreover, it contributes to enhanced flexibility and overall cardiovascular health.

To summarise, strength training serves as an all-encompassing health improvement mechanism, impacting nearly every aspect of physical well-being and equipping the body to handle life's challenges more effectively.

The prevailing guidelines[11] for physical activity endorse strength exercises for all principal muscle groups — including legs, hips, back, chest, abdomen, shoulders, and arms — at

least two times a week. A single set of 8 to 12 repetitions per workout can be effective, although some studies suggest that two to three sets might yield superior results.

Here are seven key tips to ensure that your strength training remains safe and effective…

- Always allocate five to ten minutes for warming up and cooling down. A simple walk or dynamic stretching can serve as an effective warm-up, while static stretching can effectively cool down your body.
- Prioritise form over weight. Ensuring the correct alignment of your body and smooth execution of each exercise is key. Incorrect form can lead to injuries and impede progress. Many fitness experts recommend starting strength training routines with minimal or no weight, focusing instead on slow, controlled lifts and descents while concentrating on specific muscle groups.
- Maintaining the right tempo is crucial for staying in control and not relying on momentum for strength gains. For instance, take a three-count while lowering a weight, pause, and then take another three-count while lifting it back to the starting position.
- Stay mindful of your breathing during workouts. Exhale when you are working against resistance, such as lifting, pushing, or pulling and inhale when you release.
- Keep your muscles challenged by gradually increasing weight or resistance. The right weight for you will depend on the exercise. Choose a weight that exhausts the target muscle (s) by the last two repetitions (reps) but still allows you to maintain proper form. If you cannot complete the last two reps, you should opt for a lighter weight. If it's too easy to finish, consider adding weight or an extra set of reps to your routine. If you decide to

add weight, ensure that you can still perform all the reps in good form and the targeted muscles feel tired by the last two reps.
- Consistency is key. Aim to work all the major muscles of your body two or three times a week. You could opt for a comprehensive full-body strength workout two or three times a week or divide your strength workout into upper-body and lower-body components. In the latter scenario, ensure you perform each component two or three times a week.
- Allow your muscles time to rest. Strength training induces minor tears in muscle tissue, which are not harmful. Rather, they are crucial for muscle strengthening as they heal. Ensure you give your muscles at least 48 hours to recover before your next strength training session.

Stability And Balance

The world of fitness often places heavy emphasis on strength, endurance and flexibility. While these are undoubtedly important elements in maintaining overall physical health, two other critical components are frequently overlooked: *stability and balance.* These two foundational elements not only enhance performance in any physical activity but are also the key to preventing injuries and promoting long-term health.

Here are some strategies to enhance stability and balance…

1. **Incorporate balance exercises:** Balance can be improved by practising exercises that challenge your stability. This could be as simple as standing on one leg, walking heel to toe, or more complex exercises like yoga and tai chi.
2. **Strengthen your core:** The muscles in your core — including your abdomen, back, and hips — are key to

maintaining stability. Regularly performing exercises like planks, bridges and bird dogs can strengthen these muscles and enhance your stability.
3. **Use exercise tools to challenge stability:** Equipment like balance boards, stability balls and bosu balls can add an extra challenge to your workout and help improve your balance and stability.
4. **Practise functional movements:** Functional exercises mimic movements you do in daily life and often engage multiple muscle groups and joints. These exercises, such as squats, lunges or step-ups, can help improve your balance and stability.
5. **Stay consistent:** Like any fitness endeavour, the key to improve balance and stability lies in consistency. Regularly incorporating these exercises into your routine will yield the best results.

Remember: It's not just about how strong or fast you can go, but also how well you can find your centre and maintain control. Stability and balance are not just foundational aspects of fitness; they are essential elements of a healthy life.

The fitness regimen that I adhere to, and which I believe would be beneficial for most people, involves a mix of strength training, aerobic exercises and high-intensity interval training (HIIT). Specifically, it includes two to three strength training sessions, two to four aerobic workouts, and one HIIT session each week. It's crucial to begin every workout with at least 10 minutes of warm-up to raise the core body temperature. Equally important is to conclude with at least a five-minute cool down period, where focusing on elongated exhalation can activate the parasympathetic nervous system, facilitating relaxation and recovery.

Many of my friends dislike exercising. Disliking exercise isn't some kind of moral failure. It's a common scenario. Many of us, regardless of age or background, have experienced a certain level of resistance to exercise. The thought of running on a treadmill, lifting weights, or joining a yoga class might seem far from appealing.

Unravelling Resistance

First, let's unpack this resistance. It comes from various sources and understanding its roots can help us address it more effectively.

1. **Past experiences:** Negative encounters in past physical activities or gym environments can induce a strong aversion to exercise. If we have been shamed, judged, or made to feel inadequate, we naturally want to avoid repeating such experiences.
2. **Discomfort and pain:** Exercise can sometimes exacerbate pre-existing pain or discomfort, making us reluctant to engage in physical activity. Moreover, the prospect of sweating, panting and pushing our bodies does not appeal to everyone.
3. **Intimidation:** The fitness world can seem intimidating. From highly fit gym-goers to complicated-looking equipment, these aspects can be overwhelming and off-putting for beginners.
4. **Perception of exercise:** If we see exercise as a punishment, a chore, or something we "have to do" for our health, we would likely resist it.
5. **Identity:** Some people feel that the fitness culture simply does not align with their personality or lifestyle. They might not identify as the "sporty type," making it difficult to adopt exercise as a routine.

Transforming Resistance Into Motivation

Once we understand the source of our resistance, we can begin to transform it into motivation. Here are a few strategies...

1. **Choose activities you enjoy:** Exercise does not have to mean running miles or lifting weights. It can include dancing, hiking, swimming or even gardening — anything that gets you moving. When you enjoy the activity, you would be less likely to resist it.
2. **Redefine your goals:** Instead of focusing on losing weight or gaining muscles, consider other benefits of exercise, such as better mood, increased energy or improved sleep. Shifting your goals can make exercise feel more rewarding.
3. **Create a supportive environment:** Surround yourself with positive influences. This could mean finding a workout buddy, hiring a supportive trainer or joining a fitness group with a welcoming and non-judgmental atmosphere.
4. **Start small:** Do not pressure yourself to dive into intense workouts from the start. Begin with small, manageable steps. As your confidence and fitness levels improve, you can gradually increase the intensity and duration of your workouts.
5. **Incorporate mindfulness:** Practise tuning into your body during exercise. Pay attention to how it feels to move, breathe and sweat. This mindful approach can make exercise a more enjoyable and less daunting experience.

Remember: Fitness isn't a one-size-fits-all proposition. It's a personal journey, and the most important thing is to find a path that feels right for you. Like whiskey, exercise can be an acquired taste. Some people love it at first sip, some learn to love it and others just do not enjoy it. And that's okay!

Regardless of the type, the best exercise is the one you enjoy and can incorporate regularly into your lifestyle. Remember, it's not about perfection or competing with others; it's about moving more, improving health and enjoying the journey of fitness. The key is to find a balance and routine that suits your individual needs, preferences, and goals. In the end, every step taken towards a more active lifestyle is a victory worth celebrating.

Pause & Reflect
- How does your body feel during and after different types of movement or exercise?
- Are there specific forms of exercise that you find more enjoyable than others? What could be the reason?
- How does regular movement or exercise impact your mood, energy levels or overall well-being?
- Do you notice any changes in your body's ability or ease in performing daily activities when you are regularly exercising?
- What barriers or challenges do you face in incorporating regular movement or exercise into your lifestyle?
- How do your personal health and fitness goals align with your current movement or exercise habits?
- Do you consider movement or exercise a chore, a punishment or a form of self-care? What could be the reason behind this perception?
- What role does exercise play in your self-image and identity?
- How can you make movement or exercise a more integrated and enjoyable part of your daily routine?
- How does your current environment or social circle support or hinder your ability to engage in regular movement or exercise?

🪶 PAUSE & REFLECT INSIGHTS

2.3 SLEEP, THE SILENT HEALER

"Sleep is the golden chain that ties health and our bodies together."
— **Thomas Dekker**

Throughout our childhood, we have all come across various fairy tales that have left a lasting impact on us. These enchanting stories often carry deeper messages and symbolism, and interestingly, sleep plays a significant role in many of them. Fairy tales such as *Snow White*, *Sleeping Beauty* and *The Princess and the Pea* highlight the importance of sleep, portraying it as a transformative and restorative process.

In *Snow White* and *Sleeping Beauty*, the princesses experience long periods of deep sleep that preserve their beauty and youth. These tales associate the idea of being well-rested with the concept of "beauty sleep". This enduring connection between sleep and beauty continues to captivate our imagination.

Similarly, in the epic *Ramayan,* the character Kumbhakaran, portrayed as a powerful prince, is known for his extended six-month sleep. This serves as a metaphor, emphasising the profound benefits of good sleep in building immunity and leading a healthy, disease-free life.

Sleep, an enigmatic human behaviour, consumes nearly one-third of our lives. During sleep, we refrain from work, gathering food, mating and socialising, seemingly engaging in nothingness for a crucial portion of our existence. The universality of sleep across species suggests its profound importance in life's evolution and preservation.

Within the trinity of balanced diet, exercise and sleep, the latter reigns as a pre-eminent force. Its impact reverberates through various aspects of our well-being, yielding substantial benefits.

It plays a vital role in maintaining our physical and mental health, allowing our bodies to rejuvenate, repair and regenerate. Sleep is a fundamental part of our existence, and its preservation throughout evolution reinforces its essential nature.

Sleep supports weight loss. Sleep helps improve your immune system. Sleep improves cardiovascular health and keeps blood pressure low. Sleep helps in cancer prevention. In fact, this list can keep growing. We are forced to wonder if there are any biological functions that do not benefit from a good night's sleep. Still, we do not give sleep the priority it needs. Our fast-paced life leaves us with little time for restful sleep. Despite knowing that going to bed would be the best thing to do, we prefer to watch one more episode of our favourite show, flip through social media posts, check our emails or have one last drink of the evening with friends. We fear missing out and we want to do more, see more, work more. We sacrifice our sleep in the process which is the most important element for our health.

Sleep deprivation starts at a young age, when children are pulled out of bed for school before their bodies and minds are ready to wake up. Students are pathologically tired when they are forced to get up early every school day. It disrupts their natural sleep-wake rhythm or circadian rhythm.

During my time at Rama Krishna Mission Vidyapith, my school implemented a favourable schedule that prioritised the well-being of students. With school timings from 10 am to 4 pm, we were provided with a more reasonable start time, allowing us to have sufficient sleep. Additionally, the boarding school ensured that all hostel lights were switched off at 9.30 pm, giving us the opportunity to unwind and prepare for a restful night's sleep.

In contrast, it has become increasingly common for schools to adopt early start times, some as early as 6 am. If you peep into a school bus, you will find many children still half asleep, struggling to fully wake up and engage in their day ahead.

When reflecting on the contributions of Thomas Edison, it's natural to think of his remarkable inventions and his reputation for prodigious productivity. However, we often overlook the lasting impact of his relentless work ethic and the implications it had on society's perception of sleep.

Edison's introduction of the light bulb played a significant role in making the notion of working through the night a viable option. As the founder of General Electric, he had a vested interest in promoting the idea that forsaking sleep could provide a competitive advantage. Edison went to great lengths to advocate for the merits of sleeplessness, collaborating with journalists and addressing the public at exhibitions to convey the message that sleep was a mere waste of time.

His hiring practices also reflected this preference for sleep-deprived workers. Edison sought out individuals who demonstrated a willingness to stay up and work for prolonged periods. Newspapers, captivated by his success story, readily disseminated his philosophy. An 1878 edition of the Chicago Tribune detailed Edison's tireless work ethic, emphasising how he remained awake day and night, allowing himself only brief intervals of two or three hours for rejuvenation.

Indian Prime Minister Narendra Modi has become a symbol of tireless dedication and unwavering commitment to his responsibilities. Reports[12] suggest that he devotes long hours to his work, often starting his day in the early hours of the morning and persistently engaging in various activities until late at night.

It is often claimed that he sleeps for less than four hours each day, yet he continues to maintain a demanding schedule with remarkable energy and vibrancy.

It is true that some individuals possess the ability to function on minimal sleep. However, it is important to note that such cases are exceptions rather than the norm. Most people require adequate sleep to ensure optimal cognitive function, physical well-being and overall performance.

Defining Sleep

Sleep is something that everybody intuitively grasps. We know that we need to shut down and 'power off' every night to function well during the day. Yet it's hard to define exactly what sleep is.

The nerdy definition usually goes something like this…

- Sleep is a reversible behavioural state of perceptual disengagement from and unresponsiveness to the environment.
- Sleep is a state of unconsciousness from which a person can be aroused by stimuli.

In other words, **it's a time when our brains and bodies partially 'disconnect' from what's around us.** It's something similar to when you put your phone on aeroplane mode. Your phone still works, but it's not getting any signals, so you cannot make calls, check your email or scroll social media.

Stages Of Sleep

Being asleep does not mean that our brain is completely inactive or "off". In reality, sleep takes us on a fascinating journey through various phases, each characterised by distinct levels of brain activity.

As you surrender to sleep each night, your brain embarks on a roller-coaster ride, transitioning through different stages of sleep. You may not be consciously aware of these processes, but your brain is far from idle. It engages in a multitude of activities, and each sleep stage contributes uniquely to how you will feel and function the following day.

A sleep cycle is a complex and fascinating physiological process that occurs as we sleep. Rather than sleeping in one continuous phase, our sleep is composed of multiple sleep cycles. Each sleep cycle consists of four distinct sleep stages: N1, N2, deep sleep (also known as N3), and Rapid Eye Movement (REM) sleep.

To understand this better, let's follow the story of my mentee, Irfan. He represents an "ideal average" of what a good sleeper might be. He usually goes to sleep at 10 pm and wakes up at 6 am. Throughout the night Irfan's brain and body go through several stages in a cycle. These stages are divided into two main groups:

Rapid eye movement (REM). This is when we dream. Our eyes move quickly back and forth under our closed eyelids, hence the name. REM is linked to body temperature changes caused by circadian rhythms. We spend about 25 per cent of our total sleep time in this phase.

Non-rapid eye movement (NREM). During this part of sleep, there is no rapid eye movement. We spend about 75 per cent of our total sleep time in various NREM phases. During N3 sleep, which makes up about 20-25 per cent of a night for Irfan, brain waves are strong, comprising slow delta waves. We cycle back and forth through the different stages throughout the night, though we tend to get more REM towards the end of our sleep, and most of our deep sleep (stage 3/4) at the beginning.

Let's look at how this unfolds for Irfan!

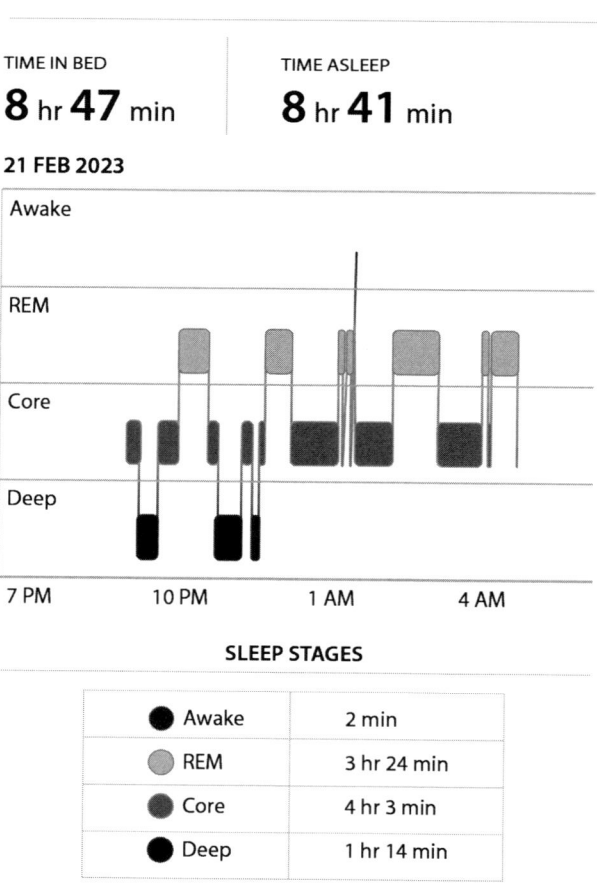

N1: Transitional sleep

As he falls asleep, Irfan drifts into NREM 1, or N1 or Stage 1. In young adults, this stage usually lasts anywhere from 1 to 7 minutes. N1 is an extremely light sleep. If someone were to wake Irfan up, he would not even think he had fallen asleep.

N2: Light sleep

Irfan then enters NREM 2, or N2 or Stage 2, and stays there for about 10 to 25 minutes. During N2, Irfan's muscles relax, and his heart rate and body temperature drop.

N3: Deep or slow-wave sleep

Irfan then enters NREM 3, or N3, which is also known as slow-wave sleep (SWS) because it is characterised by delta wave activity.

N3 is the most restful portion of Irfan's sleep. It starts about 15 to 30 minutes after he falls asleep, and continues throughout the night in progressively shorter episodes. Though it's confusingly named, N3 is actually a combination of two somewhat distinct stages of sleep: Stage 3 and Stage 4. The main difference between these stages is the percentage of slow waves over a 30-second period.

Stage 3 is relatively short, and starts with some slow wave, high-voltage brain activity. Irfan then transitions to Stage 4, and his sleep gets progressively deeper. The first time Irfan enters Stage 4, it lasts for 20 to 40 minutes. He then goes back into Stage 3, and back again into Stage 4 in a series of continuous cycles. Stage 4 gets shorter and shorter over time. Eventually, Irfan will spend the majority of his sleep in Stage 3 and no longer enters the deepest phase of sleep.

Irfan's body is also adapting to this phase of sleep. His metabolic rate slows to about 10 to 30 per cent of his waking needs. His blood pressure also goes down, and his breathing slows significantly. This is when his body will repair tissue. In N3, Irfan is so deeply at rest that it would take an extreme amount of noise to wake him up (think of sounds over 100 decibels, like a jet engine taking off 300 meters away).

If you were able to wake him up at this point, he would feel fatigued and have a mental fogginess that would leave him feeling "off" for anywhere from 30 minutes to an hour. You may have experienced this if someone has woken you from a deep afternoon nap, leaving you feeling disoriented, unsure of your surroundings and questioning what is happening.

REM sleep

REM sleep is characterised by vivid dreams. It's also accompanied by some muscle twitches and of course rapid eye movements.

Irfan does not start dreaming right away. His first cycle of REM sleep kicks off about an hour and a half after he falls asleep. As Irfan sleeps through the night, REM episodes appear more often, and for longer. By the time Irfan wakes up, he's deep in another dream. I often wake up with the dream of another failed Maths exam. REM – rich morning sleep is why you will often remember your dreams if you wake up in the morning and go back to sleep.

Sleep Cycles

Irfan does not just go through each sleep stage, one after the other, and then wake up. Instead, his sleep happens in cycles — he goes through the different stages repeatedly throughout the night.

The first cycle of sleep, from the onset of sleep to the beginning of the first episode of REM, is about 80 to 100 minutes long. After the first cycle, the remaining cycles (all NREM and REM stages together) are about 90 minutes long.

If you have ever heard of the idea that you should sleep in multiples of 90 minutes, this is why: Ideally, you are waking up at the "end" of a cycle (i.e., coming out of REM), rather than struggling awake out of a deeper sleep. The concept of sleeping in multiples of 90 minutes is often recommended, and here is the reason behind it: The goal is to wake up at the "end" of a sleep cycle, preferably after completing a REM phase, rather than abruptly awakening from a deeper sleep stage. While sleep cycles average about 90 minutes, there can be a variation in their cycle length, from 60 to 110 minutes, for different individuals.

It's worth emphasising the importance of this point: **The majority of deep sleep occurs during the first half of the night.** This is a crucial consideration when determining the ideal duration of your nightly sleep. For example, if you only sleep for four hours instead of eight hours, you do not lose 50 per cent of the restorative effects because the initial hour of sleep is especially rejuvenating.

However, this does not imply that you should aim for only four hours of sleep each night. The impact of sleep on restoration is not directly proportional or linearly tied to the number of hours you sleep. Quantity does not necessarily equate to quality.

That being said: **Each sleep stage offers its own unique benefits, and all of them work in harmony. We require all of these stages to achieve optimal well-being and functioning.**

Making Sleep Better
Good sleep pays off. Getting enough sleep makes us better. Sleep plays a critical role in nearly every one of the body's functions. It improves nearly every deep health and recovery metric we might track, ranging from pain to inflammation, to energy, to cardiovascular risk, to our mood.

I experienced severe consequences due to a lack of quality sleep before I fully recognised its significance in maintaining our overall well-being. At that time, I was working with clients across different time zones, and I had notifications enabled on my BlackBerry. Throughout the night, I would receive email notifications from clients in the USA and Europe, prompting me to immediately reach for my phone and respond. My work had become such an addiction that I would impulsively check my phone even without receiving any notifications, fearing that I might have missed something important.

This unhealthy habit took a heavy toll on my health. I would wake up feeling groggy, tired and perpetually sleepy, lacking the energy I needed to tackle the day ahead. It greatly affected my ability to focus and concentrate on my tasks during the daytime. Besides ending up tired and all the other metabolic issues, one of the most powerful effects of sleep deprivation is impaired emotional regulation — or being able to manage our moods and feelings.

When you are sleep-deprived, the impulsive, panicky, and emotional parts of your brain run amok. Although this emotional regulation can seem like a small aspect of our inner world, emotion plays a crucial role in nearly all our behaviour and decision-making. When it stops working, our ability to function goes away with it.

One of the factors contributing to my anger issues could well be my lack of quality sleep. It was only after experiencing these negative effects first-hand that I realised the profound impact of sleep on our physical and mental well-being. I learnt the importance of establishing boundaries and prioritising restful sleep in order to maintain optimal health and productivity. Making positive changes to my sleep habits became essential for regaining my energy, improving my focus and ultimately enhancing my overall quality of life.

Pre-sleep Ritual

A pre-sleep ritual is a set of behaviour that I ask my mentees to follow to improve their chances of good sleep. These helps dial down the level of stimulation of their 'amped up' sympathetic nervous system and activate their 'calm-down', parasympathetic nervous system.

You can choose your own sleep ritual, but here are a few options that I would suggest…

- Dimming the lights.
- Making the room as dark as possible.
- Taking a hot shower or bath.
- Listening to calming music.
- Turning off all stimulating electronics and screens (e.g., video games, TV, social media, computer work, phones).
- Journaling (especially doing a "brain dump", which transfers the day's worries or concerns onto paper that can be dealt with later).
- Cuddling a loved one or pet.
- Deep breathing, muscle relaxation, yoga, tai chi, or other body-calming exercises.
- Using aromatherapy such as lavender.
- Cutting off caffeine and other stimulants 8-10 hours before scheduled bedtime.

Improve Environment Cues

In addition to establishing a basic pre-sleep ritual, it's worth exploring various tools and techniques to create an environment that promotes quality sleep. This can involve adjusting factors such as…

Light levels and quality: Experiment with the brightness and type of lighting in your sleep environment. Some individuals may find dimmer, warmer lights or the use of blackout curtains beneficial, while others may prefer a softer, indirect light source. Find out what works best for you.

Environmental temperature: Find the optimal temperature that allows you to feel comfortable and cosy. Experiment with different settings on your thermostat or try using breathable bedding materials to help regulate your body temperature during the night. In general, our body temperature drops when asleep, so having a cool environment is considered sleep-promoting. However, some folks may find warmth more relaxing, and prefer a heated blanket or warm bath before bed. Again, go with what works for you.

Noise levels: Explore ways to minimise or control noise disturbances in your sleep environment. This could involve using earplugs, a white noise machine, or even gentle background music or nature sounds to create a soothing auditory atmosphere.

Tactile stimulation: Consider the textures and sensations that contribute to your sleep environment. Experiment with different types of bedding, pillows, or mattress firmness to find what feels most comfortable and supportive. Individuals with sensory sensitivities often have heightened responses to fabrics, textures and the pressure or weight of certain objects like pyjamas or blankets. For them, the choice of sheets or pyjama fabric can greatly impact their comfort and sleep quality. The "wrong" type of fabric may cause discomfort or distress, making it crucial to find materials that are soothing and well-suited to their sensory needs.

Remember: There are no rigid rules when it comes to creating a sleep-friendly environment. It's a process of trial and error. Feel free to explore different options and see what works best for you. By adapting and personalising your sleep environment, you can invite your body to embrace a restful and rejuvenating sleep experience.

Improve Biological Cues
Harness the power of your body's natural sleep-promoting mechanisms by working in harmony with them. While you may not be able to alter certain biological factors like your genetic makeup, you can optimise and support other aspects that influence your sleep. In particular, you can focus on amplifying the circadian cues and other zeitgebers that help organise waking and sleeping. These can include…

Establish a consistent sleep-wake schedule: Set a regular bedtime and wake-up time, even on weekends or days off, to align your body's internal clock.

Purposeful light or dark exposure: Expose yourself to natural light during the day, especially in the morning, to signal wakefulness to your body. Note that getting light exposure in the morning after we have hit our lowest body temperature (usually after 4 am) shifts our biological clock earlier. If you are struggling to fall asleep, then try to get light exposure as early as possible in the morning. Dim or avoid bright screens close to bedtime to encourage the release of melatonin, a hormone that promotes sleep.

Adjust your circadian phases: If necessary, gradually shift your sleep schedule by adjusting the timing of your exposure to light and darkness. This can help recalibrate your internal clock to better align with your desired sleep patterns. This can be particularly useful in the case of jet lag. Some people also use it to pre-emptively shift their circadian clock to match a future destination.

Consider your eating and nutrition: Be mindful of how your eating habits and food choices affect your sleep. Avoid heavy meals close to bedtime and limit caffeine and alcohol intake, as they can disrupt sleep. In general, here's what seems to work best for most people...

- Consume moderately sized meals no later than three-four hours before bedtime.
- Eat meals higher in carbohydrates and protein rather than high-fat meals, which seem to make sleep quality worse.

Incorporate physical activity: Regular exercise can contribute to better sleep but aim to finish your workout at least a few hours before bedtime to allow your body time to wind down.

Summary Of Points That Can Help You Improve Your Sleep – Here are some guidelines or suggestions I follow to improve my sleep quality. These are not guaranteed solutions, but they focus on creating better conditions for sleeping and allowing your brain and body to rest. It's not necessary to implement all of these, but the more you incorporate, the better are your chances of a good night's sleep.

1. Avoid alcohol altogether. If necessary, limit yourself to one drink before 6 pm. Remember, alcohol can impair sleep quality, so do not mistake its drowsiness-inducing effects for quality sleep.
2. Refrain from eating within three hours of bedtime, or even longer if possible. It's best to go to bed slightly hungry, although extreme hunger can be distracting.
3. Minimise the use of stimulating electronics at least two hours before bed. If you are having trouble falling asleep, try to avoid screens altogether. If unavoidable, use a setting that reduces the blue light emitted by your device.

4. Avoid engaging in activities that provoke anxiety or stimulation, such as reading work emails or scrolling through social media, for at least an hour before bed. These activities stimulate areas of the brain associated with rumination and worry, hindering sleep.
5. If available, spend time in a sauna, or hot tub, or take a hot bath or shower before bed. The subsequent drop in body temperature, when you enter a cool bed, signals your brain that it's time to sleep.
6. Keep your sleeping environment cool, ideally in the 18-20 degrees centigrade. Use a "cool" mattress or cooling devices for your bed, especially if you and your partner prefer different temperatures.
7. Ensure complete darkness in your bedroom. If necessary, use an eye shade to block out any remaining light. The room should be so dark that you cannot see your hand in front of your face with your eyes open.
8. Allow yourself sufficient time for sleep, known as a sleep opportunity. This means going to bed at least eight hours before you need to wake up, preferably nine hours. Without adequate sleep, the rest of these guidelines may be ineffective.
9. Establish a consistent wake-up time and stick to it, even on weekends. While you can be flexible with your bedtime, prioritise allocating at least eight hours in bed each night.
10. Avoid obsessing over your sleep, especially if you are experiencing difficulties. If you use an alarm clock, position it away from your line of sight to prevent clock-watching. Giving yourself a break from sleep tracking can also alleviate worries about poor sleep scores.

Remember: These suggestions are aimed at creating a conducive sleep environment, but it's important not to overly fixate on sleep. Each individual's sleep needs and patterns may vary, so find what works best for you.

But, What If You Can't Sleep?

Occasionally, despite our diligent attempts, sleep can be disrupted. The intricacies of sleep are vast and multifaceted. As a result, there are numerous factors that can throw us off track or give rise to sleep-related problems. If basic interventions and strategies do not seem to be effective, it may be beneficial to consult a sleep specialist, typically through your general practitioner.

Pause & Reflect

- How would you describe the quality of your sleep on a regular basis?
- Are you aware of the recommended amount of sleep for your age group? How does your current sleep duration align with it?
- What are some factors or habits that may positively or negatively impact your sleep quality?
- How do you prioritise and manage your sleep within your daily routine?
- Reflect on how you feel when you consistently get a good night's sleep versus when you don't. What differences do you notice in your energy levels, mood and overall well-being?
- Are there any specific sleep disorders or issues you have experienced or are currently facing? How have they affected your daily life?

- How do technology and screen time impact your sleep patterns? Are there any adjustments you can make to promote better sleep hygiene?
- Do you have a bedtime routine or rituals that help you relax and prepare for sleep? If not, what are some practices you could incorporate to create a more conducive sleep environment?
- Are there any stressors or worries that tend to keep you awake at night? How do you typically manage or address them?
- Reflect on the importance of sleep in your overall health and well-being. How can you make sleep a higher priority and establish healthy sleep habits?

🖎 PAUSE & REFLECT INSIGHTS

Section 3

Soothing Spring – Cultivating Emotional Health

"Your emotions affect every cell in your body. Mind and body, mental and physical, are intertwined."
— **Thomas Tutko**

As we traverse the intricate maze of life, we frequently find ourselves wrestling with an array of emotions. Fear, anger, loneliness, stress; these are but few of the many challenges that make up our emotional landscape. They shape our perspectives, decisions and relationships. Consequently, understanding and mastering these emotions is a key to fostering personal growth and nurturing meaningful connections with others. This chapter delves into the emotional terrain we navigate throughout our lives and provides insight and tools to better manage these complex feelings.

The journey begins with **The positive power of stress,** a pervasive reality in our modern, fast-paced world. Stress can be a powerful and relentless foe, draining our energy, clouding our judgment and impacting our physical health. But it does not have to be. In this section, I delve into the mechanics of stress, exploring its origins, manifestations and consequences. I offer practical, effective strategies for transforming stress from a looming threat into a manageable aspect of life; not to eliminate it, but to control and channel it into positive avenues.

Next, I tackle the often-overlooked issue of **loneliness** in the chapter **From Isolation to Illumination.** Despite our interconnected world, feelings of isolation and emotional disconnect can strike anyone, at any age. I examine the different faces of loneliness, its roots, its effects, and most importantly, its remedies. This section provides a blueprint for acknowledging and addressing loneliness, with the aim of rekindling connections with oneself and others.

The terrain shifts as we move to a **mid-life crisis** in the chapter **From Mid-life to My Life,** a misunderstood stage often characterised by self-doubt, identity confusion and a sense of mortality. Here, I deconstruct the myths and realities of a mid-life crisis, guiding you through the emotional tumult and providing advice on how to navigate this phase with grace and self-assuredness.

Our journey then takes us to confront one of our deepest fears in **Confronting Death and Celebrating Existence.** This section encourages an open, honest confrontation with our mortality, a subject often shrouded in fear and denial. I explore strategies to face and accept this inevitable reality, using it as a catalyst to live more fully, more mindfully, and with a greater appreciation for life's ephemeral beauty.

In the following section, **From Fury to Freedom,** attention shifts to one of the most potent and potentially destructive emotions: **anger**.Unchecked anger can fracture relationships, escalate conflicts and damage our self-esteem. Here, I explore the roots of anger, offering practical techniques and tools to manage and express it healthily, transforming potential confrontations into opportunities for understanding and growth.

Our final stop, **Dialogue over Discord**, equips you with the communication skills needed to handle delicate, often uncomfortable discussions. Whether it's asserting personal boundaries, addressing workplace conflicts, or navigating personal relationships, this section provides guidance on conducting these conversations with empathy, respect and assertiveness.

Navigating the emotional landscape is a life-long endeavour, but it need not be an overwhelming one. Through this chapter, I aim to provide you with a comprehensive guide to understanding and managing your emotional terrain.

The goal isn't to suppress or eradicate these feelings, but to acknowledge, understand and master them. As you turn each page, embrace the challenge and opportunity to explore, learn and journey through the fascinating world of our emotional landscape.

3.1 THE POSITIVE POWER OF STRESS

"The greatest glory in living lies not in never falling, but in rising every time we fall."

— **Nelson Mandela**

Challenges are an inherent part of our journey. They provide us with opportunities to learn, grow, change and ultimately thrive. However, it's equally important to recognise the significance of our ability to recover from these challenges. The capacity to bounce back and adapt is essential for maintaining our well-being and achieving long-term success.

Here are three important facts to understand…

1. We all experience stress.
2. We all have the capacity to recover from stress.
3. If we recover well, we can thrive.

These three facts are the basis for this chapter.

Understanding Stressors

A stressor is anything that disrupts our state of equilibrium or homeostasis. It can manifest in various forms and affect different areas of our lives.

For example, stressors can be…

- Physical – e.g., poor sleep, illness, injury, dehydration, hunger, etc.
- Mental or Cognitive – e.g., information overload, too many decisions, solving difficult problems, etc.
- Emotional – e.g., painful emotions such as guilt, sadness, anger, etc.
- Social – e.g., conflict with family and friends, loneliness, discrimination, etc.
- Existential or Spiritual – e.g., hopelessness, crises of faith or identity, etc.

- Environmental or What's around us – e.g., temperature, pollution, noise, safety, etc.

Stress is a subjective experience, with its impact differing from one person to another. What acts as a stressor for one might not affect another the same way. Recovery from stress varies, depending on unique coping mechanisms, support systems and individual resilience.

Stress does not always stem from one event or situation. It can accumulate, so the build-up of multiple stressors can compound effects on our well-being. When already under stress, handling additional stressors becomes more challenging.

Each stressor encountered adds to the existing burden. When these pile up, they hinder our coping capabilities. Thus, even minor stressors, when faced simultaneously or consecutively, can escalate stress levels and disrupt our balance.

Take driving in heavy traffic as an example. For some, this might be a mild stressor, an annoyance, that can be handled with little distress. But, introducing more stressors into this scenario increases the overall stress.

Picture being caught in traffic, running late for an important meeting, needing a restroom, and hearing a strange car noise. Each of these stressors might be tolerable alone, but together, they heighten the overall stress. This combination transforms what might be a small annoyance into overwhelming panic and anger. The added stressors intensify reactions, making the traffic seem even more bothersome and heightening frustration.

The years between 2006 and 2009 marked some of the toughest times in my life. That era was riddled with personal losses, struggles and situations that pushed my resilience to its limits. First, I lost my Guru and cherished Granddad. His passing left an indelible mark on my heart, especially witnessing his two-year battle with complications from obesity. Then, a car accident added to my challenges, causing both physical harm and emotional distress.

Concurrently, the massive US recession threatened our business, given our dependency on the North American market. We were on the edge of closing. My eldest son chose a path different from the family's expectations, causing more strain. And as if the situation was not hard enough, my father was diagnosed with throat cancer. Watching him fight the disease drained my spirit.

Amidst all this, I was grappling with a mid-life crisis, often wondering, "Why me?" and seeking my purpose. My emotional turmoil led to violent outbursts and self-harm. Seeing the depths of my distress, my wife enlisted the aid of a counsellor, marking a pivotal moment in my healing journey. Through this book, I have chronicled my transformative process from those bleak days. With therapy and introspection, I slowly overcame my anger, learning healthier coping strategies.

Engaging in therapy showed me the value of relying on others, whether it's friends, family or professionals. It was a monumental step, teaching me the importance of seeking assistance in hard times.

Although remnants of that tough period linger, they stand as a testament to my resilience and my ability to rise from adversity. These experiences moulded me, gifting me a profound sense of gratitude, resilience and empathy.

Pause & Reflect

Where do stressors show up for you in your life? Are there some areas that feel difficult or easier to manage than others? Consider each dimension of deep health:

Physical, mental, emotional, social, existential and environmental. Then ask yourself: What opportunities do I have to build my resilience and recovery capacities in these areas?

The Stress Response

A stressor prompts a stress response. A physiological stress response follows a predictable pattern.

Let's consider the example of an intense workout as a stressor and explore the physiological stress response and its predictable pattern.

Starting in homeostasis: Before the workout, we are in a state of equilibrium and familiarity. Let's say we are entering the gym feeling relaxed after a good meal.

Encounter with a stressor: The intense workout disrupts our homeostasis as we push ourselves physically.

Alarm phase: During the workout, various physiological changes occur as our body responds to the demands and challenges –

- Our body taps into available nutrients, breaking down muscle, liver and bloodstream reserves for fuel.
- Heart rate increases to supply oxygen-rich blood to tissues.
- Breathing becomes faster and deeper.
- Stress hormones like epinephrine and cortisol are released, mobilising stored fuel and activating the immune system in preparation for potential injuries.
- In particularly stressful situations, the fight-or-flight response may kick in, triggered by the sympathetic nervous system. This can result in a burst of energy, nausea or feelings of shakiness.

Immediately After The Workout –

- Fatigue sets in due to metabolic by-products, increased body temperature, temporary depletion of glucose and glycogen in blood, liver and muscles, and a natural slowdown in the muscular and central nervous systems.

- Thirst may result from water loss through sweating and increased respiration.
- The immune system experiences a brief activation followed by a temporary depression for a few hours as the body recovers.
- Micro-damage occurs in muscles and tissues, initiating protein breakdown.
- Inflammatory hormones and cytokines are released to activate the inflammatory pathway, aiding in tissue healing and regeneration.

Recovery And Rebuilding –

Over the next few days, the body undergoes a process of recovery and rebuilding, provided certain conditions are met…

- Adequate sleep and nutrient intake are essential.
- The absence of excessive accumulated stressors.
- No serious illness or health issues hindering the regenerative process.

During This Phase –

- Tissues damaged during the workout are repaired and rebuilt.
- The brain and nervous system adapt to the neurological demands of the exercise, including motor learning and skill development.
- Long-term adaptations occur, such as increased energy transfer efficiency through improved mitochondrial function, enhanced immune system strength, stronger muscles, glycogen replenishment, protein synthesis, reduced inflammation and improved movement efficiency.

New homeostasis or baseline –

As a result of recovery and adaptation, we reach a new state of equilibrium, slightly better than before. This natural pattern of stress followed by recovery promotes growth and resilience over time. By understanding the predictable pattern of the physiological stress response, we can appreciate how the body adapts and improves in response to various stressors, ultimately becoming stronger and more resilient. Stress, regardless of whether it is psychological, mental, emotional, environmental, existential, or physical, follows a similar trajectory in the way it affects us. A stressor and the resulting stress response can have both positive and negative effects.

Consider The Following –
- Are you finding this reading enjoyable?
- Does it feel like a valuable experience that has a purpose or helps you progress towards something you desire?
- Do you feel somewhat capable of meeting the demands of the task?

If your answers are affirmative, even if the task is difficult or challenging, it falls under "good stress" or eustress. If your answers are negative, it falls under "bad stress" or distress. When I read *The Bhagavata Puran* or *The Ramayan* to my Grandmom, the glucose levels would spike in my continuous glucose monitor. Determining whether stress is good or bad also depends on factors such as the duration and intensity of the stress and how you perceive the stressor. Additionally, the ability to recover from stress plays a role.

Good stress, also known as eustress, is characterised by the following…
- It is short-lived, infrequent and quickly resolved, typically lasting only a matter of minutes or hours.

- It can be a part of a positive life experience, contributing to personal growth and fulfilment.
- It motivates and inspires us to take action and overcome challenges.
- It is related to skills or challenges that align with our abilities and interests.
- It helps build resilience and leaves us in a better state than before.

However, it's important to note that even good stress can become overwhelming if experienced excessively or continuously. Say, you enjoy a roller coaster ride or your gym session but if you are asked to do it for eight hours, it becomes bad stress. Bad stress, also known as distress, is characterised by the following…

- It lasts for an extended period, becoming chronic and ongoing.
- It has a negative impact, causing feelings of depression, demoralisation and distress.
- It demotivates and paralyses us, hindering our ability to cope effectively.
- It breaks us down physically, mentally and emotionally, leaving us worse off than before.

The key factor that distinguishes good stress from bad stress is the ability to recover effectively from it. If we cannot adequately recover between stressors due to their frequency, intensity, or compromised recovery mechanisms, repeated exposure to stressors will progressively worsen our well-being.

Recovery includes elements like –
- Regular sleep
- Good nutrition
- Gentle movement
- Fulfilling activity
- Social connections

- Positive emotions
- Time in nature
- Mindfulness

Stress includes elements like –
- Poor nutrition
- Low energy intake
- Intense exercise
- Work stress
- Relationship stress
- Caregiving
- Financial stress
- Loneliness
- Negative stress
- Emotional stress
- Environmental stress
- Alcohol and drug use
- Illness and injury

It's important to find your sweet spot. Everyone has a unique "recovery zone" that determines how well they can recover from stress. Understanding how we recover is essential in finding the optimal balance of stress for each person.

What Can You Do?
Focus On What You Can Control

One exercise that can help you manage your stress, perceptions of control and expectations, is known as the **'Sphere of Control'.**

The Sphere of Control enables you to visually map out those aspects of your life that you have the greatest influence over, as well as those that are beyond your control. This exercise helps you to identify where you should realistically direct your energy to achieve the best outcome.

For example, if you are experiencing sleep issues caused by factors outside your control, such as noisy neighbours, age-related changes in sleep patterns, or the demands of being a new parent, worrying excessively about these factors proves less productive. Instead, you can focus your attention on small daily actions within your control, such as optimising your sleep environment, reducing caffeine intake, practising self-compassion and implementing other beneficial habits. By shifting your focus to actionable steps, you can enhance your sleep quality and overall well-being.

Sphere of Control

NO CONTROL
- Other People's Thoughts & Actions
- The Weather

SOME CONTROL
- Anticipating Daily Challenges
- My Shoe Size

TOTAL CONTROL
- My Actions
- My Mindset
- My Efforts

- My Schedule
- My Home & Work Environment
- My Support Team

- Sudden Traffic Jams
- The Economy
- Natural Disasters

What's Your Stress Load?

Let's use a basic test to find out our stress. This test is based on the **Perceived Stress Scale (PSS)**[13] — the most widely used stress assessment. Remember that this is an exercise for *you* and **NOT** a diagnosis. If you are worried about your well-being, then you should consult a doctor or therapist.

For each question choose from the following alternatives –

0 – never, 1 – almost never, 2 – sometimes, 3 – fairly often, 4 – very often

In the last month,

1. How often have you been upset because of something that happened unexpectedly?
2. How often have you felt that you were unable to control the important things in your life?
3. How often have you felt nervous and stressed?
4. How often have you felt confident about your ability to handle your personal problems?
5. How often have you felt that things were going your way?
6. How often have you found that you could not cope with all the things that you had to do?
7. How often have you been able to control irritations in your life?
8. How often have you felt that you were on top of things?
9. How often have you been angered because of things that happened that were outside of your control?
10. How often have you felt difficulties piling up so high that you could not overcome them?

Figuring Your Pss Score

You can determine your PSS score by following these directions:

First, reverse your scores for questions 4, 5, 7, and 8. On these 4 questions, change the scores to this: 0 = 4, 1 = 3, 2 = 2, 3 = 1, 4 = 0.

Now add up your scores for each item to get a total. My total score is __.

Individual scores on the PSS can range from 0 to 40, with higher scores indicating higher perceived stress.

Scores ranging from 0 – 13 would be considered low stress.

Scores ranging from 14 – 26 would be considered moderate stress.

Scores ranging from 27 – 40 would be considered high perceived stress.

The Perceived Stress Scale is interesting because your perception of what is happening in your life is most important. Consider the idea that two individuals could have the exact same events and experiences in their lives for the past month. Depending on their perception, the total score could put one of those individuals in the low-stress category and the second person in the high-stress category.

Physical Response To Stress

The physical response to stress involves all the body's systems, including the nervous, immune, endocrine, cardiovascular, musculoskeletal and digestive systems. When faced with stress or injury, the body coordinates multiple systems to respond. For example, if you break a leg, your nervous system alerts the brain, the immune system combats potential pathogens, the endocrine system releases stress hormones, the cardiovascular system clots the blood and increases circulation, the digestive system slows down, the reproductive system down-regulates temporarily, and the muscular and skeletal systems adapt and heal. These coordinated efforts aim to address the immediate threat and facilitate recovery.

Of course, while this is all going on, all that adrenaline is probably going to keep you wide awake. But after the ambulance sirens have died down, you are safely in a cast, and you are ready to get some rest, your sleep will likely be affected too. Once a threat recedes, your heart rate and breathing will return to normal, and you will feel calm again. But what happens when the body is subjected constantly to a situation of repeated stress? Imagine the impact on our health, if instead of healing, someone continuously hammered on a broken leg. The problem in today's modern world is "Invisible Stress". It is the stress that we are unaware of, but it's sucking life out of us. Invisible stress quietly does its dirty work beneath your level of awareness. When enough of these silent stressors add up, you face some health issues as a visible stressor.

Some of these could be…

- **Information overload and filter failure**: Many of us have jobs that require us to process huge data in the form of emails, video calls and chat messages. On top of that, we often fill our non-work hours with more electronic material and social media.
- **Noise around us:** Noise from construction in your neighbourhood, barking dogs, etc. are annoying. Some noises are almost universally stressful. For instance, honking cars in a busy street.

- **Emotional labour:** Many of us do jobs that require emotional labour and it's never appreciated – customer care, call centre, nursing, even parenting. It becomes exhausting by the end of the day.
- **Microaggressions:** Microaggressions are small, often subtle, everyday statements or actions that communicate hostile, derogatory and negative attitudes towards someone. Many females suffer physical aggression when they use public transport. These hidden stressors can be so constant that we do not register them. They are a part of the backdrop, woven seamlessly into our 'normal'. Over time, however, as they accumulate, hidden stressors can wear us down — leaving us feeling foggy, listless, tired, bloated and sore.

Stress Management

In this section, I introduce a concept that may be new to you; the idea that reducing stress is not always the ultimate goal. Sometimes, it's about effectively managing stress or even embracing and appreciating it.

Take a moment to ask yourself: *How would it feel to shift your focus from solely reducing stress to effectively managing it or intentionally seeking it out for personal growth? What skills and daily practises would you need to develop to achieve this?*

By exploring these questions, you can open yourself up to new possibilities and approaches for navigating stress in your life. Rather than solely avoiding or minimising stress, you can learn to harness its potential and use it as a catalyst for personal development and positive change.

When was the last time you experienced a challenging situation? Perhaps it was yesterday or earlier this morning. Are you feeling stressed right now? Now, let's imagine a life completely devoid of stress. Picture a life without any worries or concerns, but also without any opportunities to face challenges, undergo personal growth, or be motivated to change.

Stress itself is not inherently negative. Instead, it is our response to stressors that determines whether they have positive or negative effects on us. This response encompasses our perspective on stress, known as our stress mindset, as well as our coping mechanisms, which can either be adaptive or maladaptive. Additionally, it involves our assessment of the demands and resources involved in a stress-inducing situation, also known as our stress appraisal.

Stress Mindset

The way we perceive stress greatly influences our experiences. It shapes our actions, behaviour, and ultimately, the outcome we derive from those experiences. Our mindset regarding stress can be seen as self-fulfilling prophecies, influencing how we feel, think, and act, as well as how our bodies respond. Consider the following two questions –

- *Do you view stressors as damaging, debilitating and disruptive forces?*
- *Do you view stressors as valuable challenges that facilitate learning, growth and improvement?*

Your answer to these questions will impact your emotions, thoughts, actions and even physiological responses. This response can then create a confirmation bias, leading to a feedback loop that reinforces our perspective.

When we believe that stress can be a beneficial asset, we tend to –
- Feel, think, and act in ways that enhance our performance and foster adaptability and resourcefulness.

- Recognise evidence of our resilience, further reinforcing our belief in our capabilities.
- Cultivate deep health and fitness over time, increasing our capacity and resilience for the future.
- Embrace new stressors as opportunities for growth, firmly believing in our ability to rise to the challenge.

On the other hand, when we believe that all stress is harmful, we tend to –

- Feel, think and act in ways that undermine our resilience and make us more susceptible to the negative effects of stress.
- Focus on our negative feelings, finding ample evidence of our perceived failures and distress.
- Develop fear and anxiety about the future, doubting our capacity to cope with upcoming challenges.
- Avoid situations that have the potential to push us and facilitate personal growth.

In 2003, our company seized an outstanding opportunity when a major US enterprise entrusted us with a contract to develop 23 new products. The catch: we had only 90 days. At that moment, the technology to craft the necessary tools and dies was rare, and producing a single tool took extensive time. Crafting 23 distinct parts appeared insurmountable. Faced with these overwhelming odds, I chose to tackle the challenge head-on. Understanding the project's potential impact on our company's trajectory, with the order equating to triple our annual turnover, I recognised its invaluable nature. Consulting experts and diving into current technologies, we introduced vertical machining centres and incorporated 3D modelling.

For the next 40 days, my team and I were subsumed in relentless effort and tension. Our collective drive and tenacity powered us forward. Our hard work bore fruit, resulting in the successful development of all required dies within the given time. Impressively, we presented the initial samples well ahead of the 90-day target.

This endeavour reshaped our company's path. Beyond meeting the contract's demands, it accelerated our growth trajectory. The accomplishment showcased our dedication, unyielding spirit and talent in managing tense situations. Those pivotal, pressure-packed days now stand as a landmark moment in our company's story, elevating us to our current stature. This experience confirmed our capacity to handle, adapt and triumph over challenges, setting the stage for our enduring progress.

Stress Appraisal

Imagine this scenario: You're at the wheel of a car on a rainy day, and as you make a sharp turn, the car starts to skid.

Now, consider the following options –

Option 1: You are a student driver on your first day.

Option 2: You are a highly trained stunt driver.

With this added information, let's revisit the question: Is this situation stressful?

Your answer may differ based on the option you chose. Psychologists term this your stress appraisal of the situation, which involves evaluating two essential factors.

Factor 1: Demands
The demands of a situation encompass elements such as –
Uncertainty: Is the current situation predictable?
Effort: How challenging will this be?
Danger: What is the potential severity of the situation?
Familiarity: Have I encountered a similar situation before?

Factor 2: Resources

Our evaluation of personal resources, or our ability to cope with the situation, includes –

Internal resources: Our knowledge, familiarity and specific skills related to the situation.

External resources: Social support from family, friends, colleagues or the community.

When we believe that our available resources, whether internal or external, cannot meet or exceed the demands of a situation, our stress response is more likely to be characterised as a challenge.

During the 2008 US economic downturn, my business grappled with an intense crisis. The pre-existing company challenges paired with the strain of the downturn created a perfect storm. A notable product of ours faced field failure and recall, while steel prices, our primary raw material, soared. The US dollar's depreciation against the Indian rupee meant that I faced losses for every shipment. If this trend had persisted for six more months, my company might have met its end.

Recognising the dire situation, I decided to terminate our annual contract with our largest customer prematurely. But then, the 2008 recession hit, reducing our order book to nothing, primarily because most of our clientele was US-based. Faced with such critical conditions, I discerned I had around six months of funds to sustain the business.

Determinedly, I scoured for business opportunities outside of the US. Within four months, opportunities in Australia and Germany emerged. This shift allowed us to broaden our customer base and transact in diverse currencies, propelling us into a growth phase for the business.

The 2008 economic downturn pushed me into a pivotal stress evaluation for my business. The simultaneous emergence of several obstacles could have easily been paralysing. However, by critically evaluating our position, I took steps such as cancelling contracts and seeking alternative revenue streams.

This evaluation pushed me to diversify, to reduce reliance on a single market or currency. This perspective shift opened doors in different countries, despite the complexities and demands these new markets posed.

Adopting a challenge-driven mindset rather than seeing stress as an insurmountable barrier was transformative. It underscored the demands but also highlighted my capacities to counter them. By leaning into available resources and industry network, I transitioned from seeing the scenario as a roadblock to view it as brimming with potential. Through this appraisal, decisions were made that not only helped navigate the crisis but set the company on a path of diversification and growth. Presently, our German clientele forms our largest business segment. Transacting across multiple countries and currencies ensures our resilience against economic downturns or currency fluctuations.

Stressful Experiences Can Be Productive Opportunities For Growth, As Well As Long-Term Well-Being And Performance.

This forms the foundation for reassessing stress, which involves reconsidering and reinterpreting situations from various angles.

The process of stress reappraisal encourages us to make three significant shifts in our outlook:

- Viewing stress responses as functional and adaptive, rather than indicators of a problem.
- Recognising that stressful situations can offer valuable opportunities, rather than being inherently harmful.
- Acknowledging that it's not always necessary to reduce stress; we have the ability to modify our response instead.

In fact, when we learn to reframe or re-evaluate our stress responses, we tend to have stronger stress responses than those using avoidance-based threat responses. But those responses also drop away faster once the challenge has been met — meaning that we have more efficiently and effectively dealt with the situation. Earlier in the year, I read the book, *The Comfort Crisis* by Michael Easter[14].

Facing a turning point in his life after struggles with alcohol, Michael finally decided to quit drinking and choose the arduous path of self-growth. His quest for health took him across the world, from Bhutan to the Arctic. It also became the basis for his book, *The Comfort Crisis,* where he explores how "intelligent discomfort"— i.e., purposely seeking out certain kinds of stress in order to grow, has been a part of our evolutionary history, and something that might help ease our modern minds and bodies.

When he journeyed to Alaska, it required hopping between five or six planes, each progressively smaller than the last. The initial leg of the trip was from Las Vegas to Seattle, where he had a stopover. He genuinely disliked flying on such planes. The seating area was cramped, the onboard entertainment lacked quality, the coffee tasted off, and the bathroom was tiny. To him, it felt like the epitome of discomfort.

However, after spending a month in Alaska's freezing conditions, Michael's perspective shifted dramatically. In Alaska, basic necessities like using the restroom became a challenge due to the ever-present threat of grizzly bears. There were no conventional toilets. To fetch water, one had to trek down to a stream. With limited food supplies, hunger was a constant companion. He consumed fewer calories than he burned, leading to weight loss and an obsession with food. All these experiences were stark reminders of the genuine obstacles our ancestors might have faced.

On his return journey, the plane ride from Seattle to Las Vegas felt like a luxury. Suddenly, the same seat that he had found cramped seemed extraordinarily comfortable. Having been disconnected for a month, even the most mundane movies felt entertaining. The aeroplane bathroom, with its hot water, felt like a marvel, especially considering that he was tens of thousands of feet in the air.

This experience underscored a crucial lesson: **often, our perception of stress and discomfort is shaped by our experiences and can quickly change based on circumstances.** When we constantly seek the easiest path and gravitate towards the next convenient option, it may not necessarily lead to personal growth and fulfilment. Research[15] has shed light on a fascinating concept known as "toughening," which explores the relationship between challenges and our well-being. Surprisingly, both individuals who have faced an excessive number of hardships and those who have experienced no challenges at all tend to exhibit poor mental health outcome.

However, there exists a sweet spot in this dynamic, represented by a U-shaped curve. The key message here is not to recklessly pursue discomfort for its own sake. Becoming a better boxer, for example, does not solely entail subjecting oneself to constant punches to the face. Rather, the journey toward improvement may involve occasional setbacks and challenges that contribute to growth. It is crucial to approach discomfort strategically and not merely expose us to unnecessary harm.

The key lies in striking a balance, recognising that moderate levels of challenge and discomfort can propel us forward. By pushing ourselves beyond familiar boundaries, we open ourselves up to new experiences, opportunities for learning and the development of valuable life skills.

Ultimately, life's most rewarding moments often stem from the willingness to tackle difficult tasks and endure temporary discomfort.

We Can Use Stress To Our Advantage.
We can think of stress as a tool that allows us to push ourselves and achieve our goals.

Pause & Reflect
- Can you think of a time when stress led you to perform better or achieve a personal goal?
- How do you typically respond to stress? Do you view it as a threat or as a challenge?
- How has your understanding or perspective of stress changed over time?
- Can you identify any positive changes or personal growth that came because of a stressful experience?
- Can you think of any strategies you have developed to cope with stress more effectively?
- How has stress influenced your decision-making or problem-solving abilities?
- Have you ever sought professional help, such as therapy, to manage stress? If so, how has that experience impacted your perspective on stress?
- Can you recall any instances where stress motivated you to learn a new skill or improve an existing one?
- Do you believe that some level of stress is necessary for personal growth and development? Why or why not?
- In your life, how can you turn stress from something negative into a positive driving force for change and growth?

🌿 PAUSE & REFLECT INSIGHTS

3.2 FROM ISOLATION TO ILLUMINATION

"Loneliness and the feeling of being unwanted is the most terrible poverty."

— **Mother Teresa**

It's 3 am and I am writing this chapter from a hotel in the heart of Frankfurt. The silence is overwhelming, but I stay awake, fighting jet lag to remain in my Indian time zone. This work trip covers four countries in five days, a hectic schedule I once approached with excitement and energy. This time, I had to gather motivation to start this journey, seeing it more as a duty to my business.

I recognise now that I do not want to travel by myself. During my stay, I deeply missed my wife. As the years go by and we journey together, an evident truth emerges: we depend on each other more and more. We have forged a strong bond that offers us comfort and peace. Yet, a challenging reality hangs over us; one day, one of us will leave before the other. The idea of facing a future without my wife or her life without me fills my heart with sorrow. Such is the tough reality we all face.

It has been over 15 years since I lost both my grandfathers. I watched both my grandmas navigate this phase of life. What caught my attention was their journey of acceptance. It presented the most challenging obstacle, yet it formed the bedrock of their resilience and strength. They faced the truth of their loss, allowing grief and healing to take place. Through acceptance, they summoned the courage to move forward without their partners, meeting challenges with unyielding resolve. Their capacity to adjust and stand firm amid adversity showed me the depth of acceptance and its transformative influence on the soul.

One useful strategy to combat loneliness is to build a nurturing environment with the presence of family. Family members offer a feeling of belonging, empathy and companionship, lessening the sense of isolation. Having loved ones around brings warmth and connection, offering emotional support in lonely moments. Doing activities together, sharing meals and delving into deep talks can create a bond and diminish feelings of loneliness. After my grandfather passed on, grandma always lived with company, and her house remained full, providing her with mental fortitude.

But we just do not become lonely when we lose our partner. In today's fast-paced and digitally connected world, it may seem paradoxical that loneliness is on the rise. Loneliness has become a prevalent issue affecting people of all ages and backgrounds. Loneliness is not merely a feeling of being alone; it is a deep sense of social isolation and disconnection that can have detrimental effects on one's mental, emotional and physical well-being.

In the past few years, my Dad witnessed the loss of nearly all his friends to age-related diseases. These friends, who filled his days with shared memories and laughter, were no longer there. Suddenly, Dad faced a deep sense of loneliness. The familiar phone calls, WhatsApp messages, and shared moments disappeared, creating a gap in his daily life. His once active social circle shrank, and Dad sought ways to address the lingering emptiness.

In his search for companionship, he discovered an organisation in Mumbai. This organisation consisted of a group of senior citizens actively engaged in charity work, events, annual holiday tours, both domestic and international, tailored for their members. My parents joined, appreciating the arrangements and the company of fellow seniors. They found a renewed sense of community and conversation.

Community groups have a vital role in countering loneliness, offering a feeling of belonging, backing and social engagement. Such groups unite people with shared interests, experiences or objectives, paving the way for lasting connections and friendships. Whether a hobby club, walking group, book circle or volunteer body, these assemblies offer avenues for individuals with similar inclinations to connect. They often act as a pillar of support, granting a comfortable environment for members to express thoughts, worries and shared stories. As my parents discovered, active involvement in these groups help in forging bonds, building valuable friendships and offsetting the effects of loneliness.

Loneliness from migration is a heartfelt experience that many people endure when they depart their known environments to start anew in a foreign place. The distance from family, friends and familiar settings can evoke intense feelings of isolation and a yearning for connection. Language obstacles, cultural disparities and efforts to fit into a new society amplify this loneliness. Lacking a support system and the task of forging relationships in a new setting can heighten the emotional strain. When I moved to Faridabad from the comfort of my home in Purulia, the initial years were challenging not just due to adapting to a new locale but also because of the absence of any familiar faces.

In modern society, children often migrate overseas for education or career prospects, leaving their parents to contend with an empty nest. This notable shift can induce feelings of loneliness and affect parents' mental well-being. A close friend of mine transformed his own loneliness into a golden opportunity for bonding and sharing cherished moments. He and his wife live in Kolkata, while their offspring have made homes in the USA. When his wife embarked on a 47-day visit to be with their children, my friend faced the prospect of solitude, especially during evenings after work. He then hatched a plan to turn his alone time into an enriching experience.

He chose to invite old friends, schoolmates, former customers and even extended family to his home for dinner. Welcoming a broad spectrum of acquaintances with open arms, he discovered that, out of those 47 days, guests accompanied him on 40 evenings. These gatherings afforded him refreshing conversations and deepened relationships. Every night presented new discussions, diverse viewpoints and an array of insights from his varied guests.

What seemed like an impending phase of isolation became a boon for him. Instead of fixating on his wife's absence, he seized the chance to interact with many, unveiling connections that might have otherwise stayed dormant. Through these communal moments, he grew enriched by the narratives, wisdom and distinct tales of those he hosted. His proactive stance serves as a guiding light for individuals facing comparable circumstances.

It underscores how moments of loneliness can morph into valuable and fulfilling encounters by connecting with others, welcoming fresh relationships and celebrating the rich tapestry of human narratives. Loneliness is a subjective experience, and individuals may have different thresholds for feeling lonely. What may cause loneliness in one person may not have the same effect on another. **It's also worth highlighting that loneliness is not solely dependent on being alone.** People can feel lonely even when surrounded by others if they lack meaningful connections or a sense of belonging.

The prevalent "epidemic" of loneliness in today's society extends beyond the elderly, contrary to common belief. Surprisingly, a 2018 survey[16] conducted by the UK's Office for National Statistics revealed that young adults were the age group most likely to report experiencing feelings of loneliness. Within this millennial generation, it is often assumed that social media bears responsibility for this phenomenon. However, is social media truly the root cause of millennial loneliness, or is it merely a manifestation of deeper societal issues?

Undoubtedly, social media plays a role in exacerbating feelings of loneliness, as evident in the contemporary term "FOMO" (Fear Of Missing Out). A 2012 survey[17] highlighted that nearly three out of four young adults experienced FOMO, often triggered by witnessing the seemingly glamorous lives portrayed in other people's social media posts. Multiple studies[18] support the notion that social media can significantly impact our emotions. Facebook itself conducted an experiment[19] in 2014, demonstrating that the emotions expressed in posts can influence users' own emotional states, creating a ripple effect within vast social networks.

However, before we rush to condemn this new technological landscape, let us reflect on the lessons of history. Similar concerns were raised about the social implications of the telephone when it was first introduced. Some feared it would foster laziness and discourage face-to-face interactions. Yet, it became apparent that the telephone offered numerous benefits, particularly for isolated individuals who could now easily stay connected with others.

Ultimately, the impact of social media depends on how it is utilised and the broader context of an individual's life. Research suggests that social media use can indeed amplify feelings of loneliness, but only when it supplants offline activities.[20] If there remains a bridge between online interactions and "real-life" connections, social media does not pose any harm. The problem arises when online engagement replaces meaningful offline engagement. Perhaps social media is neither the cause nor a symptom of millennial loneliness.

It is a tool that can yield either positive or negative effects, contingent upon its integration into a person's overall lifestyle. Undeniably, it can exacerbate feelings of isolation for some individuals. Yet, it also has the potential to bring people together, foster genuine connections and facilitate real-life interactions. When harnessed effectively, social media can benefit not only millennial; but also, other demographic groups significantly impacted by loneliness, such as older individuals. It has the capacity to serve as a positive force, bridging gaps in social connection and combating isolation in various age cohorts.

The Consequences Of Loneliness

Butter, sugar and cream are essential ingredients in the diet of the Haredim, a strict Judaic community comprising around 12 per cent of Israel's population. It is unsurprising that the Haredim are seven times more prone to obesity compared to their other Israeli counterparts. Furthermore, they tend to have significantly lower incomes, with over 54 per cent living below the poverty line.

One might assume that these factors contribute to a lower life expectancy among the Haredim. However, the reality is quite the opposite. Despite their socio-economic challenges, the Haredim have a longer life expectancy. Experts attribute this phenomenon to the strength of their close-knit community. The Haredim pray, celebrate and work together. They provide support in various forms, including childcare assistance, financial aid and general advice.

The link between community and longevity is established. Consequently, it should come as no surprise that the current crisis of loneliness is taking a physical toll on individuals. Loneliness has direct implications for health and well-being. Recall a time when you felt lonely. It is likely that the experience felt subdued and quiet rather than stressful. Nevertheless, your body still produced the same stress hormones associated with the "fight or flight" response triggered during moments of threat. Consequently, your cholesterol, blood pressure and cortisol levels increased more rapidly than if you had felt supported and connected.

Over time, these fluctuations in blood pressure and cholesterol levels have lasting effects on the body. They activate stress responses in the brain and lead to persistent inflammation. When the body is in a state of inflammation, the immune system becomes overworked, leaving individuals more susceptible to various illnesses.

Unsurprisingly, studies indicate that lonely individuals are 32 per cent more likely to experience a stroke, 29 per cent more prone to heart disease and 64 per cent more at risk of developing clinical dementia.[21]

Loneliness is not merely an unpleasant feeling; it can have severe consequences on both mental and physical health. Chronic loneliness has been associated with higher rates of depression, anxiety and increased risk of developing mental health disorders. Additionally, loneliness can weaken the immune system, increase the risk of cardiovascular diseases and impair cognitive function. It is crucial to recognise the profound impact loneliness can have on overall well-being and take proactive steps to combat it.

Tools To Overcome Loneliness

Cultivate self-awareness: Understanding and acknowledging your feelings of loneliness is the first step towards overcoming it. Take time for self-reflection and identify the underlying causes of your loneliness. Reflect on your needs, values and aspirations to gain insight into the type of connections that would be meaningful for you. A good example of how to tackle loneliness is Frida Kahlo, the renowned Mexican artist.

In the book, *Frida: A Biography of Frida Kahlo*[22] by Hayden Herrera, Kahlo's personal journey and struggles, including her battles with physical and emotional pain, are explored. Kahlo's life was marked by periods of intense isolation and loneliness due to her health issues and turbulent relationships. By utilising artistic expression, journaling, and self-reflection, Kahlo harnessed self-awareness as a powerful tool to confront and address her feelings of loneliness. Her artistic and personal journey serves as an inspiring example of how self-awareness can be employed to navigate and overcome the challenges of isolation and emotional distress.

Build a supportive social network: Developing and nurturing strong social connections is a key to combating loneliness. Join social or interest-based groups, clubs, or organisations that align with your passions. Engage in activities that provide opportunities for interaction and shared experiences. Take the initiative to reach out to friends, family and colleagues, and invest time in building and maintaining relationships.

Michelle Obama, the former First Lady of the United States, in her book, *Becoming*[23] shares her personal experiences and insights, including the significance of social connections to combat loneliness. Through her personal stories and reflections, she encourages individuals to actively seek and nurture connections, engage in community activities and embrace empathy and vulnerability as tools for building strong and meaningful relationships.

Embrace technology mindfully: While technology can contribute to feelings of isolation, it can also be a powerful tool for connection when used mindfully. Utilise social media platforms, online communities and forums to find like-minded individuals and engage in conversations. However, be mindful of the potential pitfalls of excessive screen time and ensure that your online interactions do not replace meaningful face-to-face interactions. There are many books and articles by renowned social psychologists and even tech czars like Mark Zuckerberg or Steve Jobs[24] which caution us to approach technology mindfully and consciously to combat loneliness.

Volunteer and engage in community service: Engaging in acts of kindness and volunteering not only benefits others but also provides an avenue for social interaction. Seek out local organisations or community initiatives that resonate with your values and contribute your time and skills. Volunteering exposes you to diverse perspectives and allows you to form connections with individuals who share similar passions and values.

The late Diana, Princess of Wales's dedication to volunteer work and community service not only made a significant impact on the lives of others but also served as a means for her to combat loneliness. By immersing herself in philanthropic endeavours, she found purpose, formed connections, and created a sense of community, ultimately contributing to her own well-being and a sense of fulfilment.

Practise active listening: Loneliness often stems from a lack of meaningful communication and understanding. Practise active listening when engaging in conversations with others. Show genuine interest, ask open-ended questions and provide empathetic responses. By demonstrating your willingness to listen and understand, you create an environment conducive to building deeper connections. American media mogul, talk show host and philanthropist, Oprah Winfrey, emphasises many times in her shows on how active listening serves as a reminder of its transformative power in combating loneliness.

Seek professional help: If loneliness persists despite your best efforts, seeking professional help can be immensely beneficial. Mental health professionals can provide support, guidance and coping strategies to navigate through feelings of isolation. They can help address underlying mental health conditions and provide tools to develop resilience and build stronger social connections.

Practise gratitude and positive thinking: Cultivating a positive mindset and practising gratitude can help combat loneliness. Take time each day to reflect on things you are grateful for, whether it's the presence of a supportive friend, a beautiful sunset, or a personal accomplishment. By shifting your focus to the positive aspects of your life, you can enhance your overall well-being and attract more positive experiences and relationships.

Step outside your comfort zone: Overcoming loneliness often requires stepping outside of your comfort zone. Challenge yourself to try new activities, attend social events alone, or initiate conversations with strangers. Pushing past your fears and embracing new experiences can open doors to unexpected connections and opportunities for growth. Brené Brown,[25] a well-known research professor and author, has spoken extensively about the importance of stepping outside our comfort zones to combat loneliness and cultivate a sense of belonging. Brown believes that embracing our true selves, even if it feels uncomfortable or vulnerable, is the key to finding genuine belonging and combating the sense of isolation that loneliness can bring.

Loneliness is a pervasive issue that can have detrimental effects on our mental, emotional and physical well-being. However, it is not an insurmountable challenge. By employing the tools and strategies discussed here, individuals can take proactive steps to combat loneliness and foster meaningful connections.

Pause & Reflect

- Do you feel lonely? How does loneliness manifest in your life, and what are some of the underlying factors contributing to those feelings?
- Examine the quality of your relationships. Are they nourishing and fulfilling, or do you often feel disconnected, unheard or unseen?
- Do you nurture a healthy relationship with yourself, practising self-compassion and self-care? Are you comfortable being alone with your thoughts and emotions?
- What were the key elements that made you feel that way, and how can you incorporate more of those elements into your life?
- Consider the different types of loneliness, such as social, emotional or existential.
- Which type resonates with you the most, and what steps can you take to address that specific type of loneliness?
- How do technology and social media impact your experience of loneliness?
- Are there opportunities to cultivate new connections or strengthen existing ones to alleviate feelings of loneliness?

🪶 PAUSE & REFLECT INSIGHTS

3.3 FROM MID-LIFE TO MY LIFE

"Thoroughly unprepared, we take the step into the afternoon of life. Worse still, we take this step with the false presupposition that our truths and our ideals will serve us as hitherto. But we cannot live the afternoon of life according to the program of life's morning, for what was great in the morning will be little at evening and what in the morning was true, at evening will have become a lie."

— **Carl Jung**

During my period of being grounded at home following surgery and going through rehabilitation, I experienced a profound sense of dissatisfaction and introspection. Despite having built a successful and profitable enterprise and having my family around me, I had a sudden realisation that my life had been consumed by my business. The restrictions imposed by my physical condition allowed me the space to reflect on my life, leading me to recognise the significant voids that existed.

Up until that point, my life had revolved entirely around my enterprise. While I had achieved financial success and had the privilege of travelling extensively, it dawned on me that I had never truly experienced the joys of being a tourist. My life lacked meaningful hobbies or skills beyond the realm of running my business. Moreover, my social circle had dwindled to the point of non-existence. In essence, I had failed to fully embrace the beauty that the world had to offer and had neglected the love and companionship of my family and friends.

The realisation of my own mortality hit me with great force. I became acutely aware that my time on earth was finite and that I had been squandering it on a single pursuit. It was a sobering thought that if the car accident I witnessed had involved me instead of the vehicle ahead, my life would have abruptly ended.

This wake-up call served as a catalyst for a profound transformation in my perspective. I felt an overwhelming urgency to rectify the imbalances in my life and to seize the opportunities that lay before me. I yearned to fully immerse myself in the experiences that I had neglected for far too long.

In 1965, Elliot Jaques,[26] a prominent social scientist and psychoanalyst, made an intriguing observation while studying the lives of famous individuals and working with his patients. He noticed that middle age often marked a transformative period in their lives. For instance, the great Italian poet, Dante experienced a metaphorical state of being "lost in a dark woods" at the age of 35, just before he embarked on writing *The Divine Comedy*. Similarly, renowned Italian artist, Michelangelo painted very little between the ages of 40 and 55. Recognising the significance of middle age for both extraordinary and ordinary individuals, Jaques penned an influential essay titled *Death and the Mid-Life Crisis,* which sparked the widespread use of the term "mid-life crisis".

Today, the characteristics of a mid-life crisis are familiar to most of us. Not everyone goes to extremes of say buying a motorcycle, changing careers, or getting a divorce, but most do experience a newfound sense of dissatisfaction around the age of 40. Why does this happen? As we reach middle age, we are often confronted with harsh realities. It becomes necessary to acknowledge that many of our childhood and adolescent dreams may never materialise. We must come to terms with our lives as they truly are and grapple with the fact that disappointment and boredom are sometimes unavoidable.

Beyond these gradual disappointments, a more profound realisation awaits us: middle age is when many people truly grasp their own mortality. While we intellectually understand the inevitability of death even when we are young, the physical signs of ageing, such as backaches, wrinkles and health concerns, make our mortality feel more tangible and urgent. The notion of mid-life dissatisfaction is not mere speculation; substantial research supports this observation.

In 2008, economists David Blanchflower and Andrew Oswald conducted a study on lifetime well-being and found that happiness levels tend to follow a U-shaped curve throughout our lives.[27] We start out relatively happy, experience a period of increased dissatisfaction in middle age, and then gradually regain happiness in our later years.

I, once engrossed in the routine of business, was driven by the desire for a richer and more fulfilling life. This led to a transformative journey from being a hurried businessman to an eager traveller, exploring the different corners of India, the wildlife of Africa, the scenic beauty of Australia and New Zealand, and the cultural history of Europe. Each trip was more than a vacation; it was a path to self-discovery and personal growth.

Parallel to these voyages, I dived into diverse hobbies, ranging from music and painting to culinary arts, finding both self-expression and joy. I stepped out of my comfort zone and made efforts to reconnect with old friends, facilitated by social media platforms like Facebook and Orkut. The path was not always smooth; it demanded introspection, re-evaluation and the re-establishment of boundaries within my business. But this deliberate transformation led to a holistic understanding of life's priorities and a realisation that success is as much about personal experiences and relationships as it is about professional achievements.

The Feeling Of Missing Out Is Inevitable In A World Full Of Divergent Values.

The trek to Mt Everest base camp you dreamt of, the motorcycle trip to Ladakh you wanted to take, the home you want to build and retire in the hills... suddenly you realise that these dreams may never be fulfilled. This realisation can be disheartening, causing us to reflect on the decisions that have shaped our current path.

Fortunately, this process is not inevitable, and there are philosophical insights that can help make mid-life easier to navigate. Philosopher Friedrich Nietzsche emphasised the importance of finding a sense of purpose and meaning in life.[28] By discovering our "why" and pursuing meaningful goals, we can better cope with the challenges of mid-life. It is important to acknowledge that this feeling of missing out is a natural consequence of living in a world with diverse values and possibilities. Even if we are generally content with our lives, it is human nature to look back with a sense of longing and ponder the alternate paths we could have taken.

Consider This Perspective –

In a single lifetime, we are bound to confront difficult decisions, where choosing one path means forgoing another. Should we pursue a career in music or law? Should we embrace a career path or dedicate ourselves to being a stay-at-home parent? Should we embark on a new relationship or rekindle an old one?

These choices are undoubtedly challenging, as they require us to make trade-offs. Devoting ourselves entirely to becoming a doctor, for example, may mean sacrificing the opportunity to pursue a legal career. Even if we believe we have made the right choices, it is only natural to wonder about the roads not taken.

The world is replete with valuable experiences and worthwhile paths, many of which are fundamentally different from one another. In philosophical terms, these choices are often incommensurable. In other words, they are not easily compared or measured against one another.

Remember the famous dialogue from the hit movie, *Yeh Jawaani Hai Deewaani*[29]: *"Jitna bhi try karo Bunny, life mein kuch na kuch toh chutega hi, toh jahan hain wahin ka maza lete hain."*

THIS SCENE! THIS DIALOGUE! JUST NEVER GETS OLD!

Practising Gratitude And Mindfulness Can Also Be Valuable Tools For Coping With Mid-Life Challenges

Taking the time to appreciate the present moment and cultivating gratitude for what we have, can shift our focus from what we lack to what brings us joy. Engaging in mindfulness practices, such as meditation or journaling, helps us develop a deeper understanding of ourselves and our desires, enabling us to make more intentional choices.

As I reflect upon my life before the car crash, I find myself questioning whether I would want to change anything. Surprisingly, the answer is likely no. During that time, my unwavering focus and priority were to build a successful career, ensure financial stability for my family and provide the best possible life for my children. It was through this singular dedication that I achieved success.

Now in the stage of life I find myself in, I can bask in the fruits of my labour and enjoy the rewards alongside my beloved family. As I embarked on this journey, there were sacrifices to be made along the way. Time and energy were invested wholeheartedly into my professional pursuits, leaving little room for extraneous endeavours. Hobbies were set aside, personal ambitions took a back seat, and my social circle gradually diminished. There was not enough time to spend with my sons. The path I had chosen demanded undivided attention and an unwavering commitment.

There Are Good Reasons Not To Regret So-Called Mistaken Decisions

The sacrifices I made were not in vain. Through my single-minded devotion and perseverance, I witnessed the gradual blossoming of success. The seeds I sowed in my career took root, steadily growing into a flourishing enterprise.

And now, as I stand in this stage of life, I find myself able to revel in the rewards of my hard work. My sons surround me, their presence a constant reminder of the love and joy that permeate our lives.

It is essential to recognise that a mid-life crisis can also be an opportunity for growth and self-discovery. Many individuals have used this phase to explore new passions, re-invent themselves professionally or strengthen their relationships. By embracing change and facing the discomfort head-on, we can emerge from the mid-life crisis with a renewed sense of purpose and fulfilment.

Philosophy Can Help Us Deal With Death

This stage of life marks a significant turning point for many individuals, as we often witness the inevitable passing away of our parents or grandparents. It is during this time that we are confronted with the reality of mortality and the impermanence of life. As children, we often view our parents and grandparents as invincible figures who will always be there to provide guidance, support and unconditional love. However, as we reach middle age, the circle of life reveals itself, and we come face to face with the fragility of existence.

I lost my Grandfather at the peak of *'the mid-life crisis'* period I was going through. Babuji, as I used to call him, was my Guru, my guide, my light. The person I was closest to in my life. And seeing him suffer with his obesity and illness and ultimately death was a depressing phase.

The loss of a loved one, especially a parent or grandparent, is a deeply poignant experience. It serves as a reminder of our own mortality and forces us to confront our own fears and uncertainties surrounding death.

This stage of life acts as a catalyst for introspection and self-reflection. We begin to question our own purpose and legacy, contemplating the mark we will leave behind when our time comes. The awareness of mortality prompts us to re-evaluate our priorities, assess the quality of our relationships and reconsider the significance of our accomplishments.

The Roman poet, Lucretius found solace in Epicurean[30] philosophy, which encouraged a perspective of indifference towards death. He posed a thought-provoking question: Why should we fear death? How does being dead differ from the time before we were born? In this light, Lucretius suggested that death might be "more peaceful than the deepest sleep." This perspective, often referred to as the "symmetry argument," treats the state of being unborn and being dead as mirror images of each other. While this line of thinking may provide comfort to some, it is not without its critics.

Consider A Scenario –

Would you prefer to remember having been hit by a car in the past, or to know with certainty that you will be hit by a car tomorrow? Given our inherent bias towards our future well-being, the obvious choice would be to have experienced the incident in the past rather than face it in the future.

This same bias towards the future applies to our perception of death. We naturally care more about the non-existence that lies ahead than the non-existence that preceded our existence in distant history. Likewise, while it would be appealing to avoid death, there is no reason to worry when we lack the ability to achieve immortality any more than we lack other superhuman powers. Accepting the inevitability of death can lead to a more balanced perspective, allowing us to focus on living a fulfilling and meaningful life in the time we have.

Learn To Love The Process, Not The Goal

As we reach middle age, a feeling of dissatisfaction can often overshadow us once we achieve the goals we have pursued for decades. Reflect on the last time you obtained something you truly desired. It could have been a promotion at work or a luxurious vacation. Initially, you probably experienced a surge of pure joy upon realising that your goal was within reach. After investing your efforts and practising patience, you have finally succeeded.

However, what happened once that initial wave of delight subsided? If you are like most people, you likely found yourself just as dissatisfied as before. This realisation formed a cornerstone of Arthur Schopenhauer's philosophy[31], as he was known for his pessimistic outlook on life. Arthur was a German philosopher who developed a unique philosophical system that combined elements of idealism, metaphysics and pessimism.

By the time we reach mid-life, we may have achieved several significant milestones, whether it's becoming a partner at a law firm or marrying the person of our dreams. So why do many of us still find ourselves asking, *"Is this all there is?"* Arthur's advice was to relinquish desires altogether. After all, unfulfilled desires lead to suffering, and even when we attain what we want, satisfaction is often fleeting. Arthur believed that it would be better to simply stop desiring.

We do not necessarily have to adopt Arthur's perspective. Instead, we can distinguish between two types of activities: telic and atelic. Telic activities are those aimed at completion, such as writing a book, getting a promotion or getting married. These activities often leave us feeling disappointed and unsatisfied. The term "telic" comes from the Greek word "telos," meaning "end".

On the other hand, atelic activities are without end. Listening to music, spending time with loved ones, and enjoying sunsets are some examples of atelic. The solution lies in making more time for atelic activities. Alternatively, you can change your attitude toward everyday life. Instead of fixating solely on the prize, pay attention to the process itself. Over time, you may find yourself genuinely enjoying the journey rather than solely focusing on the destination.

Mid-life presents challenges, but they do not have to dismay us. Learning to deal with regret, find time for pleasures, and appreciate the atelic can help us offset some of our middle-aged angst.

Remember: Mid-life challenges can be opportunities for growth, self-reflection, and embracing the richness of life. By focusing on the present, finding joy in atelic activities and appreciating the intricacies of your reality, you can offset middle-aged angst and cultivate a sense of fulfilment.

Pause & Reflect

- Are you satisfied with the life you lead currently?
- What are your biggest regrets thus far? How can you learn from them?
- Have you been neglecting certain aspects of your life, such as health, relationships or personal interests?
- What dreams or aspirations have you not yet fulfilled?
- What changes can you make to ensure the second half of your life is more aligned with your values and desires?
- How would you define success in life at this stage? Is it different from how you used to define it?
- Have you given enough time to your personal interests and hobbies?
- Are you nurturing your relationships effectively, or have they taken a backseat due to your work or other commitments?
- Do you feel connected to the world around you or do you often feel isolated and alone?
- How are you taking care of your physical and mental health? What improvements can be made?
- What kind of legacy do you want to leave behind?
- Is there something you have always wanted to do but never had the courage or time to pursue? What's stopping you now?
- What can you do to bring more joy and fulfilment into your daily life?
- Are you living true to yourself, or are you living up to societal expectations or roles?

✎ PAUSE & REFLECT INSIGHTS

3.4 CONFRONTING DEATH AND CELEBRATING EXISTENCE

"Life begins at the end of your comfort zone. When you push past your fears and embrace the unknown, you discover the extraordinary possibilities that await you."

— **Neale Donald Walsch**

In November 2018, I made a special 15-day trip to New Zealand to challenge myself and confront my fear of mortality. I wanted to perform every adventure that I feared of. I did skydiving, bungee jumping, altitude hiking in snow and jet boating amongst others. These thrilling activities provide a unique opportunity to face my fears head-on and experience a sense of empowerment and liberation. The most thrilling of all was bungee jumping in Queenstown. When I stood at the edge of the approximately 134-metre drop, I wanted to give up. **I was facing my life's greatest fear — confronting the possibility of my own mortality.**

The thought of stepping off that edge sent shivers down my spine. Yet, amidst the mix of excitement and terror that coursed through my veins, I realised that this was an opportunity to tackle my fears head-on. The words etched on the jump board caught my attention: **"Live more. Fear less."** With my heart pounding and my body trembling, I allowed myself to be strapped to the ankle and perched on the edge.

As I stood atop the jump board, a surge of conflicting emotions engulfed me. The four seconds that followed felt like an eternity, filled with the most intense moments I had ever experienced. As soon as I came back on the board after the exhilarating jump, tears streamed down my eyes. The initial terror gradually transformed into an overwhelming sense of euphoria. At that moment, I gained a profound understanding — **the fear I had harboured for so long was not as terrifying as it had seemed.**

It was an eye-opening realisation that became one of the defining moments of my life.

I came to comprehend that life truly begins at the end of our comfort zones. Now, whenever I hear that apprehensive voice within, cautioning me against taking risks or facing new obstacles, I pause and take a deep breath. I remind myself that things are often not as scary as they appear. With this newfound perspective, I push myself further away from my comfort zone, step by step.

It is through these courageous endeavours that we grow, learn and ultimately discover the limitless potential that lies within us. For the longest time, I held a deep fear of speaking in front of unfamiliar faces, especially from a stage. The mere thought of it would render me silent and apprehensive in the presence of strangers. Determined to overcome this fear, I embarked on a journey to cultivate courage and let go of concerns about judgement. Starting small, I gradually accepted public speaking assignments before modest-sized audiences.

Then, in early 2023, I was invited to address a colossal crowd of 3000 people. With no safety net of a pre-written speech, I took the leap and delivered my talk. To my astonishment, the audience responded with nearly five minutes of thunderous applause and a standing ovation.

This experience taught me the profound power of facing our fears head-on. By stepping outside my comfort zone and embracing vulnerability, I not only conquered my fear of public speaking but also discovered an inner strength I never knew existed.

Fear is a natural and instinctual response deeply ingrained in the human psyche. Humans experience anxiety, fear and worry due to a combination of biological, psychological, and environmental factors. These emotions have evolved as adaptive responses that served a survival purpose throughout human history. Among the multitude of fears that exist, the fear of death stands out as one of the most primal and universal fears. This fear is rooted in our evolutionary design, crafted by nature to protect us from situations that could potentially harm us. However, it is in facing and overcoming our deepest fears that we often find significant growth and transformation.

As we embark on the second innings of our lives, a stark reality begins to unveil itself before our eyes — the realisation that our time in this world is limited. It is during this phase that we often witness the passing of our beloved seniors, one by one, within the confines of our homes.

I have a calendar that shows me the number of weeks I am left with. Taking into consideration my health and average age, I have calculated that I have 1204 Sundays left in my life as I write this chapter. As the realisation dawns upon me that my time on the earth is limited, I find myself contemplating how I would like to spend my remaining time — the precious moments that remain in my journey. These years left represent an opportunity to shape the culmination of a life well-lived, where I can prioritise experiences that bring me joy, connection and fulfilment.

In the first 57 years of my life, I have seen only two deaths of someone close, of both my grandfathers. However, as I look ahead to the remaining 25 years, I anticipate a significant increase in the number of such heart-wrenching episodes, with more than 15 expected losses of cherished family members. In light of this realisation, my foremost desire is to dedicate as much time as possible to these dear souls, embracing the opportunity to learn from their wisdom and cultivate profound happiness in their presence.

The prospect of impending loss has ignited a sense of urgency within me — an intense longing to seize the moments we have left together. Each interaction with my close family members becomes an invaluable opportunity to absorb their knowledge, experience and life lessons. I yearn to immerse myself in their stories, to listen intently as they share the wisdom they have gathered over the years.

Their unique perspectives and lived experiences serve as treasures, offering guidance and inspiration for my own journey. I aim to maximise my own happiness by fostering deep connections with these dear family members. I recognise the significance of their presence in my life, and I am determined to nurture and cherish our time together. Whether through shared laughter, engaging conversations or creating lasting memories, I want to ensure that our bond grows stronger with each passing day.

In the face of impending loss, I am also driven to cultivate a deeper appreciation for the circle of life. As I accompany my family members on their final journey, I am confronted with the brevity of our existence and the importance of embracing the present moment. It is within these moments that I find solace, strength and a renewed determination to make a positive impact on the lives of others.

As we approach our 40s, our fears are not just about death and mortality. A few examples of fear, anxiety, and worry that individuals in their 40s and beyond may encounter –

- **Career transitions:** Fear of starting over or changing careers can lead to anxiety about financial stability, job security or the fear of being perceived as too old in a new field.

- **Financial concerns:** Worries about retirement savings, investments, paying off mortgages or supporting children through higher education can cause significant anxiety.
- **Health issues:** As we age, health concerns become more prominent. Fear of developing chronic illnesses, worries about maintaining a healthy lifestyle, or anxiety related to age-related changes can arise.
- **Ageing parents:** Many individuals in their 40s and beyond face the worry and responsibility of caring for ageing parents. Concerns about their health, well-being and managing their needs can be overwhelming.
- **Empty nest syndrome:** When children leave home for college or to start their own lives, parents may experience feelings of sadness, loneliness and anxiety about their new phase of life.
- **Fear of missed opportunities:** There can be a sense of urgency and worry about missed opportunities, unfulfilled dreams or the fear of not accomplishing certain goals by a certain age.
- **Relationship challenges:** Fear of loneliness, anxiety about finding love or maintaining long-term relationships, or worries about growing apart from partners can arise during this phase of life.

In the midst of your busy life, it is crucial to pause and reflect on the pervasive emotions of fear, anxiety and worry that often accompany you on your journey. These emotions can be powerful and overwhelming, affecting your mental and physical well-being. Taking a moment to introspect allows you to gain insight into the nature of these emotions and explore strategies to navigate them more effectively.

What Can You Do?

Some powerful exercises to practise to navigate fear, anxiety and worry are as follows…

- **Mindful reflection:** Find a quiet and comfortable space where you can dedicate uninterrupted time for reflection. Close your eyes, take a few deep breaths and centre your attention on the present moment.
- **Explore emotions:** Allow yourself to fully acknowledge and experience the emotions of fear, anxiety and worry. Without judgement or resistance, observe how these emotions manifest in your body and mind. Notice any specific thoughts or triggers that contribute to their intensity.
- **Question the validity:** Begin questioning the validity of these emotions. Ask yourself whether the fears and worries are based on real threats or if they are driven by assumptions or future projections. Challenge any irrational beliefs or exaggerated scenarios that contribute to these emotions.
- **Reframe perspectives:** Consider alternative perspectives and interpretations of the situations that trigger fear, anxiety and worry. Look for evidence that contradicts or diminishes the intensity of these emotions. Encourage yourself to adopt more balanced and realistic viewpoints.
- **Cultivate self-compassion:** Extend compassion and kindness towards yourself as you navigate these tumultuous emotions. Recognise that fear, anxiety and worry are common experiences shared by many individuals. Embrace the imperfections and uncertainties of life, knowing that growth and resilience often emerge from facing and overcoming these emotions.

- **Implement strategies:** Explore and experiment with coping strategies that resonate with you. This may include deep breathing exercises, mindfulness practices, journaling, seeking support from loved one or seeking professional guidance if necessary. Develop a toolbox of techniques that empower you to manage and navigate fear, anxiety and worry effectively.

Find Some Tools To Embrace Life Outside Your Comfort Zone –

- **Confront your fears:** To embark on a journey beyond your comfort zone, it's essential to confront and understand your fears. Acknowledge the fears that hold you back, whether it's fear of failure, rejection or the unknown. By facing them head-on, you can gradually expose yourself to these fears and realise that they are not as insurmountable as they may seem. Take small steps to conquer your fears, and with time, you will gain the confidence to overcome even the most daunting challenges. J K Rowling once said, *"It is impossible to live without failing at something, unless you live so cautiously that you might as well not have lived at all, in which case you have failed by default."*

- **Embrace novelty:** Break free from the monotony of your routine by embracing new experiences. Step out of your comfort zone by trying something new — a hobby, an adventure, or exploring uncharted territories. Embrace the unfamiliar and open yourself to the possibilities that lie beyond your comfort zone. By stepping into uncharted territory, you may discover hidden passions, forge new connections and create memories that will last a lifetime.

- **Embrace uncertainty:** Life is filled with uncertainty and embracing it can be liberating. Instead of clinging to the familiar, be open to the unknown. Embrace the unexpected twists and turns that life presents, for they often lead to valuable lessons and personal growth. Taking chance on new opportunities, even if they seem daunting, can lead to remarkable discoveries about yourself and the world around you.

- **Surround yourself with positivity:** Surrounding yourself with positive influences is crucial when stepping outside your comfort zone. Seek out individuals who uplift and support you on your journey. Their encouragement and belief in your abilities will fuel your confidence and provide a safety net when faced with challenges. Positive relationships and support systems create an environment that fosters personal growth and resilience.

- **Celebrate milestones:** Celebrate your successes along the way. Recognise that stepping outside your comfort zone is an ongoing process of growth and self-discovery. Every step you take, no matter how small, deserves acknowledgement and celebration. Whether it's overcoming a fear, achieving a goal, or simply trying something new, take the time to appreciate your progress and reflect on the lessons learnt. Celebrating milestones boosts your self-esteem and motivates you to continue embracing life outside your comfort zone.

Pause & Reflect

- What specific situations or thoughts tend to trigger feelings of fear and anxiety in you?
- How do fear and anxiety manifest in your body and mind?
- Are your fears based on actual threats or are they driven by perceived or imagined scenarios?
- What coping mechanisms or strategies have you found effective in managing fear and anxiety?
- Would reframing your perspectives or adopting alternative viewpoints help you manage fear and anxiety?
- How can confronting death change the way you live your life and what steps can you take to embrace this perspective?
- How do you differentiate between genuine concerns and overblown worries?
- Who or what serves as your anchor during anxious moments?
- Does the idea of mortality motivate or hinder your daily life choices?
- How have experiences with the mortality of loved ones shaped your understanding or feelings towards your own mortality?

✒ PAUSE & REFLECT INSIGHTS

3.5 FROM FURY TO FREEDOM

"Anger, if not restrained, is frequently more hurtful to us than the injury that provokes it."
— **Lucius Annaeus Seneca**

Sometime in 2008, a series of distressing incidents brought to light the deep-seated anger and frustration that had taken hold of my life. These events, characterised by intense displays of violence, served as wake-up calls, propelling me on a journey of self-reflection and personal growth.

One such incident occurred when my sister came to visit, and we made plans to go out for a pleasant dinner together. Little did we know that the evening would take an unexpected turn. As we sat in our car, waiting patiently at a traffic signal on our way to a restaurant, a sudden jolt from behind shattered the tranquillity of the moment.

Another vehicle had collided with ours, abruptly disrupting the serenity of the evening. Instantly, my heart raced and a surge of anger coursed through my veins. Fuelled by a potent combination of shock, frustration and a distorted sense of justice, I leapt out of the car, my actions reminiscent of a dramatic scene from a Hindi movie.

Without taking a moment to think about the potential outcomes, I impulsively yanked the negligent driver out of his vehicle, giving in to an overwhelming surge of anger that drove me to unleash my fury upon him. I mercilessly battered him, struck blow after blow. Finally, drained both physically and emotionally, I left him there, his body battered and bloodied. It was a scene of chaos and brutality that I could hardly fathom in the aftermath.

Regrettably, this incident was not an isolated occurrence. Another distressing event unfolded after a peaceful family dinner, when my cousin, upon reaching the car park, realised that he had inadvertently left his cell phone behind in the café where we just had dinner. We panicked and quickly retraced our steps, desperately trying to find the lost device. Our fears were confirmed when we failed to find the phone on the table where it had been left. Our attempts to call it proved futile, as it was switched off.

During our frantic search, my attention was drawn to one of the café employees, whose demeanour and body language suggested a deeper involvement in this unfolding drama. In a moment of misguided certainty, I convinced myself that he must have stolen the phone. Driven by an unchecked rage and without seeking any confirmation or engaging in dialogue, I violently attacked the employee without holding back. With each blow, I unleashed the full force of my anger, his body colliding with the kitchen slab, creating a scene of brutality that had the potential to end a life.

Inexplicably, my actions were met with his accepting his crime. He confessed to the theft and promptly returned the stolen phone. It was only later, as the storm of my anger began to recede, that the full gravity of my actions crashed down upon me. I was confronted with the terrifying realisation that I had strayed far from the path of rationality, indulging in acts of aggression that could have resulted in irreversible harm or even death. The weight of the consequences threatened to crush me, leaving behind an indelible stain on my conscience.

Reflecting upon these incidents, I came to understand that my life had become an embodiment of anger and frustration. It was a tumultuous existence where negative emotions reigned supreme, wreaking havoc on my relationships, my well-being and my sense of self. The stress and pressures of my professional life served as fertile ground for the proliferation of my anger, causing it to seep into every aspect of my being.

For years, my anger had been festering beneath the surface, growing in intensity and influence. It had reached a point where it found expression through destructive behaviour, culminating in the wanton destruction of property within the confines of my home. I was no longer in control of my own actions, a slave to the relentless rage that threatened to consume me. The toll it took on both my own mental and physical health, as well as the well-being of those around me, was immeasurable.

My anger had far-reaching negative impacts that went beyond the immediate consequences of my violent outbursts. It affected every aspect of my life, damaging relationships, instilling fear and anxiety in my family and pushing away the people I cared about. The mere idea of facing my explosive anger filled those who loved me with fear, leading them to avoid any direct confrontation with me.

It was amid this chaos and despair that my wife and I realised that a change was necessary. We recognised that I could no longer afford to ignore the destructive force that had taken hold of my life. A decision was made to seek professional help, to embark on a journey of self-discovery and healing, with the hope of reclaiming the joy and tranquillity that had been lost amidst the tumult of anger.

Together we chose the path of seeking guidance from a counsellor, fully aware of the challenges that lay ahead. The initial step was one of hesitancy and apprehension, as I confronted the painful realities of my behaviour and acknowledged the unacceptable nature of my actions. The early sessions proved to be arduous and emotionally draining, as I delved into the depths of my psyche, exploring the origins of my anger and its myriad triggers.

Through the unwavering support and expertise of the counsellor, I gradually gained a better understanding of my emotional landscape. Techniques and coping mechanisms were imparted to me, empowering me with the tools to manage my anger and prevent it from spiralling out of control. Deep breathing exercises, visualisation techniques and the practice of mindfulness became integral to my daily routine, allowing me to regulate my emotions and prevent their escalation into destructive outbursts.

Communication emerged as a crucial aspect of my journey towards healing. I learnt how to effectively express my feelings, articulating the emotions that once festered beneath the surface and fuelled my anger. The counsellor guided me in cultivating healthier and more constructive communication patterns, enabling me to engage in open and honest dialogues rather than succumbing to the explosive release of pent-up frustration.

The path to redemption was not an easy one. It demanded unwavering commitment, personal accountability and a willingness to confront the darkest aspects of my being. In the 12 weeks of intensive counselling, I began to witness the gradual emergence of a transformed individual. I let go of the suffocating behaviour of anger and frustration, embracing a fresh sense of freedom and inner peace.

This transformation extended beyond my personal growth. My changed behaviour touched every aspect of my life, repairing broken relationships that had suffered due to my destructive actions. Healing was not only about fixing the emotional wounds I caused but also about rediscovering my own identity. Realising the pain and fear I had inflicted on my loved ones motivated me to approach them with humility, remorse and a steadfast dedication to change. The act of seeking help and acknowledging the need for change was, without a doubt, the most profound decision I had ever made.

During the US Open 2020, Novak Djokovic steadily extended his winning streak as he outclassed Germany's Jan-Lennard

Struff 6-3, 6-3, 6-1 in a routine third-round victory. He looked unbeatable and his 18th major title seemed certain. In the next match against Carreno Busta, Novak had three set points. The set would have been over but for an incredible challenge. Down 0-40, Carreno hit a forehand that was called out, but the Hawkeye replay showed it was a hair's breadth inside the baseline.

Carreno fought through that game to keep the set on serve. Novak started showing signs of frustration. Trailing 5-6 in the tie-break, Novak struck the ball wildly in anger. The ball ricocheted back and unintentionally stuck a lineswoman on the throat. Novak, the World No.1, immediately realised that he had made a grave error and rushed over to check on the shocked lineswoman. But the damage was done. Tournament officials went by the rulebook and the match was awarded to Carreno and Novak was disqualified from the tournament.

Our Ancient Mythologies Are Full Of Stories About Anger And Its Effects –

A story that stands out in the *Mahabharat* about the devastating effects of anger is that of King Dhritarashtra. When the Pandavs came to meet him after defeating the Kauravs, Dhritrashtra was seething with anger, especially against Bheem for killing his son, Duryodhan.

Dhritrashtra asked Bheem to come closer to be embraced, ostensibly to congratulate him. Krishna, ever wily and wise, held Bheem back. Instead, he placed before the blind Dhritrashtra, a solid metal statue of Bheem and the powerful hug, arising from the pent-up anger of the old man, reduced the statue to rubble. Such was the strength of the anger that burnt inside Dhritarashtra. And when he realised what he had done he broke down like a child.

If history is any indication, leaders, generals and athletes, who are driven by anger, either become failures or remain miserable all their lives. Napoleon Bonaparte was known for his fiery temper and often made decisions based on anger and emotion rather than rational thinking. This impulsive behaviour ultimately led to his downfall, as he made several costly military mistakes and was eventually exiled to the island of Saint Helena.

Mike Tyson was a successful boxer in his prime, but his aggressive and confrontational behaviour outside of the ring often landed him in trouble with the law. His anger issues ultimately contributed to his decline as a boxer and his subsequent struggles with addiction and mental health. A recent example is former US President, Donald Trump. Trump's anger and impulsiveness were on full display during his presidency, leading to a number of controversial decisions and policies. He was impeached twice and ultimately lost re-election, leaving a divisive legacy in American politics.

Anger is a weakness. Losing your temper can sometimes mean losing respect, co-operation and the love of friends and family.

Like most of us, I used anger as a weapon to 'control people'. This resulted in an unmotivated, anxious team. Employees were anxious, stressed and uncertain about what was expected of them, leading to lower job satisfaction and higher turnover rates. In a fit of anger, I fired our head of design and lost a great resource without whom many projects got delayed. On another occasion, I fired our cook of over 10 years. He cared for my boys during their growing-up years. (It's another story that a few months down the line, I apologised and had both of them back).

We forget that while it is not possible to control people, it is easy to influence them. Influencing people is always simpler

and can be done with peace and love and maintaining cordial relations.

- Anger blocks us from whatever goal we are trying to achieve.
- Anger can never make us content and happy.
- Anger is counterproductive.
- It often comes from an overblown sense of self-importance.
- We often get angry simply to draw attention to ourselves.

You may work out regularly. As a health freak, you routinely consume protein, vegetables and have a healthy diet and get a good seven to eight hours of sleep each night. Despite all the care, your body develops bouts of illnesses. Most wonder – *What more should I do to lead a healthy lifestyle?* We need to be aware that our feelings and thoughts create a subtle energy shift in our bodies. While diet, sleep and exercise influence physical health, clean energy is needed to sustain a perfect physical body. Emotional stress and anger can manifest as illness.

Release past hurts. Forgive people to heal yourself. Remain calm and stable to cleanse the body. We have the power to create a healthy mind, which then creates a healthy body and a happy life. To create a happy and fulfilling life, it's essential to let go of past hurts and forgive those who have wronged us. By doing so, we release the negative emotions and energy that hold us back and open ourselves up to healing and growth.

When we remain calm and stable, we can cleanse our bodies of stress and negativity, creating a foundation for optimal health and well-being. By taking charge of our thoughts and emotions, we have the power to create a healthy mind, which then translates into a healthy body and a happy life.

Here are five things that you can do to reduce your anger…
1. **Write a journal or log whenever you get angry.** You will be surprised by what it reveals. Monitor every episode of anger, from fleeting moments of frustration or impatience to extreme rage. For each one, note down the facts, and the intensity of your anger 0-10 (where 0 = no anger, and 10 = maximum rage). This habit of systematically describing your angry outbursts is often all someone needs in order to gain a little perspective.
2. **Watch yourself being angry.** Roger Federer used to throw his racquet in anger during his earlier days and says watching himself throw tantrums put him off them for life. The angry are often proud of their anger. Even if they leave a scene having achieved nothing like shouting at another driver through the closed windows of their car. Re-imagine the scene again. You will feel embarrassed.
3. **Take care of yourself.** Most of the time you will find you are angry because of alcohol, hunger, stress, fatigue, unmet needs, PMS. Get some sleep; take some time off; streamline your week; delegate; relax; improve your diet. If you feel yourself becoming angry, take a break from the situation and give yourself some time to cool down. Take some deep breaths, go for a walk, or take up a relaxing activity like meditation or yoga. In short, look after yourself.
4. **Be less judgmental.** In life, most factors are subjective rather than objective. Your personal views on public displays of affection may not be shared by everyone, as there are always people who will agree or disagree with your opinion. When we consider the various customs and traditions that people follow around the world, it's unreasonable to criticise others for not adhering to our

own way of life. Instead, it's helpful to acknowledge the vast array of behaviours and practices that exist across different cultures and societies.

5. **Understand that anger is a problem.** Anger is an ineffective way of working in this world. It will mostly backfire and ruin relationships. Studies say that 80 per cent of the time people direct their anger against their family and friends. These are not the people you wish to antagonise. Understand that having a warm relationship is the key to emotional health and well-being. And if you can't sort it out yourself, seek professional help like I did. There is no shame in going to a doctor to sort it out. Treat anger like any other disease.

Anger is counterproductive. Anger hurts not just us but many other people as well. Always look at the bigger picture. Replace anger with love, gratitude and purpose. You will be a winner. You will build a solid foundation to reboot your life.

Pause & Reflect

- What are the common triggers or situations that tend to provoke anger in you?
- How does anger manifest in your body and mind?
- Are there any underlying emotions or unmet needs that might fuel your anger?
- What are your typical responses or coping mechanisms when you feel angry?
- Are there alternate ways to express or channel your anger constructively?
- Would changing your perspective or reframing situations help in managing anger?

✒ PAUSE & REFLECT INSIGHTS

3.6 DIALOGUE OVER DISCORD

"Our lives begin to end the day we become silent about things that matter."

— **Martin Luther**

During the rapid expansion phase of my company, I became a spectre in my own home, absent more often than present. My professional responsibilities led me on an unending journey, either travelling across cities or buried under late-night meetings, even when I was in town. This constant chase of corporate growth turned me into a stranger to my family, specifically my wife and children.

My wife craved for shared moments that were increasingly becoming rare — the quiet dinners, the joyous family outings, the simple comfort of our shared space. She yearned for my presence in our boys' lives, longing for me to attend their school events, cheering from the sidelines, celebrating their achievements and simply being a dad.

However, my continuous absence gave birth to frustration and disappointment, often surfacing as sarcasm in our interactions. Her words, laced with bitter humour, reflected the distance that had grown between us – "I feel closer to my friends on Facebook than you." Ironically, her criticisms, intended to signal her discontent and bring about change, were counterproductive. They triggered a defensive instinct within me, pushing me to withdraw even more. The more she remarked on my prolonged absence, the more I found myself staying out late, timing my return to the silent house long after she had retired to bed. It was as if I was inadvertently fuelling the very situation, we both wanted to avoid.

We were ensnared in a vicious cycle, a self-destructive loop. Her attempts to express her longing for more time and closeness with me were only driving me further away. As a mentor, I have had the opportunity to engage with a myriad of individuals, each carrying their unique set of circumstances and life stories. One such tale that struck me profoundly involved a mentee of mine and it resonated closely with my experiences.

During our discussions about his declining health, marked by alarming blood test results and increasing physical symptoms, we delved deeper to identify the root cause. To my surprise, it was not merely a physical ailment we were confronting, but a complex inter-play of professional stress and personal strain that had taken a toll on his health.

This individual was in the ascendant phase of his career, embarking on a journey of exponential growth and success. However, as his career graph saw an uptick, his personal life seemed to dip in inverse proportion. His intense professional commitment left him with little time to dedicate to his spouse and children, resulting in a growing chasm in his family life. To evade the uncomfortable reality of his neglect towards his family, he found himself spending even more time away from home. His prolonged absences became the norm, causing his personal life to suffer more significantly.

To compound the situation, his spouse often expressed her discontent and loneliness through sarcastic comments or avoided talking to him to show her displeasure, underscoring his lack of presence in their lives. If he had initiated an open, honest dialogue with his wife about his professional commitments, their shared expectations, and possible ways to strike a balance, the damaging impact on their relationship, and subsequently, his health, could have been mitigated.

What happens when you avoid addressing the issues you are experiencing with your boss, your partner, your neighbour, or

your colleague? Will these concerns simply vanish into thin air? Far from it. Rather than disappearing, these issues transform into the prism through which you view these individuals. The way you perceive them inevitably colours the way you interact with them. Any lingering resentment, unspoken and unresolved, manifests in your behaviour towards them.

For instance, you might find yourself lashing out at them unexpectedly, deliberately reducing the time spent together, or quickly jumping to conclusions about their intentions, accusing them of being deceitful or selfish. You might even withhold crucial information or affection, all because of the unaddressed issue between you.

This problem, instead of resolving itself, only exacerbates over time, straining an already delicate situation further. The longer you continue to express your feelings through counterproductive actions rather than discussing them openly, the more harm you inflict on both your relationships and the outcome you desire.

In essence, neglecting crucial conversations does not alleviate issues; it compounds them, perpetuating a cycle of miscommunication and misunderstanding that can have lasting, damaging effects.

What's A Crucial Conversation?

In our daily lives, we have numerous conversations with people. Most of these discussions are routine and occur without any significant impact. But then, there are those special dialogues, the critical, high-stakes conversations that can change the course of our lives or have substantial impacts on relationships, projects, or the bottom line in businesses. These are the 'crucial conversations'.

Whether it's talking about poor performance with an employee, discussing dissatisfaction in a relationship, or navigating through conflicts, knowing how to handle these situations effectively can mean the difference between a successful outcome and a disastrous one. Every day, we encounter situations that demand crucial conversations, yet we often sidestep them or mishandle these interactions, negatively impacting our relationships.

Consider a colleague who is underperforming, adversely affecting your shared project. Instead of addressing the issue directly, you might harbour resentment, causing team dynamics to sour. Or think about dealing with a rebellious teenager. As tempers flare and emotions run high, important discussions might devolve into shouting matches rather than constructive dialogue. This can damage the parent-child relationship and leave the issues at hand unresolved.

Consider those quirks of your spouse or family member that have gradually morphed from mildly irritating to downright annoying. Rather than having an open conversation about it, you might snap or react passive-aggressively, which only serves to strain your relationship further.

Imagine a situation where you need to ask a friend to repay a loan. The fear of jeopardising the friendship might cause you to avoid the conversation entirely, leading to financial stress and silent resentment.

Or picture a scenario at work where you feel your boss is impeding your professional growth. Instead of seeking a discussion about your career aspirations and concerns, you might suppress your dissatisfaction, leading to decreased job satisfaction and potential burn-out. In all these instances, the importance of handling crucial conversations with care and skill cannot be understated. Navigating these situations effectively is crucial for maintaining healthy relationships and achieving desired outcomes.

The distinguishing factor that elevates these conversations from mere annoyances, fears, or frustrations to the status of 'crucial' is the significant potential impact of their outcomes. These outcomes could affect your relationships or results in ways that significantly influence your life. In each of the instances mentioned above, an aspect of your everyday life could be permanently modified, either for better or worse. However, the scenario need not always be so bleak.

Armed with the knowledge and skills to navigate "Crucial Conversations", you can confidently engage in challenging discussions on almost any topic and arrive at a resolution. Maintaining healthy crucial conversations is instrumental for your overall well-being. Remember the insights we gleaned from the chapter on stress and the immune system? When you experience intense psychological stress, often originating from social interactions, your sympathetic nervous system is activated.

The results? Increased heart rate, blood pressure, cortisol levels and inflammation. Beta-adrenoreceptors alter the expression of cell adhesion molecules, which impacts the 'stickiness' of your immune cells. Consequently, immune cells start to behave erratically, adhering to various elements such as endothelial walls. Plasma fibrinogens rise, leading to increased coagulation. While these responses can be beneficial in a life-or-death situation, they spell trouble in the long run.

When we lack effective mechanisms to articulate our thoughts, particularly during stressful social situations, we internalise and then embody the stress. In simpler terms, our bodies become the 'home' for this stress. If we encounter a succession of stress-inducing incidents without an emotional 'release valve', we essentially transform into walking vessels of potential ailments.

Mastering the art of engaging in difficult conversations is not a panacea, but it's a critical part of expressing our needs and feelings in a manner that allows emotional pressure to dissipate. Therefore, nurturing the ability to navigate through tough discussions can serve as an essential tool in our stress management kit, contributing positively to our overall health.

At the core of most persistent issues in relationships, teams, organisations and even nations are crucial conversations that people either shy away from or handle poorly. The health of relationships can be gauged by measuring the time taken to resolve issues from when they are first identified. This 'lag time' is a crucial indicator of overall health and functioning. The lag time between identifying a problem and effectively resolving it grows because either we do not address it at all, or we address it poorly and the problem persists.

I had once tweeted, *"A goal of healthy living is acceptance of life events and the appreciation of each new day."* I received a direct message from someone I have known for quite some time. She wrote, *"What if the acceptance of events is not making you happy? What if you had expected a life that is totally different from what you are living?"* As I had known her very well, I started further communicating on this with the motive to help her and within a few minutes, I could make out that there was zero communication between her and her husband Raj (name changed), a successful interior designer. He is often absorbed in his work and brings it home, leading to less quality time spent with her. She notices this but decides not to bring it up immediately, fearing it might upset Raj or that she may come across as unsupportive.

As time passes, the issue of her husband's preoccupation with work continues, and her resentment grows. This resentment manifests itself in various ways — occasional irritability, withdrawal from shared activities and less communication. Instead of a direct conversation about the issue, her dissatisfaction seeps into other aspects of their relationship, causing unnecessary friction.

In this instance, the lag time between recognising the issue (Raj's work taking up personal time) and addressing it (having a crucial conversation about it) is prolonged. As this lag time increases, so does the tension between them. Their relationship, which once was marked by open communication and mutual support, is now fraught with unspoken grievances and mistrust.

Despite the critical role of crucial conversations, we frequently shy away from them out of fear that initiating such discussions might exacerbate the situation. Thus, we inadvertently become experts at dodging difficult dialogues.

While avoiding crucial conversations is one issue, another common pitfall is handling these conversations ineffectively. Frequently, during such challenging moments, we exhibit our least desirable behaviour — we may overreact, raise our voice, become withdrawn, or utter words that we later regret. The unfortunate irony of crucial conversations is that when the stakes are the highest, we often falter the most.

When asked about the reasons for break-ups in romantic relationships, most people would point to differences of opinion. They might suggest that disagreements over financial management, maintaining romance, or raising children are the primary culprits. It's true that all couples argue about significant issues, but not all end up parting ways. **The manner in which couples argue is the crucial determining factor.**

Consider the research conducted by psychologist Howard Markman[32]. He studied couples during their heated debates and observed that people usually fall into three categories;

those resorting to threats and name-calling, those reverting to silent resentment, and those who express their views openly, honestly and effectively. After hundreds of hours observing these couples, Howard and his research partner, Clifford Notarius made predictions about the couple's relationships over the next decade. Astonishingly, they correctly predicted nearly 90 per cent of the divorces that occurred.

The most significant finding was that by teaching couples how to engage in crucial conversations more effectively, they could reduce the chances of relationship dissatisfaction or separation by over half.

Pause & Reflect

Consider your own relationships. Are there crucial conversations that you are currently avoiding or mishandling? Do you retreat from some topics only to plunge head-first into others? Do you suppress negative opinions only for them to spill out as sarcastic comments or low blows? When the stakes are highest (these are your beloved ones, after all), do you find yourself behaving poorly?

If the answer to any of these questions is yes, then learning to manage crucial conversations effectively is certainly a skill you stand to benefit from.

Identifying Crucial Conversations

Recognising a crucial conversation can sometimes be challenging, yet it's vital for managing high-stakes dialogues effectively. Signs such as a stalled conversation, palpable tension, or discomfort, which might show through extended silences, increased volume or evasive eye contact, can hint at the conversation being crucial. High-stake topics, like important family disagreements, are also indicators. Finally, heightened emotions are a clear sign of a crucial conversation that may necessitate a shift in communication strategies to reach a positive resolution.

Consider a scenario where your teenage daughter has always been an excellent student and is very open with you about her life. Recently, however, you have noticed a drop in her grades, and she has become more withdrawn and secretive, spending a lot of time alone in her room. In this situation, you might find yourself heading towards a crucial conversation with her. The signs are there: there is an uncomfortable tension when you try to talk about her school life, the stakes are high since her academic performance and mental well-being might be at risk, and your concern for her well-being is causing your emotions to run high.

Despite the discomfort this conversation may bring, it's vital not to avoid it. It's a crucial conversation that, when approached with care and openness, could help you understand what she is going through, offer support and work on solutions together.

Adopting The Right Mindset

It is crucial to remember that there are no winners or losers in any conversation, especially high-stake ones. Everyone brings something valuable to the table. Approaching each dialogue with a mindset geared towards mutual solutions, devoid of pre-conceived judgments and assumptions about others' intentions, lays the groundwork for finding common ground.

Imagine that your spouse has recently started a new job that requires more of his time, leaving you to deal with most of the household chores and responsibilities. You are feeling overwhelmed, and this imbalance has led to some tension between the two of you. Now, adopting the right mindset before initiating a crucial conversation about this issue is key. You might initially feel that he is being inconsiderate or that he's "winning" by escaping household duties, while you are "losing" by taking on extra responsibilities. This mindset can lead to conflict and resentment.

Instead, approach the conversation with the mindset that there are no winners or losers. Recognise that both of you are navigating a change. He is adjusting to a new job, and you are adapting to a shift in household responsibilities. Everyone involved is experiencing challenges and has something valuable to contribute to the conversation. Instead of seeing him as the adversary, view him as a partner in finding a solution.

Revisiting Points Of Disagreement

'Circling back', or revisiting contentious points after a period of time, helps ensure that everyone feels acknowledged and respected throughout the process. This approach encourages open communication, fostering effective solutions even when differing views are in play.

My wife and I once found ourselves at odds over our holiday plans. She was keen on visiting her family, while I yearned for the tranquillity of a beach resort. Our differing preferences ignited a heated discussion that, at the time, yielded no consensus. However, rather than letting this disagreement fester, we decided, after a few days, to revisit our conversation.

In our second discussion, we approached the issue differently. Both of us came to the table with the intent to understand the other's viewpoint, as opposed to solely championing our own desires. My wife empathised with my need for relaxation, considering the intensity of my health coaching classes. She also candidly expressed her feelings of missing her family and the emotional significance they held for her.

On my part, I reciprocated her understanding by acknowledging the depth of her familial bonds. I also shared my concerns that the hustle and bustle typical of her family gatherings might not afford me the relief I sought from this vacation.

By taking the time to revisit our disagreements and look deeper into our individual perspectives, we were able to find a mutual resolution. We agreed to divide our holiday time, spending the initial few days with her family in Bengaluru and then driving down to a serene beach resort in Puducherry for the rest of our vacation.

Maintaining A Safe Atmosphere

Safety is paramount in any conversation. A lack of it can cause a rational dialogue to deteriorate into heated disputes, hampering productive communication. Establishing a safe atmosphere requires mutual respect and a shared purpose. If participants do not feel respected, their behaviour can quickly become aggressive.

Let's say you and your brother, Amit, have recently inherited a family property. You would like to sell it and divide the proceeds, but Amit wants to keep it in the family. This disagreement has the potential to become a heated argument if not handled properly.

To maintain a safe atmosphere during this crucial conversation, you could do the following:

- Begin by expressing your respect and love for Amit, reinforcing that the discussion isn't about winning or losing but about finding a solution that respects both of your perspectives.
- As you explain your point of view, use 'I' in statements to communicate how you feel, instead of 'you' statements which might feel accusatory. For instance, say, 'I feel

that selling the property would be beneficial because...' rather than, 'You do not understand that selling the property is the best idea...'

- Ask Amit to share his perspective and listen actively. Validate his feelings and show that you understand his viewpoint, even if you disagree.
- If the conversation starts to heat up, pause and remind both of you about the common ground you share — your love for each other and your shared history as a family. This can help to de-escalate emotions and keep the conversation productive.
- Make it clear that it's okay to take a break from the discussion if it becomes too emotional. Agree to return to the conversation later when both of you are calmer and able to engage more constructively. Mastering crucial conversations can lead to improved personal and professional relationships.

By ensuring mutual respect, validating interpretations of behaviour before reacting, and focusing on shared solutions, these conversations can be less daunting and more constructive. With the right preparation, crucial conversations can enhance communication, foster stronger relationships and enable creative problem-solving. Effective communication is, indeed, key to personal and professional success.

Pause & Reflect
Before The Conversation –
- What is your primary goal for this conversation?
- Why do you find this topic challenging or uncomfortable?
- What assumptions are you making about the other person's perspective or reactions?

- How are you feeling physically and emotionally? Are these feelings likely to influence your approach?
- What are the potential outcomes, both positive and negative, of this discussion?

During The Conversation –
- Are you truly listening, or are you formulating your response while the other person speaks?
- How is the other person likely feeling right now?
- Are there non-verbal cues or body language signs that you need to be aware of, either from the other person or from yourself?
- Is the conversation staying on track, or is it veering into unproductive areas?
- If emotions are escalating, can you take a moment to breathe and refocus?

After The Conversation –
- What went well in that conversation, and what could you improve next time?
- Did you reach a resolution or mutual understanding, even if you did not agree?
- How do you feel now, both physically and emotionally?
- Do you need to follow up on anything after this conversation?
- What did you learn about yourself and the other person during this dialogue?

✒ PAUSE & REFLECT INSIGHTS

Section 4

Crystal Clear Waters – Fostering Mental Clarity

"One small crack does not mean that you are broken. It means you were put to the test and you did not fall apart."
— **Linda Poindexter**

Fostering mental clarity is akin to navigating a vast, unexplored wilderness. It's a journey that requires patience, understanding, and most importantly, an inward gaze. In our modern, fast-paced world, it's easy to lose ourselves in external noise, daily chores, responsibilities and digital distractions. The key to finding our way back to clarity lies within our own minds. Every individual has a unique mental landscape, filled with thoughts, beliefs, memories and emotions. Each of these elements plays a crucial role in shaping our perception, behaviour, and ultimately, our life experiences. Therefore, gaining insight into our mental landscape is the first step towards fostering mental clarity.

Inner Echoes: The Role Of Thoughts And Beliefs In Mental Health

Our thoughts and beliefs are not just passing notions or fleeting ideas; they are the architects of our reality. They shape our perspectives, guide our decisions and can influence our emotional responses. Negative thought patterns can distort our perceptions and affect our mental health, leading to stress, anxiety or depression. On the other hand, nurturing positive beliefs and maintaining an optimistic outlook can enhance our mental resilience, promote well-being and provide clarity.

Calm In Chaos: Harnessing The Potential Of Mindfulness

Mindfulness, the practice of being fully present and engaged in the current moment, serves as a haven of tranquillity in the midst of life's constant hustle. By focusing on the 'here and now', we can manage stress, reduce anxiety, improve focus and gain a deeper understanding of our emotions and reactions. Mindfulness allows us to respond, rather than react, to situations, leading to better decision-making and greater mental clarity. Regular mindfulness practices such as meditation, mindful eating, or simply taking a few mindful breaths throughout the day can greatly enhance our journey towards mental clarity.

Joyful Journey: Embracing Happiness As A Choice

Happiness can be influenced by external circumstances, but it is also a state of mind that we can consciously choose. When we choose to focus on the positives, express gratitude, and find joy in the mundane, we cultivate a sense of contentment and inner peace. This choice to be happy, despite life's challenges, strengthens our mental resilience and promotes mental clarity. It does not mean ignoring difficulties, but to try and find ways to remain hopeful and optimistic amidst them.

Beyond Work: The Joy And Journey Of Having A Hobby

Our professional lives can often consume a significant part of our identity and time, but having a hobby offers a vital balance. An hobby provides an outlet for stress, stimulate our creativity and add joy to our lives. Whether it's gardening, painting, playing an instrument, or hiking, a hobby can contribute to our self-expression and personal growth. It give us something to look forward to outside of work, enhancing our overall happiness and mental clarity.

4.1 INNER ECHOES

"The mind is everything. What you think, you become."
— **Linda Poindexter**

Have you ever experienced the curious phenomenon where something you like, or desire seems to manifest more frequently in your surroundings? For instance, you find yourself enjoying a particular song, only to realise that it's playing on multiple radio stations. Or perhaps you have set your sights on purchasing a specific car, and suddenly you start noticing that model everywhere on the road. This intriguing occurrence can be attributed to a combination of psychological and perceptual factors, shedding light on the influence of our thoughts and beliefs on our perception of the world.

The concept at play here is known as selective attention or the frequency illusion, also referred to as the *Baader-Meinhof phenomenon*.[33] It occurs when our minds unconsciously prioritise certain information while filtering out other stimuli. In the examples mentioned, your affinity for the song or the car has heightened your awareness of their presence, making them appear more frequently in your perception.

Selective attention is closely tied to our thoughts and beliefs. Our minds naturally gravitate towards things that align with our interests, preferences and desires. When we develop a positive association with a particular song, our thoughts and emotions create a cognitive bias that directs our attention towards it. Consequently, we notice it more readily, increasing the perception of its frequency. Similarly, when we have a strong desire to own a specific car, our mind becomes attuned to its distinctive features, making it more salient in our surroundings.

This phenomenon highlights the powerful interplay between our thoughts, beliefs and perception. Our mental constructs shape how we interpret and interact with the world around us. Our thoughts and desires act as filters that influence our attention and focus. What we choose to think about, believe in, and attach significance to affects what we notice and how we perceive our reality.

The influence of thoughts and beliefs extends beyond the frequency illusion. They also impact our overall mindset and outlook on life. Positive thoughts and beliefs can enhance our well-being, boost our confidence and attract opportunities that align with our aspirations. Conversely, negative thoughts and beliefs can limit our potential, hinder our growth, and create a self-fulfilling prophecy of failure or dissatisfaction.

Therefore, cultivating a positive and empowering mindset becomes crucial. By consciously nurturing thoughts and beliefs that support our goals and well-being, we can enhance our perception of the world and manifest positive experiences. This involves cultivating self-awareness, challenging and reframing negative thoughts and intentionally focusing on what brings us joy and fulfilment.

Carver and Scheier (1987) introduced the term *dispositional optimism.*[34] They argued that it is the presence of positive traits that increases the chances of something good happening to us. The dispositional theory of optimism suggests that optimism leads to positive consequences in life and pessimism leads to stressful outcomes and increased dissatisfaction.

I have an uncle who has always impressed me with his unwavering cheerfulness and happiness. Even during some of life's toughest moments, he manages to maintain a positive outlook. Intrigued by his perpetual optimism, I once asked him the secret behind his happiness. His response was filled with profound philosophy. He said, *"There is a concept called Brahma muhurat, a special time that occurs every day but remains unknown to us. It is believed that whatever you wish for during that time comes true. So, I always strive to keep my thoughts positive. 'Pata nahi kab Brahma Muhurat hai' (Who knows when it's Brahma muhurat),"* he would say with a smile. Whenever someone asks him how he is doing, his response is always *"Bam Bam,"* which signifies a fantastic state of being.

Throughout our lives, we encounter numerous individuals who, even in the best of circumstances, remain pessimistic. They seem to dwell on negativity and perceive the world through a lens of doubt and despair. In stark contrast, my uncle's approach to life is a shining example of the profound influence that thoughts and beliefs can have on our overall well-being and perception of reality.

His belief in the mysterious Brahma muhurat reflects his understanding of the power of timing and intention. By aligning his thoughts with positivity, he aims to seize the opportune moment when the universe is receptive to his desires. Although the concept of Brahma muhurat may be metaphorical, it serves as a reminder to be mindful of our thoughts and the energy we emit into the world.

My Uncle's choice to embrace a positive mindset is not determined by external circumstances alone but is an intentional decision he makes every day. He understands that dwelling on negativity will not alter or improve a situation. Instead, he chooses to focus on the brighter aspects of life, maintaining hope and optimism even when faced with challenges.

Life is anyway full of challenges, and when we reach mid-life, the demands seem to multiply. We find ourselves striving to grow in our professions, while also juggling the responsibilities of raising teenagers and caring for ageing parents. The pressures can be overwhelming, and stress tends to reach its peak during this phase. However, amidst the chaos, there is a guiding light that can help us navigate this complex terrain with grace and resilience: optimism and positivity.

Maintaining an optimistic outlook becomes essential as we navigate the multiple roles and responsibilities that mid-life brings. Optimism allows us to view challenges as opportunities for growth and transformation. It enables us to approach each situation with a sense of possibility, rather than being weighed down by the pressures and demands.

The origin of the word **'optimism'** can be traced back to the Latin word **optimum**, which means 'the best'. In the realm of psychology, optimism, or dispositional optimism, refers to a set of beliefs and traits that enable individuals to focus on the positive aspects of life rather than dwelling on the negative ones. It encompasses a personality pattern characterised by resilience and personal strength.

You may have come across individuals who exude an upbeat demeanour even in the face of challenging circumstances, and you may find yourself wondering, "How do they do it?" However, a more pertinent question to ask is, "Can I cultivate that mindset too?"

The power of optimism extends beyond merely being happy. It involves leveraging this mindset to bring about positive changes in one's life. Optimistic individuals typically hold the belief that with the right approach and appropriate actions, they can overcome obstacles and improve their circumstances. This perspective empowers them to tackle problems head-on and embrace a proactive mindset.

Optimism acts as a catalyst for personal growth and development. By cultivating an optimistic outlook, individuals gain the confidence to explore new possibilities, take calculated risks and pursue their goals with unwavering determination. It fosters a belief in one's ability to navigate obstacles and find solutions, even in the face of adversity.

It's not clear exactly how optimism affects health. Researchers have considered both biological and behavioural mechanisms. For example, optimistic people tend to have lower levels of inflammation and healthier cholesterol levels compared with less optimistic people.

They are also inclined to embrace healthy habits, including regular physical activity, balanced eating, refraining from smoking and avoiding excessive alcohol consumption. Optimistic individuals tend to be more open to taking risks, exploring new ventures, and welcoming fresh opportunities. They tend to be more resilient in the face of setbacks, as they hold the belief that positive outcomes can arise from any challenge or adversity.

Optimism comes with a plethora of advantages. Research indicates that optimists often enjoy longer lives in comparison to pessimists, primarily because they exhibit lower levels of stress hormones, such as cortisol, in their systems.[35] Furthermore, optimistic individuals tend to express higher levels of satisfaction in their relationships, achieve more success in both academics and careers, experience better physical health, and maintain an overall heightened sense of well-being. Archimedes, the great scientist and mathematician of ancient Greece, famously posited, *"Give me a lever long enough and a fulcrum on which to place it, and I shall move the world."* Our brains, too, operate according to the Archimedean formula.

Let's Imagine Two Scenarios…
Scenario One: Take, for example, a seesaw. On a seesaw, the fulcrum is set at the exact centre between the two seats. If

two kids, each weighing 30 kg, sit the same distance from the fulcrum on opposing seesaw seats, they will balance each other.

Scenario Two: Now, imagine two kids, 'A' weighing 30 kg and 'B' 60 kg, in the same situation. 'A' is going to hang in the air until 'B' either pushes off with his feet from the ground or jumps off and lets 'A' crash earthward. But what if we move the fulcrum?

The closer we move the centre point, i.e., the fulcrum, towards 'B', the easier he is to lift. If we keep moving the fulcrum in that direction, eventually 'A' will effectively weigh more than 'B'. Move the fulcrum close enough to 'B' who weighs 60 kg, and 'A' can climb off his seat and use the seesaw lever to move 'B' up.

In other words, by shifting this point around which energy is applied, we can effectively turn the seesaw from a balancing scale into a powerful lever. That was exactly Archimedes' point. If we have a long enough lever and a good place to stand, a fulcrum point, we can move the entire world.

What I realised is that our brains work in precisely the same way. Our power to maximise our potential is based on two important factors –

1. **The length of our Lever – How much potential power and possibility we believe we have, and**
2. **The position of our Fulcrum – The mindset with which we generate the power to change.**

What this means, in practical terms, is that whether you are a student striving for better grades, a junior executive aiming for better pay, or a teacher hoping to inspire students, you do not need to try so hard to generate power and produce results. Our potential is not fixed. The more we move our fulcrum (or mindset), the more our lever lengthens and therefore the more power we generate.

Simply put, if we move the fulcrum to a negative mindset, we never rise off the ground. Move the fulcrum to a positive mindset, and the lever's power is magnified, ready to move everything up.

This means that by changing the fulcrum of our mindset and lengthening our lever of possibility, we change what is possible. It's not the weight of the world that determines what we can accomplish. It is our fulcrum and lever.

How To Move The Fulcrum?

Begin by observing your thoughts and identifying negative patterns. Notice the impact of negativity on your emotions, actions and overall mindset. Awareness is the first step towards change. **Question your negative beliefs and assumptions.** Are they based on facts or just fears? Replace them with positive affirmations and realistic perspectives. Challenge yourself to see new possibilities and reframe negative situations. **Cultivate a gratitude practise to shift your focus from what is wrong to what is right in your life.** Regularly acknowledge and appreciate the positive aspects, no matter how small. This trains your brain to seek out the good.

Shah Rukh Khan, often referred to as the 'King of Bollywood', has had a remarkable journey in the entertainment industry. However, his path to success was not without its share of challenges and setbacks. In many of his interviews, Shah Rukh Khan has exemplified the power of self-awareness in transforming a negative mindset into a positive one.

Negative self-talk fuels anxiety, depression and low self-esteem. Our inner critic can be merciless, and the more we give in to their demands, the worse our mental health becomes. John Milton, the famous English poet, wrote, *"The mind is its own* *place, and in itself can make a heaven of hell, a hell of heaven."* Negative self-talk can make life a living hell. But the good news is we can reframe our thoughts and overcome our inner critic. Indian mystic and philosopher, Jiddu Krishnamurti believed that our beliefs and thoughts create the world we live in and that by changing our thoughts, we can change our reality.

Create a mental image of your best possible self. Where do you see yourself in five or 10 years?

This exercise helps you address three essential questions –

What are you doing now?

What is important to you?

What do you care about and why?

The answers can help you focus on new goals and areas of improvement you have always wanted to pursue, but could not because of other responsibilities and priorities, like work and raising kids. This can help you turn your attention toward something stimulating and exciting, which can increase your sense of great possibilities and a more positive future.

Start each day with positive affirmations. Choose a mantra that resonates with you and repeat it throughout the day to keep your spirits high.

Surround yourself with positive people who inspire and motivate you. Spend time with people who support your growth and lift your spirits when times are tough.

Take it one day at a time. Remind yourself that today is all that matters and take small steps in the right direction each day. I just finished the book, *The Choice: A True Story of Hope* by Edith

Eger.[36] It's an amazing story of living every day to survive during Hitler's time. At the age of 16, Edith Eger was sent to Auschwitz. Hours after her parents were killed, Nazi officers forced Edith to dance for their amusement and her survival. Edith was pulled from a pile of corpses when the American troops liberated the camps in 1945. One line from the book that describes Optimism and which has gone into my list of best quotes is *"I survived today. Tomorrow I will be free."*

Have faith in yourself and your ability to overcome obstacles. Believe that everything happens for a reason, even if it does not make sense at first. One of the learnings that I took from my Babuji (Grandfather) was, *"Jo hota hai ache ke liye hota hai (Whatever happens, happens for good)."*

So, the next time you find yourself experiencing the frequency illusion — where that beloved song seems to follow you or that desired car appears everywhere —take a moment to think about the power of your thoughts and beliefs. Recognise that your mind has homed in on these aspects due to your affinity for them. Embrace this as a reminder of the profound influence your thoughts and beliefs hold over your perception and the potential to shape your experiences. Use this awareness to foster positivity, set intentions and manifest the reality you desire.

Pause & Reflect

- How does your general outlook on life shape your thoughts and actions?
- Are you more inclined towards optimism or pessimism?
- When faced with challenges or setbacks, do you tend to view them as temporary obstacles or insurmountable barriers?

- How do your current thoughts and beliefs influence your perception of the world around you and your responses to various situations?
- Can you identify any recurring negative thoughts or limiting beliefs that could affect your mental health?
- How often do you consciously cultivate positive thoughts and beliefs? How do these impact your mood and overall mental state?
- How can you use mindfulness or other techniques to become more aware of your thoughts and beliefs in the moment?
- How have your beliefs changed over time? Have these changes positively or negatively impacted your mental health?
- How do your beliefs about mental health influence your behaviour and attitude towards it?
- Are there any beliefs you hold that might create barriers to seeking help or improving your mental health?

PAUSE & REFLECT INSIGHTS

4.2 CALM IN CHAOS

"Mindfulness is the only virtue. To be aware means to be in control; not of the outside, but of the inside."
— **Osho**

Since my college days I have been a follower of Osho Rajneesh's teachings. His wisdom had a profound impact on my life. In one of his sermons, he narrated the following story…

"Once upon a time, a senior monk and a junior monk embarked on a journey together. In their path, they encountered a river with a swift current. As they prepared to cross, they noticed a young and beautiful woman who also sought to cross the river. The woman approached them and asked for their assistance. The two monks hesitated, as they had taken vows not to touch women. However, without uttering a word, the senior monk gracefully picked up the woman, carried her across the river, and gently placed her on the other side.

The younger monk was astonished by this act, for it seemed to contradict their vows. Silently, they resumed their journey, and an hour passed in silence between them. Another hour went by, then three, as the younger monk struggled to contain his confusion and curiosity. Finally, he could no longer withhold his thoughts and blurted out, "As monks, we are forbidden to touch women. How could you carry that woman on your shoulders?" The senior monk looked at his companion and calmly replied, "Brother, I set her down on the other side of the river. Why are you still carrying her?"

The young monk was struck by the profound truth in his companion's words. The incident at the river had passed, and yet he continued to carry the weight of it in his mind. It was a reminder of how easily we cling to the past, allowing it to burden us with grievances and wounds that no longer serve us.

The act of holding onto the past only perpetuates suffering, drains our energy and hinders our ability to find happiness in the present moment."

Life swiftly passes by, and it is our responsibility to extract every drop of joy and happiness from the time we possess. When we catch ourselves dwelling on the past, revisiting memories that no longer serve us, we must remember the wisdom of the two monks and let go. Putting down the unnecessary baggage of the past allows us to cultivate a new habit — an inclination to live fully in the present moment, where peace and contentment reside.

In June 2001, our lives took an unexpected turn when my mom was diagnosed with cancer. The conversation with the doctor was heart-wrenching as we asked the dreaded question: "How long does she have?" The doctor's response was disheartening; he had not witnessed any patient in a similar condition survive beyond six months. It came as a shock to us that reverberated through our entire family.

But amidst the devastation and uncertainty, we made a collective decision to embrace the present moment and make the most of the time we had together. We realised that we could not change the prognosis or alter the course of the illness, but we could choose to approach each day with love, strength and determination to create happy memories. This conscious choice to live in the present moment echoes the essence of mindfulness.

It involves accepting the reality of the situation without judgement or resistance and fully immersing ourselves in the here and now. Rather than succumbing to despair or allowing fear to consume us, we recognised that the only way to truly support our mom and one another was to appreciate the preciousness of each passing moment.

With mindfulness as our guiding light, we embarked on a journey of love, laughter and connection. We let go of regrets about the past and worries about the future, focusing instead on the beauty and joy that could be found in the present. We created a sanctuary of love and support, where we celebrated milestones, shared stories and cherished the simple pleasures of everyday life.

The practise of mindfulness allowed us to find strength in the face of adversity. It did not mean that we ignored the pain or denied the challenges; rather, it provided a framework for navigating them with grace and resilience. Mindfulness taught us to approach each day with gratitude, to savour the small moments of happiness, and to find solace in the bonds we shared as a family.

As the months passed, we discovered that time is not defined by numbers on a calendar, but by the depth of the connections we forge and the memories we create. Our mom exceeded the doctor's six-month prediction, and she still enriches our lives with her presence. Though the path had its challenges, we stayed dedicated to embracing life to the fullest.

Mindfulness is the basic human ability to be fully present, aware of where we are and what we are doing, and not overly reactive or overwhelmed by what is going on around us.

You have heard of mindfulness. Maybe you have even tried practising mindfulness or read about its role in helping to manage stress. Mindfulness is meeting the moment as it is, moment after moment after moment, wordlessly attending to our experience as it actually is. One of Buddha's teachings is that, as humans, we create suffering and problems in our own minds. Deep health cannot be achieved without being mindful.

For the most part of my life, I found myself caught in a perpetual cycle of mindlessness, constantly fixated on the past and future. Anxiety held me tightly in its grip, and my own thoughts tormented me incessantly. However, I remained oblivious to the root cause of my distress, unaware of the source of my suffering.

My mind wandered ceaselessly, replaying past events with regret and longing, or projecting into an uncertain future filled with worry and apprehension. I was trapped in a relentless cycle of rumination, unable to break free from the chains of my own thoughts. The present moment slipped through my fingers, unnoticed and unappreciated. My first exposure to mindfulness happened sometime in 2010 when I was listening to some Osho sermons on a CD player, recouping from my car crash and surgery thereafter.

Till then, I held the belief that mindfulness was intrinsically tied to religion — a practice reserved for those who engaged in prayer while sitting cross-legged in serene meditation. It seemed inaccessible and distant, something that belonged to a specific spiritual path rather than a universal human experience.

But, as I listened to Osho, a realisation began to dawn upon me. Mindfulness was not confined to the realms of religion or the rigid confines of a particular practice. It was an innate capacity within each one of us — an invitation to embrace the present moment, to be fully aware and engaged in our experiences, regardless of our background or beliefs. Mindfulness, I learnt, was the practice of being fully present and aware, without judgement or attachment.

It was about cultivating a conscious relationship with our thoughts, emotions and sensations as they unfolded in the here and now. It was an invitation to engage with life wholeheartedly, to savour the richness of each moment, and to awaken to the beauty that often went unnoticed in the busyness of our daily lives. Mindfulness is often defined as *"the awareness that arises by paying attention, on purpose, in the present moment, and non-judgmentally."* — Jon Kabat Zinn. The concept of mindfulness can initially seem overwhelming for those who are new to the practice. However, at its core, mindfulness can be best described as the state of simply 'noticing things'.

Yes, it truly is as straightforward as that. When you engage in the act of noticing things, you are actively practising mindfulness. When you grasp the science underlying mindfulness and meditation, it can be a powerful motivation to cultivate these habits. But it's especially helpful if you are the kind of person who wants evidence of efficacy before embarking on a new goal.

The human brain is a complex organ that can be loosely categorised into three main regions: the reptilian brain, the limbic brain and the cortex. Each of these regions plays a unique role in shaping our thoughts, emotions and behaviour.

Reptilian brain: The reptilian brain, also known as the primitive or primal brain, is the oldest and most evolutionarily preserved part of the human brain. It includes structures such as the brainstem and the basal ganglia. This region is responsible for basic survival functions and instinctual behaviour. It regulates vital processes like breathing, heart rate and body temperature. The reptilian brain is primarily focused on self-preservation, instinctual response and basic survival instincts.

Limbic brain: The limbic brain, sometimes referred to as the emotional brain, is located above the reptilian brain and consists of structures such as the amygdala, hippocampus, and hypothalamus. This region is involved in processing emotions, memory formation, and the regulation of basic drives such as hunger, thirst and sexual behaviour. The limbic brain plays a crucial role in our emotional experiences, social interactions and the formation of long-term memories. It also influences our motivation, learning and decision-making processes.

Cortex: The cortex is the largest and most developed part of the human brain. The cortex is further divided into different lobes, including the frontal, parietal, temporal and occipital lobes. These lobes are associated with specific functions such as motor control, sensory perception, language processing, visual processing, and executive functions like reasoning, problem-solving and decision-making.

The cortex allows us to think, plan, learn, communicate, appraise danger and engage in abstract thinking. The cortex, the reptilian brain and the limbic brain collectively work together. They are interconnected by complex neural pathways (white matter) that have developed to influence one another.

I remember a few years back I was walking in the paddy fields at Kanha where my friend, Vipul runs a wonderful NGO, Earth Focus. I saw something that looked like a snake. The stored memories in the hippocampus reminded me that I fear snakes. This lights up my amygdala — the fear centre of the brain — which activates the hypothalamus. The hypothalamus then sends a signal to my pituitary glands, which in turn, sends a message to adrenal glands releasing cortisol throughout my bloodstream.

Cortisol is the primary stress hormone, which prepares the body for fight or flight response, and I started to run. The villagers, who were guiding me through the field, did not panic. In fact, the snake turned out to be a rope. When I became aware of it, the cortex deactivated the amygdala, which in turn inhibited the secretion of cortisol via the hypothalamus, thus bringing the body back into homeostasis.

I often wonder what my rational mind, the cortex, was doing during this time. Why did I panic and not the villagers? My anxiety, which resulted from childhood trauma when one of my schoolmates died because of a snake bite, had hijacked my bodily sensations. Ever since I can remember, I have been terrified of snakes and that is why I have never done any reptile photography though I have been invited to visit Amboli and other snake parks.

Have You Ever Felt Completely Shaken And Overcome By Fear?

This phenomenon occurs when a stimulus in your environment triggers a stress response within you. It could be a situation wherein your partner raise their voice, a colleague criticises you at work, a close call occurs while driving, or even a sudden fright caused by someone or something.

From a neuroscientific perspective, when a visual or auditory stimulus is detected, it is relayed to the respective cortex in your brain, such as the visual cortex for visual stimuli or the auditory cortex for verbal stimuli. Subsequently, a message is transmitted to your amygdala, which plays a key role in processing emotions, particularly fear and stress. As a result, a stress response is activated, preparing your body to cope with the perceived threat.

Traditionally, this is how most people experience stress, and it has been an evolutionary response in our species. However, in today's fast-paced and demanding world, the stress response is increasingly triggered by our own minds rather than external circumstances. This internal activation of stress comes in two distinct forms: ruminating about a past that cannot be changed and worrying about an imagined future.

These internal stressors are particularly challenging to manage. While external stressors may come and go, the battle within your own mind becomes a constant struggle. It's like forgetting to fully turn off the cortisol tap in the bathroom — drip, drip, drip — the stress response persists.

Recognising the power of these internal stressors is crucial for effectively managing stress. By cultivating mindfulness and developing an awareness of our thought patterns, we can gain greater control over our minds. Mindfulness allows us to observe our thoughts without judgement, creating space for self-reflection and acceptance.

Let me accompany you on a journey through a typical workday, offering guidance on how you can approach it with mindfulness. By embracing mindfulness, you can navigate the demands and challenges of your workday with a greater sense of calm, focus and well-being.

1. **Drive to work mindfully:** Before getting into your car, take a moment to breathe deeply and ground yourself. Silence your phone to minimise distractions. As you start driving, consciously notice your surroundings — the sights, sounds and sensations. If faced with traffic or an aggressive driver, observe any arising emotions without judgement. Use stops as opportunities for deep, calming breaths. Once you reach your destination, take a moment to sit and take three deep breaths, fully releasing each exhale.

2. **Practise transition breathing:** Instead of rushing into work, allow yourself a mindful moment of transition. Take a few conscious breaths before shifting gears, mentally preparing yourself to approach your work with calmness and centeredness.

3. **Clear your desk:** Clearing and organising your desk can be a mindful activity. As you decide where to place items and what to keep or discard, focus on the task at hand. This brief moment of mindful de-cluttering can enhance your productivity and bring a sense of calm to your workspace.

4. **Focus on your work purpose:** Even if you find your work challenging or uninspiring, infuse it with purpose and love. Discover the underlying reasons for your efforts and cultivate a positive mindset. By finding meaning in your work, you can reduce negativity and foster a more fulfilling experience.
5. **Decrease distractions:** Distractions can fragment your attention and hinder productivity. Recognise that distractions seek to take control of your focus and resources. By cultivating mindfulness, you can resist immediate gratification and maintain concentration for longer periods, enhancing your ability to accomplish tasks.
6. **Be present with peers:** Interactions with colleagues can be a significant source of stress. By practising presence and mindfulness, you can contribute to a more emotionally intelligent work environment. Engage in active listening, empathy and mutual respect, fostering better relationships and personal well-being.
7. **Create mindful meetings:** Meetings often drain energy and productivity. Transform your perspective by approaching meetings with mindfulness. Prepare yourself mentally before the meeting and maintain a beginner's mindset. Advocate for mutual respect and offer positive feedback, contributing to more valuable and engaging discussions.
8. **Stand, stretch and get moving:** Prolonged sitting can have negative effects on your health. Incorporate moments of standing, stretching and movement throughout the day. These mindful breaks serve as a reset for your body, revitalising your energy and focus.

9. **Show appreciation:** In the busyness of work, we often overlook the support and assistance provided by others. Take the time to express gratitude and appreciation for your colleagues' contributions. By showing appreciation, you signal their presence and acknowledgement of their value, fostering a positive work atmosphere.

10. **Mindfully end your workday:** Instead of mindlessly rushing out of the door, bring closure to your workday mindfully. Take ten minutes to review your accomplishments, tie up loose ends and prepare for the next day. This conscious transition allows your mind to relax and sets the stage for a more peaceful and productive start tomorrow.

Our lives are busier than ever before. Between work, chores and the endless distractions provided by our digital gadgets, it often seems like there isn't any time to relax and simply enjoy the present moment. Living life on autopilot isn't a sustainable approach. Over time, stress and anxiety can take a toll on our well-being unless we take proactive steps to counter their effects.

This is where meditation plays a significant role. With its roots in ancient practices and backed by scientific evidence, meditation has been shown to enhance both our physical and mental health, leading to greater happiness. It offers a powerful means of clearing the cluttered mind and rejuvenating the weary body. The best part? You can begin integrating this transformative practice into your daily routine starting today.

Make becoming mindful a habit. Ingrained habits can be challenging to break, and this poses a problem when it comes to negative behavioural patterns that contribute to many of society's issues today, such as smoking, overeating or excessive online usage. Why is it so difficult to change our habits? According to economist Steven Levitt and journalist Stephen Dubner, it all boils down to incentives and consequences.

In their renowned bestseller, *Freakonomics*,[37] Steven and Stephen illustrate this point through a study on hand-washing habits among medical staff at Cedars Sinai Hospital in Los Angeles. Initially, when asked about their adherence to hospital hand-washing rules, doctors and nurses reported a compliance rate of 73 per cent. However, hidden cameras revealed a different story; handwashing occurred in just nine per cent of cases. What was the underlying issue? The hospital administration had failed to provide sufficient incentives for following the rules or consequences for disregarding them.

If we want to cultivate positive habits like mindfulness, we need to nudge ourselves in the right direction. Small but effective strategies can make a significant impact. Setting realistic goals, such as dedicating just five minutes a day to mindfulness practice, makes it feel more attainable. Another valuable tip is to create a supportive environment conducive to your new habit. Designate a tranquil corner free from electronic devices that invites mindful meditation.

Additionally, it's essential to tune into the feedback your mind provides. Take a moment to acknowledge how you feel after a mindfulness session and compare it to the emotional state when you have skipped your daily five-minute meditation. Reflecting on both experiences helps establish a supportive feedback loop, motivating you to persist with your practice.

Focusing on your breathing is a great way to become more mindful and beat stress. We have all experienced those frustrating moments. You are already running late, and suddenly, the traffic ahead comes to a painful halt. As frustration builds, you can feel your breathing quicken, your heart rate rise and your blood pressure soar. How can you find calm in the midst of it all?

One effective approach is to focus on your breathing, which serves as a fundamental aspect of many meditation practices. Here's a simple technique to try: When you feel stress overwhelming you, take a moment to close your eyes and find a comfortable position. Direct your attention to your breath. It's not necessary to analyse every minute detail of your diaphragm's movement at this stage. Instead, aim to centre your mind and focus on the sensations of each breath.

Recognise that breathing impacts various parts of your body, so take the time to pay attention to each of these areas in sequence. Begin with your stomach, observing how it rises and falls with each inhalation and exhalation. Gradually shift your focus upward to your chest and ribcage, noticing their subtle movements. Finally, concentrate on the sensation of the air as it passes through your nostrils.

Remember, mindfulness centres around being fully present in the current moment. If you find your mind wandering to other thoughts or concerns, gently guide it back to your body and breathe, without judgement or frustration. This isn't a competition; the goal is simply to immerse yourself in the present moment.

Practising mindful breathing may require some time to become accustomed to, but with persistence, you will be amazed at how it can transform a stressful experience into a tranquil oasis. And here's an added bonus: regular focus on your breath has been shown to enhance concentration levels. So, by nurturing this habit, you are not only finding inner peace but also, boosting your ability to concentrate.

Transform mundane moments into memorable experiences. One of the simplest ways to cultivate mindfulness is by taking a walk. You do not need to venture far; find a quiet room with enough space to walk 10 or 15 paces in a straight line, and you are ready to go. Here's how it's done:

Begin by walking back and forth along your designated path a few times. As you settle into the rhythm, shift your attention to the sensations in your body. Notice the weight of your feet as they lift off the ground and the solidness of the floor as they make contact. Explore these sensations by shifting your weight from one foot to the other.

Continue walking and experimenting with different paces. Try walking briskly, slowly, and at your usual pace. Pay attention to which speed helps you focus on the present moment and your movements. Like mindful breathing, this exercise requires practice, and initially, your thoughts may wander. The key is gently bringing your attention back to the present and giving it another try. Once you find your rhythm, you will be amazed at how quickly time seems to fly by.

But that's not the only way to infuse the mundane with mindfulness. Another powerful technique is the body scan meditation. Here's how it works: Find a comfortable position and begin by scanning each part of your body, noting the sensations you encounter. Remember, the goal is not to judge yourself but to simply observe. If you encounter any tension, resist the urge to create a narrative about anxiety; instead, acknowledge it and move on.

Start from the top of your head and gradually move downward, exploring the sensations in your face, neck, shoulders, arms, and so on. Scan your entire body in this manner, absorbing as much detail as possible. Like the walking meditation, this practice serves as a grounding force, anchoring you in the present moment.

You do not need to retreat to a monastery in the mountains to discover the miracle of mindfulness.

Pause & Reflect
- How often do you practise mindfulness in your daily life?
- How does practising mindfulness affect your mood and overall well-being?
- In what situations do you find it most challenging to remain mindful?
- How can you incorporate more mindfulness into your daily routine?
- What barriers prevent you from practising mindfulness, and how can you overcome them?
- How does your mindfulness practice affect your interactions with others?
- How has your understanding and practice of mindfulness evolved over time?
- Are you carrying unwanted baggage in your mind?
- Are there resentments, regrets, or worries that no longer serve you?
- Are you holding onto past hurts or anxieties about the future?

✎ PAUSE & REFLECT INSIGHTS

4.3 JOYFUL JOURNEY

"Happiness is not something ready-made. It comes from your own actions."

— **Dalai Lama**

Mo Gawdat's LinkedIn profile reads like a how-to playbook for success. He worked for IBM and Microsoft; he was a VP at Google and then chief business officer for Google X, the famously secretive "moonshot" factory known for innovative tackling of some of the largest problems affecting the world. He is renowned for his involvement in ground-breaking projects like self-driving cars and balloon-powered global internet.

In 2014, Mo, faced a devastating loss when his beloved son, Ali Gawdat, tragically passed away. Ali, at the young age of 21, full of dreams and aspirations, had a bright future. The circumstances surrounding Ali's death added to the profound sorrow experienced by Mo and his family. It was an unexpected loss that occurred during a routine appendectomy.

The suddenness of the tragedy amplified the pain, leaving a lasting impact on Mo's life. In one of his conversations in Dr Ranjan Chatterjee's podcast[38], I listened to him say, *"The departure of our beloved son, Ali, was a result of a seemingly straightforward surgery to treat appendicitis, one of the simplest procedures in the realm of medical science. However, as humans, we are fallible, and mistakes can occur even at the hands of skilled surgeons. This time, tragically, the surgeon's error cost my son his life. It is a sombre reminder that imperfections are an inherent part of our human existence.*

In the wake of this devastating loss, I found myself facing a profound choice. Would I allow grief to consume me for the rest of my days, or would I seek another path? While I knew that I could never bring Ali back, I realised that within the realm of my choices, there was an opportunity to keep his memory alive and share his profound philosophies with the world. In doing so, I could preserve a fragment of his essence, allowing his wisdom to continue to inspire others.

Amidst the pain and sorrow, I recognised that even in grief, there is room for reflection and finding solace in the positive aspects of life. Losing a child is an unfathomable tragedy, but it also signifies the immense privilege and blessing of having had a child in the first place. Ali's presence in our lives, although unplanned and unexpected, was an extraordinary gift — a gift that we cherished for 21 remarkable years.

Ali's time with us became a testament to the preciousness of life and the indelible impact one soul can have on those around them. He brought immeasurable joy, love and wisdom during his all-too-brief existence. While I could not alter the finality of his passing, I could choose to focus on the gratitude for the years we shared and the profound influence he had on my life. In honouring Ali's memory and legacy, I embarked on a journey to share his philosophies and teachings with the world. By doing so, I not only keep a part of him alive but also offer the opportunity for others to benefit from his insights and the wisdom he bestowed upon us.

In the face of unimaginable loss, I discovered that within the depths of grief, there is a flicker of light — the power to choose how we navigate the pain, how we remember and honour our loved ones, and how we find meaning in the face of adversity. While the ache of loss remains, I strive to embrace the positive, to find solace in the memories, and to carry forward the profound lessons Ali taught me during his time on Earth.

In choosing to celebrate Ali's life and the impact he had on us, I am reminded of the extraordinary gift of parenthood and the enduring love that transcends the boundaries of life and death.

Mo, a man who had achieved considerable success and possessed material wealth, found himself grappling with a new reality — one that shattered his previous perception of happiness. In the face of such immense loss, he discovered that no amount of external success or possessions could fill the void left by the absence of his son. The depth of his grief challenged his understanding of happiness, prompting a profound shift in his perspective.

Dr Edith Eger's[39] remarkable life story serves as a powerful testament to the resilience of the human spirit and the transformative power of choice. As one of the last remaining Holocaust survivors, she shares her experiences in a deeply moving and inspiring memoir.

At the tender age of 16, Edith, a talented ballet dancer and gymnast, was tragically sent to Auschwitz, one of the most notorious Nazi concentration camps. It was within the confines of this horrific place that she would face unimaginable loss and suffering. Shortly after her arrival, Edith endured the heart-wrenching separation from her parents, who were sent to the gas chambers, never to be seen again.

In an extraordinary twist of fate, Edith found herself caught in the clutches of the infamous Nazi officer, Dr Josef Mengele's, known as the "Angel of Death". Forced to dance for Mengeles amusement, Edith danced with the desperate hope of securing a loaf of bread — her only means of survival. The loaf she received became a lifeline, as she selflessly shared it with her fellow prisoners, an act of compassion that would later have significant implications.

Edith's story underscores the power of choice even in the most harrowing circumstances. Amidst the unimaginable horrors of the Holocaust, she discovered that she still possessed agency over her thoughts and actions. Despite the dehumanising environment, she made a conscious decision to hold onto her humanity, to show kindness and empathy to those around her.

As she endured unspeakable suffering, Edith's remarkable resilience and determination to survive began to shape her outlook on life. She understood that while she could not control the external circumstances, she could choose how she responded to them. This realisation became a guiding principle, enabling her to find inner strength, even in the face of immense adversity.

Mo and Edith's stories exemplify the strength and resilience that can be found even in the darkest of times. Their message of choosing compassion, forgiveness and self-love serves as an important reminder that no matter the circumstances, we have the power to shape our own lives and find hope and healing.

We all go through various phases in life where external and internal challenges overpower us. These phases and challenges can sometimes feel overwhelming. External challenges such as career setbacks, financial difficulties, health issues or relationship problems can have a significant impact on our well-being. Internal challenges such as self-doubt, fear, anxiety or negative thought patterns can also create obstacles in our path to happiness.

Happiness is a state of mind that everyone desires to achieve. It is a feeling of contentment, satisfaction and joy that radiates from within. Often, people believe that happiness is dependent on external circumstances or material possessions. However, the truth is that happiness is a choice we make, independent of our surroundings.

In this chapter, we will explore the power of choosing happiness and how it can positively impact our lives. To comprehend the concept of happiness as a choice, we must first understand what happiness truly means.

Happiness is not a constant state of euphoria or an absence of negative emotions. It is a dynamic and ever-changing emotional experience that encompasses both positive and negative feelings. Happiness is not solely derived from external factors such as wealth, success or relationships, but it is an internal state of being.

The Power Of Perception

The way we perceive the world and interpret events has a significant influence on our happiness. Our thoughts, beliefs and attitudes shape our reality and affect our emotional well-being. Two people can experience the same event, yet have completely different emotional reactions based on their perception. Therefore, it becomes crucial to recognise that our happiness is not determined by external circumstances, but rather by how we choose to perceive and respond to them.

Imagine two individuals, Sarah and Saheel, who are both faced with the same challenging situation at work. Their company is going through a restructuring process, and as a result, their positions are being eliminated. Sarah perceives this situation as a devastating setback. She sees it as a personal failure and feels overwhelmed with fear, anger and self-doubt. She believes that her career is ruined and that she will struggle to find another job.

On the other hand, Saheel perceives the same situation differently. He sees it as an opportunity for growth and change. Instead of dwelling on the negative aspects, he focuses on the possibilities that lie ahead. Saheel views the restructuring as a chance to explore new career paths, learn new skills and perhaps even start his business.

While both Sarah and Saheel are faced with the same external challenge, their perceptions shape their emotional responses and subsequent actions. Sarah's negative perception leads to feelings of despair and inaction. She becomes trapped in a cycle of self-pity and remains stuck.

In contrast, Saheel's positive perception empowers him to take proactive steps. He starts networking, updating his resume and exploring various job opportunities. His mindset of seeing the situation as an opportunity opens doors that he might not have considered otherwise.

The power of perception lies in the fact that it shapes our reality. How we interpret and frame a situation influences our emotions, actions and outcomes. Sarah's negative perception limits her options and holds her back, while Saheel's positive perception propels him forward and opens up new possibilities.

Taking Responsibility For Our Happiness

One of the most empowering realisations in life is understanding that we are responsible for our own happiness. We have the power to choose our thoughts, attitudes and actions. It is easy to fall into the trap of blaming external factors for our unhappiness, such as our job, relationships or past experiences. However, by taking ownership of our emotions and realising that we have control over our reactions, we can actively choose happiness.

One of my mentees, Devyani (name changed), was feeling unhappy and unfulfilled in her current job. She constantly found herself complaining about her work environment, colleagues and tasks. She realised that her constant negativity was affecting her overall well-being and preventing her from experiencing happiness in her career.

During my mentoring calls with her, I suggested and guided her that instead of dwelling on her unhappiness and blaming external factors, she should take responsibility for her own happiness. We started by reflecting on what aspects of her job and work environment contribute to her dissatisfaction and identified that she lacks a sense of purpose and feels unchallenged in her current role.

Devyani took proactive steps to address these issues. First, she engaged in self-reflection to understand her values, passions and long-term goals. We discovered that she has a keen interest in social entrepreneurship and making a positive impact on society. Next, she explored opportunities within her current job to align her work with her passions and values. She identified projects and initiatives that allowed her to contribute meaningfully to causes she cared about. By taking on these projects and infusing her work with purpose, Devyani began to find more fulfilment in her day-to-day tasks.

Devyani took the initiative to seek out learning opportunities and professional development. She attended relevant workshops, conferences and networking events to expand her skills and knowledge in the areas she was passionate about. She actively invested in her growth and recognised the importance of maintaining a positive mindset and cultivating gratitude. Devyani started practising daily gratitude exercises, expressing appreciation for the positive aspects of her job and life. This shift in perspective allowed her to focus on the things that bring her joy and fulfilment, leading to an overall increase in her happiness.

To choose happiness, we must cultivate a positive mindset and change our perspective on life. This involves shifting our focus from what is lacking to what we already have.

Gratitude plays a vital role in this process. By practising gratitude, we train our minds to appreciate the small blessings and positive aspects of our lives. Instead of dwelling on what we lack, we learn to cherish the present moment and find joy in the simple pleasures.

Negativity can be a significant obstacle in the path to happiness. It drains our energy, hinders our growth and limits our potential. To choose happiness, we must let go of negativity in all its forms; negative thoughts, self-criticism, grudges and toxic relationships. This requires self-awareness and a conscious effort to replace negative with positive thoughts and actions.

By embracing forgiveness, practising self-compassion and surrounding ourselves with uplifting influences, we create a positive environment that nurtures our happiness. Life is filled with challenges, setbacks and uncertainties. However, our response to these difficulties determines our level of happiness. Resilience is the ability to bounce back from adversity and maintain a positive outlook. By developing resilience, we strengthen our emotional well-being and increase our capacity for happiness. Resilience is built through self-care, building a support system, practising mindfulness and reframing setbacks as opportunities for growth.

Another crucial aspect of choosing happiness is living in alignment with our values. When our actions and choices reflect our core values, we experience a sense of purpose and fulfilment. This authenticity brings a deep and lasting happiness that cannot be achieved through external validation or material possessions. By identifying our values and aligning our lives accordingly, we create a solid foundation for sustainable happiness.

Embracing Mindfulness And Presence

Mindfulness is the practice of being fully present in the current moment, as we saw in the previous chapter, without judgement or attachment to the past or future. It allows us to appreciate the beauty and richness of life as it unfolds. By cultivating mindfulness, we enhance our ability to choose happiness.

Mindfulness enables us to observe our thoughts and emotions without being consumed by them. It frees us from the grip of negative thinking and empowers us to make conscious choices that align with our happiness. I am highly influenced by the life and preaching of Gautama Buddha. His realisation and subsequent teachings formed the foundation of Buddhism, emphasising the importance of mindfulness in the pursuit of happiness and spiritual awakening. The practice of mindfulness meditation became a central aspect of Buddhist practice.

In his book, *Solve for Happy: Engineering Your Path*, Mo Gawdat, introduces the concept of the "Happiness Equation",[40] a mathematical model that challenges common misconceptions about happiness. He proposes that happiness is not a result of external circumstances, but rather an internal state of being that can be cultivated and nurtured. The equation, which he elaborates on throughout the book, consists of the perception of events, the gap between perception and reality, and the biochemicals that influence our emotions.

Central to the approach is the understanding that happiness is a choice. I encourage you to take responsibility for your own happiness, regardless of your external circumstances. Amidst the ebb and flow of life's challenges and triumphs, we hold the power to shape our own experience. It is in the moments of pause and reflection that we realise the profound truth that our happiness is not dependent on external circumstances, but rather on how we choose to perceive, respond and navigate the world.

Happiness is not a destination to be reached, but a state of being we can actively create. It requires courage, self-awareness and a commitment to personal growth. It demands that we release the notion that external factors hold the key to our joy and instead recognise that true happiness emanates from within.

The stories of Mo or Edith teach that even in the face of adversity, we can choose resilience, optimism and inner peace. Their life resonates with people from all walks of life, reminding us that regardless of the circumstances we face, we have the power to choose our attitudes, responses and the path that lead to healing and happiness. We have the power to rewrite our stories, transcend limitations and find joy in the smallest of moments.

Pause & Reflect
- What does happiness mean to you personally?
- Are there specific activities or experiences that consistently bring you joy and contentment?
- How often do you consciously make choices that prioritise your own happiness?
- What are some obstacles or negative patterns that may hinder your ability to choose happiness?
- Are there any areas of your life where you can make changes or take actions to cultivate more happiness?
- How do your relationships and connections with others contribute to your overall happiness?
- Are there any limiting beliefs or expectations that may prevent you from actively choosing happiness?
- What are some small, daily habits or practices you can incorporate to enhance your happiness?
- How does your perspective on challenges and setbacks influence your ability to choose happiness?
- Reflect on a recent situation where you consciously chose happiness. How did it impact your overall well-being?

✒ PAUSE & REFLECT INSIGHTS

4.4 BEYOND WORK

"Choose a job you love, and you will never have to work a day in your life."

— **Confucius**

April 10, 2010, Ranthambore National Park, Rajasthan

I was on the first wildlife trip of my life. It was five months after my surgery and I was recouping well. The constant pain on the left side of my body bothered me for which I was prescribed nerve relaxing pills and painkillers. The doctors had told me that I had to live my whole life with this pain as the damage to some nerves was irreparable. I was wearing a thick neck collar to protect me from the jerks of the wildlife safari.

I had never been to a jungle before. In fact, I had never heard of Ranthambore National Park. One of our Canadian customers was visiting and happened to be a wildlife photographer. He wanted to go to Ranthambore National Park and I decided to accompany him. Through a common friend, I got in touch with the owner of a resort who arranged everything for us.

We spent two wonderful days there doing four safaris. Though we did not see any tigers, the trip was magical for me. The pain that I used to suffer from 24x7 just vanished. I did not even take my painkillers and other medicines. I had a small camera and I took whatever pictures it was capable of. I also knew nothing about photography. I could not differentiate between a Deer and a Sambar. But those two days made me realise that I could lead a pain-free life too.

This was my first ever jungle trip and I think it's fair to say that I was now completely hooked onto the wonder that is wildlife and photography. I was genuinely happy. Maybe for the first time in many years. This became the first hobby of my adult life.

The first thing I did on my return was to buy a new camera and long lens suitable for wildlife photography. The weekends took on a new meaning as they transformed into exciting trips to nearby bird sanctuaries such as Okhla, Sultanpur, Dadri and Bharatpur. There, among the beauty of nature's creations, I found solace and inspiration. As my passion for wildlife photography deepened, I recognised the need to expand my knowledge about the natural world. I immersed myself into books and articles on our natural history, eager to understand the intricate connections and the delicate balance that sustains life on this planet.

I found a few mentors and reached out to them and they were all very helpful to teach and fine-tune my photography skills. Going to various jungles became a monthly routine and I visited almost all parks in India and Africa over the years. These trips to the park worked like therapy. In a couple of years, I was almost off the painkillers and consumed them only a few times in a year. I have been completely off them for almost six years now.

My hobby cured me of the pain I was told I had to live with all my life. This transformation also had a profound impact on my perspective of the future. Where uncertainty once loomed, a sense of optimism and hope began to take root. Armed with newfound strength and resilience, I became more adept at navigating life's challenges, knowing that nature had bestowed upon me the tools to weather any storm. In the serene embrace of nature, I found a connection that transcended the physical world.

As I roamed the jungles with my camera in hand, it was not just wildlife I was capturing, but a profound sense of spirituality and oneness. I felt at peace, at home with myself, and in the presence of a greater power. When I ventured into the jungle, it was an opportunity to be with myself, in complete harmony with the world around me. My camera acted as a bridge between the moments I cherished and the tangible memories I could preserve forever. Each click of the shutter was a testament to the beauty of life, a reminder of the interwoven tapestry of existence.

Thanks to the power of social media, my photographs began to gain significant attention and exposure. They were shared widely, re-posted, and liked by thousands of people. Eventually, my work was noticed by various national and international magazines, who reached out to me and offered to publish my images.

The satisfaction of seeing my photographs in print was immense, but what made it even more rewarding was the fact that my hobby was now also making me some money. I began to receive offers for paid assignments and commissions, which allowed me to pursue my passion and earn a living from it.

As my work gained more recognition, I also began to receive awards and accolades. In 2014, I was honoured with the prestigious DJ Memorial Photography Award, which was a huge boost to my confidence as a photographer. The following year, I won the ICICI Camaraderie Award, which came with a substantial prize package including a car and a holiday to Australia. The feeling of accomplishment and pride that came with these awards was indescribable.

In addition to these major awards, I also received honourable mentions in various international and national photography competitions. Each recognition was a testament to the time, effort and dedication that I had put into my hobby. It also served as motivation to continue improving my skills and pushing the boundaries of what I thought was possible.

What did I gain from having a hobby?
- It cured me of my pain.
- It fetched me recognition.
- I made new friends who also had wildlife photography as a hobby.
- It boosted my confidence which helped me be more productive at work.
- It rejuvenated me and removed negative stress.
- It helped me develop professionally too, as some of the skills I learnt came in handy at my work.

If you look at all the famous people, they all were avid hobbyists. Former US President Franklin Roosevelt enjoyed hunting, boxing, horseback riding, hiking, reading and writing. Physicist Albert Einstein was an avid sailor. Actors Brad Pitt does pottery, Julia Roberts knits, Tom Cruise does fencing, singer John Lennon collected stamps.

Business magnate Warren Buffett plays Bridge, ex US President Donald Trump plays golf, and former British Prime Minister Winston Churchill did more than 500 paintings. Closer home; Rajnikant is an avid reader, Shah Rukh Khan is into gaming, Anil Ambani is a marathon runner and Alia Bhatt is a charcoal painter. If all these busy people can have time for hobbies, so can you.

The benefits of having a hobby are often understated. Engaging in an activity that we enjoy can have numerous positive effects on our physical, mental and emotional well-being. In fact, studies have shown that having a hobby can help in curing certain diseases.[41]

The act of engaging in a hobby can be meditative, allowing individuals to enter a state of relaxation that helps reduce stress levels. Research has linked high levels of stress to a variety of ailments, including heart disease, hypertension and diabetes.[42] Engaging in activities such as gardening, painting, playing an instrument or reading a book can help individuals reduce their stress levels, leading to improved overall health.

Hobbies that involve physical activity can also have a significant impact on an individual's physical health. Participating in activities such as hiking, biking or swimming can help improve cardiovascular health, reduce the risk of obesity and increase overall energy levels. Engaging in physical activity can also help improve mood, reduce anxiety and depression and promote a sense of well-being.

People who suffer from chronic pain conditions such as arthritis, fibromyalgia or migraines may find relief by engaging in a hobby. Studies have shown that participating in activities such as knitting, painting, or playing an instrument can help distract the mind from pain and promote feeling of relaxation.[43] Hobbies that involve repetitive motions can also help improve joint mobility, reducing the severity of chronic pain conditions.

Hobbies that involve social interaction can also have a positive impact on an individual's mental health. Engaging in activities such as joining a book club, taking a dance class, or participating in a sports league can help individuals build connections and foster a sense of community. Social interaction has been linked to improved mental health, reduced feelings of loneliness and isolation, and increased overall happiness.

Engaging in a hobby can also help individuals with cognitive decline or neurodegenerative diseases such as Alzheimer's or Parkinson's. Hobbies that involve problem-solving, such as puzzles or games, can help improve cognitive function and slow the progression of its decline. Hobbies that involve physical activity, such as gardening or yoga, can also help improve balance and coordination, reducing the risk of falls and other accidents.

It is important to note that while hobbies can have numerous positive effects on an individual's physical and mental health, they should not be used as a replacement for medical treatment. Individuals should always consult with their healthcare provider before making any changes to their treatment plan.

In addition to the physical and mental benefits of having a hobby, engaging in an activity we enjoy can also promote a sense of purpose and fulfilment. Hobbies can provide individuals with a sense of accomplishment, boost self-esteem and confidence. Pursuing a hobby can also provide a sense of structure and routine, which can be particularly beneficial for individuals who struggle with anxiety or depression.

Finding a hobby that resonates with an individual's interests and personality is crucial to reaping the benefits of engaging in an activity. Hobbies should be enjoyable and promote feelings of relaxation and fulfilment. Some individuals may find that they enjoy hobbies that are more solitary, such as reading or painting, while others may prefer activities that involve social interaction, such as joining a sports team or volunteering in the community.

A hobby is needed to rest the mind that is often wearied by the stresses of life. As a professional even 24 hours in a day seem too short a period. Hobbies and passions tend to take a back seat. You will burn out which is why it is important to have some hobby outside your day job. Gardening, reading, running, collecting stamps, photography, whatever it is, let the hobby relax you and give you peace. A hobby brings stillness to life. It helps live a balanced life. A hobby is an investment. It gives you fulfilment and joy.

Schedule Them. Cultivate Them. Take Out Time.
Pause & Reflect

- How often do you make time for your hobbies in your daily routine? Are there any hobbies that you have been wanting to try, but have not found the time for?
- Have you ever noticed how engaging in a hobby can help you forget about the stresses of daily life and promote relaxation? What hobbies do you find particularly calming or meditative?
- Reflect on how hobbies can provide a sense of structure and routine in your life. Do you find that having a regular hobby helps you maintain a sense of balance and purpose?
- Have you ever considered how engaging in physical hobbies, such as hiking or dancing, can have a positive impact on your physical health? How do you incorporate physical activity into your hobbies?
- Do your hobbies align with your personal goals and passions, or do they serve as a form of escapism?
- Reflect on how you can incorporate your hobbies into your daily life in a more intentional way. Are there any small changes you can make to prioritise your hobbies and reap the benefits they offer?

✑ PAUSE & REFLECT INSIGHTS

Section 5

Deep Wells of Wisdom – Cultivating Spiritual Health

"The mind can go in a thousand directions, but on this beautiful path, I walk in peace. With each step, the wind blows. With each step, a flower blooms."
— **Thich Nhat Hanh**

Spiritual health is a fundamental facet of our well-being that too often is overshadowed by the physical and mental dimensions. It encompasses our connection with the profound, our sense of purpose, and our alignment with our core values and beliefs. It might seem elusive, but it is every bit as concrete and essential as physical vitality and mental clarity. This chapter delves into the essence of the eternal through the lenses of Transcendent Trust and Resurgence, essential elements that enable us to cultivate spiritual health.

Transcendent Trust: The Belief In A Supreme Power

One of the core components of spiritual health is the faith in something greater than ourselves, a supreme power that underpins the universe and the myriad life forms within it. This is not limited to religious contexts; atheists, agnostics and those who follow non-theistic paths can also nurture a transcendent trust.

For some, this supreme power may take the form of god or goddesses. For others, it may be a force that governs natural laws, or it could be the interconnected web of life itself. Regardless of the form, the common thread is a sense of reverence, humility and respect for that which is beyond our comprehension and control.

A trust in this supreme power encourages a shift in perspective, allowing us to embrace the world and its happenings from a vantage point of understanding and acceptance. It also nurtures an awareness of the interconnectedness of all beings, fostering empathy, compassion and an intrinsic sense of ethics.

Ultimately, transcendent trust liberates us from the futile pursuit of absolute control. It helps us surrender to the flow of life, offering a profound sense of peace and serenity. It's akin to boarding a boat and trust the river's current to carry us towards our destination, rather than attempting to push against the tide.

Resurgence: The Reality Of A Second Life

The concept of a second life or resurgence is another crucial aspect of spiritual health. This does not necessarily imply reincarnation or an afterlife, although it certainly can for some. Rather, it is about the spiritual rebirth that takes place within this life, as we evolve and transform.

Each one of us experiences moments of profound change, where old aspects of our lives or ourselves are shed to make way for the new. These moments can occur in the aftermath of crises or during periods of intense introspection. They may feel like a phoenix rising from the ashes or the blooming of a lotus from the muddy depths.

Resurgence underscores the innate capacity we have for growth and transformation. It reminds us that it is never too late to change, to improve or to start afresh. This belief in personal evolution and renewal can give us the strength to persevere through challenging times and to pursue our aspirations with resilience.

The concept of resurgence offers hope, a reassurance that while we may stumble and fall, we always have the potential to rise again. It nurtures a growth mindset and fosters a deeper understanding of the cyclical nature of existence.

In the grand scheme of life, we are explorers charting the course of our existence, powered by trust in the supreme power and our ability to evolve. As we navigate this journey, may we cultivate a spiritually healthy life, allowing us to experience the profound peace and understanding that comes from connecting with the essence of the eternal.

5.1 TRANSCENDENT TRUST

"Embrace your spiritual side and believe in the presence of a greater power. Through this connection, you will unlock the boundless strength and wisdom that resides within your soul."

— **Deepak Chopra**

Life can be overwhelming, and in those moments, it can feel like we are alone and hopeless. But what if I told you that there's a superpower that can guide you through tough times? It's not magic; it's spirituality. Being spiritual means believing in something beyond yourself, whether it's god, the universe, or your higher self. Embracing your spiritual side can help you find peace, purpose and happiness.

In March 2001, I embarked on a business delegation trip representing small and medium Indian engineering industries. This trip, arranged by the Engineering Export Promotion Council, was meant to explore potential business opportunities in the United States. During my visit, I had the privilege of meeting with a renowned tier-one auto components manufacturing company headquartered in Troy, MI, USA. Our encounter proved to be highly fruitful, resulting in a proposal for a joint venture between our respective companies.

The proposed joint venture entailed the establishment of a new venture in India, with equal shareholding, focused on manufacturing products for export to their global facilities. The scope of this ambitious project necessitated substantial investment and debt, including the import of machinery and technology from the United States. Recognising the potential of this collaboration, we proceeded to sign the joint venture agreement in June 2001, envisioning a promising future for our partnership.

However, fate had other plans, and soon after signing the agreement, an unexpected turn of events compelled me to return urgently to India, where I received the devastating news of my mother's advanced stage of cancer. The following weeks were filled with consultations, medical tests and emotionally challenging decisions about her treatment.

Faced with the gravity of the situation, I realised that my family's well-being had to take precedence over any professional endeavours. In light of my mother's health crisis, I gathered the courage to reach out to Mark, the director of our partner company. I humbly explained the significantly changed circumstances and the urgent need for me to focus on my mother's well-being. With sincere understanding and empathy, Mark graciously agreed to postpone the joint venture, demonstrating not only their professionalism but also their compassion towards my personal situation.

As I navigated the challenges posed by my mother's illness, unforeseen global events further complicated the joint venture's prospects. The tragic September 11 attacks shook the world, causing a significant downturn in the US automobile market. The repercussions of this unprecedented event reverberated across various industries, and our American partner was not exempt from its impact. The company faced severe setbacks, ultimately leading to its unfortunate declaration of bankruptcy.

Reflecting on the events during that period when I first learnt about my mother's illness, I often found myself questioning why our family had to face such a difficult situation. It seemed like an overwhelming burden to bear. However, little did I know at the time that my mother's cancer diagnosis would inadvertently spare me from the potential hardship of bankruptcy and legal prosecution.

Had I proceeded with the joint venture as planned, I would have incurred significant debt to finance the project. The financial strain could have pushed me to the brink of bankruptcy, with potentially devastating consequences for my personal and professional life. The weight of these financial obligations, combined with the unexpected closure of my customer's business, would have made it virtually impossible for me to fulfil my export obligations.

In such a scenario, I might have faced legal repercussions due to my inability to meet the export requirements against the duty-free import of machines. Prosecution under these circumstances, with strict laws and regulations in place, could have further compounded the challenges I was already facing. Ironically, it was my mother's illness that altered the course of events and shielded me from these potential pitfalls. The urgency and gravity of her condition prompted me to reassess my priorities and make the difficult decision to put the joint venture on hold. By redirecting my focus and resources towards my mother's health and well-being, I unintentionally avoided the financial risks that loomed over the project.

While the initial shock and anguish of my mother's illness were overwhelming, her diagnosis inadvertently served as a blessing in disguise. It protected me from the burdensome debt that could have led to bankruptcy, and it spared me from the legal consequences of failing to fulfil my export obligations. Looking back, I cannot help but recognise the mysterious ways in which life unfolds. What seemed like an unfathomable challenge at the time ultimately became a saving grace.

My mother's illness, as difficult as it was, served as a catalyst for change and redirection. Today, as I see my mother's health restored and witness the positive outcomes that emerged from this tumultuous period, I am filled with gratitude. It is a reminder that even in the darkest moments, there may be hidden blessings and unforeseen paths that lead us away from the precipice of despair.

In the aftermath of the 2010 earthquake in Haiti, a teenage girl named Darlene Etienne was rescued after spending 15 days trapped under rubble. When she was finally pulled from the site, she told rescuers that she had survived by praying and singing hymns throughout her ordeal. During the Holocaust in Second World War, many Jewish people who were imprisoned in concentration camps turned to their faith to survive. They prayed, shared their beliefs with others and found comfort in their connection with a higher power. This belief offered them hope and helped them keep going even when conditions were incredibly difficult.

In a world full of chaos and uncertainty, embracing your spiritual side can help you find peace, purpose and happiness. Whether you believe in god, the universe, or your higher self, there's something within you that's connected to something greater than yourself. Embracing your spiritual side means believing in something beyond yourself, being mindful, connecting with your higher self, nurturing your relationships and finding purpose and meaning in life. Hence, take a step back, breathe and embrace your spiritual side.

There's something that unites us all, and it's our innate desire to believe in something more significant than ourselves. Whether it's a god or a higher purpose, we all need something to believe in. Believing in a superpower gives us a sense of purpose and meaning in life. It helps us feel connected to something greater than ourselves, and as a result, we experience a sense of peace and inner calm.

Embracing your spiritual side is all about mindfulness. It's about being present in the moment and being aware of your surroundings. When we are mindful, we are more in touch with our emotions, thoughts and feelings. We are more in tune with what's happening within and around us. Mindfulness helps us stay grounded and centred in the present moment, which promotes mental, emotional and physical well-being.

Mindfulness can be cultivated through various formal and informal practices. Formal practices include meditation techniques such as focused attention on the breath, body scan, loving-kindness meditation and mindful movements like yoga or Tai Chi. These practices encourage individuals to anchor their attention in the present moment, observing their experiences with an open and non-judgmental attitude.

Detailed tools on mindfulness are covered in the chapter, *Calm in Chaos* of this book. When we believe in a superpower, we are essentially connecting with our higher self. Our higher self is the part of us that's connected to something beyond ourselves. It's the part of us that's intuitive, wise and compassionate. When we are connected with our higher self, we are more in tune with our purpose and what we are meant to do in life. We are more open to receiving guidance and support from the universe, and we are more confident in our decision-making abilities.

There is a difference between religiosity and spiritualism. While religiosity is often associated with organised religions and adhering to established doctrines and rituals, spiritualism can be practised both within and outside of religious frameworks. Spiritualism allows individuals to explore their own unique paths and beliefs, drawing from various traditions, philosophies and practices. It can be a more flexible and inclusive approach to spirituality, as it encourages personal interpretation and the integration of diverse spiritual teachings.

It's important to note that religiosity and spiritualism are not mutually exclusive. Many individuals may engage in religious practices while also pursuing a personal spiritual journey. However, the distinction lies in the emphasis placed on external religious structures and practices in religiosity, compared to the internal exploration and connection with the divine in spiritualism.

Embracing your spiritual side can also help you nurture your relationships. When we believe in something beyond ourselves, we are more inclined to be kind, compassionate, and understanding towards others. We are more likely to see others as equals and to treat them with respect and kindness. When we practice mindfulness and connect with our higher self, we are more in touch with our emotions, which help us communicate better with others. We are better able to express our feelings and needs, listen actively and respond with empathy and understanding.

Ultimately, embracing your spiritual side can help you find purpose and meaning in life. Believing in a superpower gives us a sense of direction and meaning. It helps us see that our lives are part of something greater than ourselves. Embracing spirituality means living a life of purpose, where we are connected to our innermost desires and values. It means knowing what we are meant to do in life and pursuing it with passion and dedication.

Pause & Reflect

- What does believing in a superpower mean to you personally?
- How does your belief in a higher power or a superpower impact your daily life and decision-making?
- Have you experienced moments or events that have strengthened your belief in a superpower?
- How does your belief in a higher power provide comfort and support during challenging times?
- Do you think believing in a superpower enhances your sense of purpose and meaning in life? Why or why not?
- How does your belief in a higher power influence your interactions with others and your perspective of the world?
- Have you ever questioned or doubted your belief in a superpower? If so, what led to those moments of doubt and how did you navigate through them?

🖎 PAUSE & REFLECT INSIGHTS

5.2 RESURGENCE

"It may be when we no longer know what to do, we have come to our real work, and that when we no longer know which way to go we have begun our real journey."

— **Wendell Berry**

It's rare for one to encounter their own obituary while they are still among the living. Such was the unusual experience of Alfred Nobel when he perused a Paris newspaper in April 1888. The publication had mistakenly printed his obituary instead of his brother Ludvig's, who had passed away on April 12, 1888 at the age of 56. With a startling headline, "The merchant of death is dead",[44] the newspaper highlighted Alfred's infamy as the inventor of dynamite.

This grim narrative of his life shook Albert. It presented the repulsive notion that one of the wealthiest men on earth might be remembered solely as a purveyor of death. It provoked him to ponder how he could leave a more positive and idealistic legacy. As a result of this jarring wake-up call, Albert resolved to devote a lion's share of his extensive wealth to a cause that would offer a lasting and positive impact on the world. This self-reflection ultimately inspired him to create the Nobel Prize, a symbol of worldwide acclaim for progress in peace, literature, science, and medicine.

Vipul Gupta, a cherished friend of mine, carries a life story I affectionately refer to as **"The tale of the entrepreneur who sold his Jaguar."** As a first-generation entrepreneur, he embarked on his journey with practically nothing and went on to establish a rapidly expanding enterprise. His company comprises five manufacturing units, employing a workforce of 750 people, and successfully exports products to over 70 countries, with an enviable EBITDA (Earnings before Interest, Taxes, Depreciation, and Amortisation), a long list of marque customers and enough headroom to grow into a highly profitable large-scale business.

Once in a gathering of esteemed business leaders, he had to introduce himself. Apart from mentioning his role as the managing director of his company, he realised he had nothing substantial to add to it. At that moment, he had a profound realisation that his identity seemed to be solely derived from his professional title and the business he represented. In his own words, *"My introduction, my very essence seemed to be solely tied to the name of the company I represented. I began to question whether building businesses was truly my sole and ultimate purpose in life. What would be the legacy I leave behind?"*

Standing at a crossroads, he faced a pivotal choice. Should he continue down the path he had been on for most of his adult life, which involved building commercial businesses, or should he venture into uncharted territory, exploring new possibilities? **Or start his second life.**

Every year, we pass our death anniversary without knowing the precise date. It serves as a reminder that the true measure of a person's life is not determined by their personal achievements, but rather by the impact they have had on others. *"Jo bhi karna hai, kar guzar... kya khabar barson ki ya lamha ki hai zindagi"* (Whatever you want to do, go ahead and do it... who knows whether life would go on for years or last just a moment.)

Vipul adds, *"I decided to halt for a bit and engage in deep reflection. Through days, weeks, and months of contemplation, I eventually stumbled upon a simple truth that held profound value.* **Focus on significance rather than success and make the rest of your life the best of your life.***"*

And that newfound realisation became his life's guiding principle, his new north star. He made the decision to prioritise living with intention rather than relentlessly pursuing wealth and fame. He chose to build something that would extend far beyond his own lifetime — a blueprint for a new, thrilling, vibrant, purposeful and service-oriented life.

At the age of 55, he decided to step back from his business ventures. He restructured the operations of his businesses and let the professionals run it and concentrated all his efforts on Earth Focus, a non-profit Section 8 company. This marked the birth of the Earth Focus Foundation (https://www.earthfocus.in/), an organisation dedicated to working with the most marginalised tribal communities in the buffer areas of Kanha National Park in central India. Their vision is to create a Kanha landscape where both people and nature thrive in harmony. Their primary focus revolves around education, as well as the restoration of degraded land, which ultimately paves the way for nature-based livelihood. In three years, Earth Focus is a case study on sustainability and social entrepreneurship.

A few years ago, on a flight from Mumbai to Delhi, I found myself seated next to a Bollywood superstar from yesteryears. In his younger days, he was adored universally for his romantic movies. His female fans would go into a frenzy upon catching a glimpse of even his parked car; even I, during my youth, admired him greatly. However, as time passed, his movies began to flop one after another. Despite his desperate attempts to retain his status as the beloved romantic hero, age was not on his side, and the audience no longer embraced his films.

During our conversation on that flight, he nonchalantly mentioned that he was no longer liked by anyone. The same people who adored him then, now do not even bother to stop and take a picture with him. He never realised that this party could not last forever. He should have seen the signs that it was coming to an end. Instead, he refused to accept this and kept working harder and harder and the more he tried, the more he failed.

Arthur C. Brooks calls this **'strivers curse'**[45] in his book, *From Strength to Strength*. People who strive to be excellent at what they do often wind up finding their inevitable decline terrifying, their success increasingly unsatisfying and their relationships lacking. At the age of 22, Charles Darwin, embarked on a momentous scientific expedition aboard a royal ship, dedicating five years to traversing the globe and collecting extraordinary samples of plant and animal life. This remarkable journey secured his esteemed place in history.

By the age of 27, Charles formulated the theory of natural selection, which revolutionised our understanding of evolution by proposing that the most adaptable organisms thrive through the principle of survival of the fittest. At 50, he achieved a milestone in his career with the publication of his ground-breaking work, *On the Origin of Species*,[46] a best-selling magnum opus that forever altered the landscape of science.

However, despite his extraordinary achievements, Charles passed away considering himself a failure. Why? Like many accomplished professionals, he struggled to accept the decline of his career as he advanced in age. Publishing *On the Origin of Species* at 50, marked the pinnacle of his professional journey, leaving him with the daunting realisation that there seemed to be no greater heights left to reach.

From the age of 50 to 73, Charles found himself trapped in a period of creative stagnation, devoid of further scientific breakthroughs or industry-defining publications. This meant a loss of purpose for Charles. His professional decline was completely normal and predictable. Whether dancer, doctor, painter, engineer, or pilot, one thing is sure: one day, you will face a similar decline in your career.

As we age, our abilities change. But contrary to popular belief, that isn't a bad thing. In fact, the second half of life can be even more promising than the first. With the right strategies and a positive mindset, it is possible to discover success and enduring fulfilment as one embraces the process of ageing, steadily progressing from strength to strength.

Why Do We Decline?

The occurrence can be attributed to alterations in brain structure, specifically the shifting functionality of the prefrontal cortex, located in the frontal lobe of the brain. This region matures during childhood and experiences the earliest decline in adulthood. Its primary function is associated with working memory, which involves filtering out irrelevant information while focusing on the current task. As individuals reach middle age, the prefrontal cortex gradually loses its efficiency, leading to difficulties in rapid analysis. Additionally, multitasking becomes challenging, and recalling names becomes increasingly arduous.

In 1971, Raymond Cattell made a significant discovery regarding human intelligence, identifying two distinct types that vary in abundance during different stages of life: **fluid intelligence and crystallised intelligence**.[47]

Fluid intelligence, as defined by Raymond, refers to *the capacity for reasoning, flexible thinking and problem-solving in novel situations.* This type of intelligence plays a crucial role in solving complex mathematical equations and fostering innovative thinking for devising new inventions. Here's the interesting part:

Fluid intelligence reaches its peak during early adulthood but experiences a significant decline starting in one's 30s and 40s. As time goes on, the capacity for fluid intelligence gradually diminishes, eventually reaching a point where it may no longer serve as reliably as before.

Raymond defined crystallised intelligence as *"a person's knowledge gained during life by acculturation and learning"*. Crystallised intelligence, in contrast, relies on accumulated knowledge and continues to increase throughout one's 40s, 50s and 60s, without experiencing a significant decline until much later in life. This implies that while young individuals possess the ability to think quickly and recall information, older individuals have a unique advantage in comprehending and effectively applying that knowledge.

In youth, there is a propensity to generate a wealth of factual information, while in old age, there is a greater understanding of the meaning behind those facts and how to utilise them. By adapting your professional role to emphasise the utilisation of crystallised intelligence while reducing reliance on fluid intelligence, you can significantly postpone the onset of cognitive decline. Shifting the focus towards leveraging accumulated knowledge and expertise allows for a longer preservation of cognitive abilities, delaying the decline until much later in life.

Around seven years ago, my eldest son decided to join my business. He expressed a strong desire to implement significant changes in the organisation and work processes, which initially met resistance from me. Being accustomed to the tried-and-tested methods that had brought me previous success, I was hesitant to embrace his ideas. However, after numerous arguments and discussions, I finally relented and allowed him to proceed with his vision.

Remarkably, over the course of the past seven years, our business has experienced an impressive fourfold growth. It became evident that if I had stubbornly adhered to my old approaches, we would have faced the possibility of bankruptcy and eventual closure. The decision to embrace my son's fresh perspective and adapt to new methods proved to be a pivotal moment for the prosperity and survival of our business.

Human beings are inherently wired in a way that prevents us from savouring our achievements for an extended period. The satisfaction derived from success seems fleeting, fleeting like a passing moment. We find ourselves unable to pause and fully relish the sense of accomplishment we have attained. It's as if we are constantly running on a treadmill, fearing that if we stop, we will lose our balance and stumble.

Thus, we keep pushing forward, hoping that the next achievement will finally grant us the lasting satisfaction we yearn for. Our lives often resemble that of a lab rat on a treadmill, tirelessly chasing after the elusive cheese placed on the spinning wheel. Even when the cheese is taken away by the scientists, the rat continues running, trapped in an endless cycle. It's crucial to ponder — are we also running aimlessly on life's treadmill? Are we caught up in a relentless pursuit without a clear purpose or direction? Taking a moment to introspect can help us break free from this repetitive cycle and find meaning in our actions.

First century BC Roman statesman, Marcus Tullius Cicero writes about vocation in the second half of life in an open letter he wrote to his son titled, *De Officiis.*[48] Marcus shares three insightful perspectives on old age. Firstly, *he emphasises that this phase should be dedicated to serving others*, implying a sense of selflessness and contributing to the welfare of society. Secondly, Marcus regards *wisdom as the greatest gift one can attain in later years,* which should be shared and used to enrich the lives of others. Lastly, he highlights that during this stage of life, *our inherent ability lies in mentoring, advising, and teaching,* without seeking worldly rewards such as wealth, power or prestige.

Marcus's wisdom encourages the notion that the later years are an opportunity to make a meaningful impact by offering guidance and knowledge to others, transcending materialistic pursuits. Recognising the decline of my fluid intelligence, I made a conscious decision to shift my focus towards mentorship, teaching and sharing wisdom. As a part of this transformation, I began writing weekly newsletters for my subscribers, covering diverse topics related to personal growth. Additionally, I expanded my engagement by participating in various conferences where I delivered talks on a wide range of subjects, ranging from business and health to photography. Through these endeavours, I embraced a new direction in my professional profile, leveraging my accumulated knowledge and experience to inspire and educate others.

Dedicate the latter half of your life to selflessly serving others, imparting your wisdom and sharing the values you hold dear. Embrace the process of ageing by disseminating the things you believe are of utmost importance. Remember, true excellence lies in its own intrinsic value, and this is how you can truly excel during this stage of life. By focusing on sharing your knowledge and experiences, you can make a significant and meaningful impact on those around you, fostering personal growth and leaving a lasting legacy.

Success often means knowing when to walk away. In the pursuit of achievement, there are three factors that can hold us back from embracing new paths: *attachment to worldly rewards, addiction to work and success and fear of decline.* These factors tend to keep high-achieving professionals tethered to their past successes, making it challenging to transition into the next phase of their lives. However, recognising and addressing these barriers is crucial for personal growth and fulfilment.

Across industries and around the world, many individuals are wired to crave continuous success. They thrive on the adrenaline rush that comes from reaching new heights and accumulating material rewards. This addiction to success can become problematic, leading to workaholism. Workaholics depend on the dopamine hit that results from receiving money, power or prestige. They become trapped in a cycle where the pursuit of these external validations becomes their primary source of happiness. Unfortunately, these chemical highs are short-lived, leaving individuals constantly chasing the next achievement in an endless quest for fulfilment.

As we age, our abilities naturally decline. The skills and capacities that brought us success in our earlier years may no longer be as reliable or effective. This shifting landscape challenges our perception of success. The fear of decline often emerges, prompting us to cling to past achievements and resist change. However, finding lasting happiness and contentment requires us to adapt and embrace the new realities of our later years.

Rather than deriving our entire sense of worth from professional success, it is essential to cultivate a well-rounded life. Success that is solely measured by career accomplishments may leave us feeling empty and unfulfilled. Instead, we can turn to outlets that will never fail us; our relationships, personal passions and spiritual or philosophical beliefs. These facets of life provide enduring sources of joy and meaning, unaffected by the transient nature of external accolades.

Leading a balanced life of fulfilment requires us to shift our perspective and redefine success. It entails recognising that working until we exhaust ourselves and neglecting all other aspects of life is not a true measure of achievement. It necessitates making room for the things that truly matter to us, such as spending quality time with loved ones, pursuing hobbies and interests and nourishing our spiritual or emotional well-being.

When one opportunity comes to an end, it opens the door for another to begin. Finding our purpose in the second stage of life requires us to embrace change and willingly tread new pathways. It may demand courage to step outside our comfort zones, leaving behind the familiar and venturing into the unknown. However, it is through this process of exploration and growth that we can uncover new passions, contribute to our communities in different ways and find a renewed sense of purpose.

Ageing isn't something to be feared. With the right roadmap, you can make the second half of life even more meaningful than the first — finding lasting fulfilment in the present rather than wistfully living in the past.

Our ancient Hindu advice for perfect existence, divides life into four stages of 25-year spans –

- Brahmacharya (student)
- Gṛihastha (householder)
- Vanaprastha (forest walker/forest dweller)
- Sanyasa (renunciate)

The first phase of life is called *Brahmacharya*, which is the student life. It means the time when you learn, absorb; the time when you are a sponge for human capital and ideas.

Then around age 25, you enter *Gṛihastha,* which is typically when a person would get married and start a household. This is called the householder phase and that's career, marriage, children, success, sexual relationships and all the worldly rewards of money, power, pleasure and fame that we get addicted to. It's fun, good, and it's hard and tiring.

The passing out of *Gṛihastha* into the third phase occurs around 50; *Vanaprastha* is from age 50 to 75 and that's a really critical and interesting phase. It's hard to get into because it requires wanting less. It requires chipping away. It requires a reverse bucket list. *Vanaprastha* comes from two Sanskrit words, *van* and *prastha,* meaning to retire into the forest (obviously, metaphoric).

The whole point is to retire away from plenty aspects of *Gṛihastha.* You are still going to work, you are still going to do your thing, but you are going to have a different focus. You are going to be focused on other people and on teaching. This is the second curve. This is where it all comes together. You are becoming less involved in your own success, but more involved in the success of other people. Now that might carry you to great glory. But it's not primarily that aspect alone, if you are going to be in the happy, successful quadrant.

The last Āśrama, which is at age 75 years and beyond, is called *Sanyasa.* A Sanyasi is somebody who is an enlightened one. This is where you are fully dedicated to spiritual enlightenment. In ancient times, Hindu men of some means would take leave of their families at the age of 75, and go to the Himalayas and sit at the foot of their master until death.

Vanaprastha, the stage of life that precedes *Sanyasa,* serves as a preparation for the renunciation. As we enter this phase, it becomes essential to reassess our priorities and reconsider our bucket list. Take a moment to pull out your list and examine it with a critical eye. Ask yourself a fundamental question: *Which items on this list are primarily driven by the pursuit of worldly rewards, and which have the potential to bring about lasting happiness and fulfilment?*

In the second half of life, it is crucial to ignore those items that fall into the first category, the pursuit of transient external validations. Instead, focus your attention on the items that resonate with a deeper sense of purpose and meaning. These are the aspirations and experiences that have the potential to bring about lasting happiness and fulfilment. Worldly rewards, such as money, power or social status, may hold a certain allure, but they are often fleeting and fail to provide enduring contentment. They can distract us from the things that truly matter; nurturing meaningful relationships, exploring our passions and aligning with our core values. It is these aspects of life that have the potential to bring about genuine fulfilment.

Pause & Reflect

- What do you envision for yourself in the second innings of your life?
- Are there any changes or adjustments you need to make in your priorities?
- How can you find a balance between personal fulfilment and making a positive impact on others?
- How can you leverage your unique skills, experiences and wisdom to create a positive impact on others and leave a lasting legacy?
- What activities, passions or pursuits bring you a deep sense of joy and fulfilment?

- How can you incorporate more of these into your life during this second stage to enhance your overall well-being and fulfilment?
- How can you foster meaningful connections and relationships?
- How can you prioritise nurturing these relationships and creating a support network that enhances your overall well-being?

✎ PAUSE & REFLECT INSIGHTS

Section 6

Gathering Grounds – Understanding Environment, Connections and Family

"The strength of a nation derives from the integrity of the home."

— Confucius

Life is an intricate tapestry woven with threads of diverse experiences, relationships and environments. In this vast expanse of existence, three elements stand out for their profound impact on our lives: our environment, our connections and our family.

Shaping Spaces, Shaping Self: The Impact Of Your Environment On Growth And Stress

Our environment, both physical and socio-cultural, acts as a powerful mirror reflecting our identity and significantly influencing our growth and stress levels. A cluttered room can induce feelings of overwhelm, while a serene park can evoke calm and peace. Similarly, a supportive and inclusive socio-cultural environment fosters personal growth, while a hostile one can trigger stress and anxiety.

We are not passive recipients of our environment; we have the power to shape it to benefit our mental and emotional well-being. Keeping our living spaces tidy and vibrant, creating a work environment that promotes focus and creativity, or fostering an inclusive culture in our community are ways we can positively influence our environment. Remember, we shape our spaces, and in turn, our spaces shape us. Hence, its crucial to invest time and effort in creating an environment that nurtures our well-being and growth.

Network Of Strength: Harnessing The Power Of Connections

Connections, whether they are friendships, professional networks or communal ties, are integral to our human experience. They provide us with a sense of belonging, help us navigate challenges and significantly contribute to our growth.

Investing in our connections is not merely about expanding our network; it is about nurturing relationships that empower and uplift us. These are the connections that form our network of strength, our safety net that we can rely on during life's ups and downs. Actively seek to build and maintain relationships with individuals who resonate with your values, who inspire you and who are willing to support you when needed. Harness the power of these connections, and you will find a reservoir of strength, encouragement and wisdom to draw upon.

Together In Joy: The Blueprint For A Happy Family

Family is not just about shared genetics or a common last name; it is a bond defined by love, mutual respect and shared experiences. A happy family can serve as an anchor in our lives, providing stability, warmth and unconditional support. However, building a happy family does not happen by accident. It requires intentional effort, open communication and mutual understanding. Prioritising quality time together, fostering a culture of empathy and respect and navigating conflicts with love and patience are vital in creating a blueprint for a happy family.

Never underestimate the joy and fulfilment that comes from a supportive and loving family environment. It can profoundly impact our mental and emotional well-being and infuse our lives with a sense of purpose and connection.

6.1 SHAPING SPACES, SHAPING SELF

"Your personal environment plays a huge role in your overall well-being. The spaces where you live and work influence your behaviour, mood and stress levels."

— **Marie Kondo**

I have travelled to Europe over 100 times, but it has always been for work. In November 2022, my wife and I embarked on our first European holiday together, exploring Switzerland, Italy and France. Our initial six days in Switzerland were fantastic, allowing us to freely roam even late into the night. The atmosphere was friendly and we thoroughly enjoyed ourselves.

However, as soon as we arrived in Milan, Italy, I noticed a sudden change in my wife's behaviour. She began holding my hand tightly while walking the streets and she expressed discomfort with venturing out at night or taking solitary walks. She found solace in staying within the confines of our hotel rather than exploring the outdoors. Her apprehension stemmed from the numerous stories of snatchings and muggings that we had come across in travel blogs about Italy and France. Sadly, this shift in perception drastically altered the mood and enjoyment of our holiday.

This experience serves as a simple example of how one's environment can have a lasting impact on us. Even if the perception of potential danger was not entirely accurate, my wife's fear took hold, making the subsequent seven days in Italy and France stressful and devoid of enjoyment. The relationship between stress and the environment we live in is a significant aspect of our overall well-being.

Our environment, including our physical surroundings and the social context in which we exist, can greatly influence our stress levels and overall quality of life. Just as my wife's perception of safety in Italy and France affected our enjoyment of the holiday, the environment we inhabit on a daily basis can have an acute impact on our health.

Take A Moment To Observe Your Surroundings Completely...

- Listen attentively and take note of the sounds around you. Breathe deeply and pay attention to any scents in the air.
- Shift in your chair and assess your level of comfort. Are you at ease or feeling discomfort?
- Consider the temperature. Is your environment warm or cool? Can you feel a gentle breeze or is the air stagnant?
- Take note of the lighting. Is it bright and well-lit, or is it dim and shadowy?
- Now, tune in to the overall energy of the place you are in. Does it feel lively, peaceful, chaotic or something else?
- Reflect on your ability to concentrate. Can you easily focus on the task at hand, or do distractions pull your attention away?
- Consider your ability to relax. Are you constantly interrupted or feel the need to look over your shoulder? Are you constantly checking the time?
- If you have your phone nearby, grab it. (I know, it's right next to you.) Now, set a timer for 3 minutes and use that time to jot down as many details as possible about your surroundings. Take note of everything you observe, from the smallest features to the most significant elements.
- What do you observe about your surroundings? Record as many characteristics as possible.
- Now, take a few more moments to reflect...

- How do you think those environmental features might affect what you think, feel and do? Remember to carry your observations with you as you proceed through the rest of this chapter. Being aware of your environment is a valuable practice that can extend beyond this moment.
- Now put your phone away, or turn it off completely (aeroplane mode!) and continue with the rest of the chapter with full focus.

As You Go Through This Chapter, Start To Notice...

- How your environment affects you?
- How can you act on your environment to help yourself do what you want to do?

The Elephant, The Rider And The Path

Whether you notice it or not, your environment shapes your health, thoughts, feelings and behaviours in countless ways.

The "elephant, rider and the path" story is a metaphor used to explain the interplay between our emotions, rational thinking and the circumstances or context in which we find ourselves. It illustrates how these elements interact and influence our behaviour and decision-making.

Imagine a rider sitting on top of an elephant, both travelling along a path. The rider represents our conscious, rational mind, while the elephant represents our emotions and instincts. The path represents the circumstances and environment in which we navigate through life.

The rider, being logical and rational, believes that they are in full control and should direct the elephant along the path. However, the reality is that the elephant, driven by its emotions and instincts, holds immense power and influence over the journey.

In this story, the rider symbolises our conscious thoughts, reasoning and intentions. It represents our ability to plan, analyse and make logical decisions. The rider may have a clear direction in mind and attempt to steer the elephant accordingly.

The elephant, on the other hand, represents our emotional impulses, desires and automatic responses. It embodies our instincts, intuitions and deeply ingrained patterns of behaviour. The elephant's strength and size often overpower the rider's attempts to control its movements.

Lastly, the path signifies the external circumstances, situations and environments that we encounter in life. It includes the social, cultural and physical context that influences our thoughts and emotions. The path can present obstacles, distractions or opportunities that impact the relationship between the rider and the elephant.

Let's repeat that last part again: The path can affect the elephant's movements more easily than the rider can. In other words, one of the best strategies for adjusting our behaviour patterns is to create a situation where the ideal choices are the obvious (or only) option. You can shape the path or adjust your environment in ways that help promote wanted actions.

When the sudden lockdown was imposed in March 2020, all of us found ourselves confined within the walls of our homes. As someone who thoroughly enjoys going to the gym, this abrupt halt to my fitness routine was disheartening. Determined to stay active, I reached out to the owner of my gym and requested to borrow some basic equipment such as dumbbells, barbells and weight plates, in order to set up a temporary gym at home.

Over the course of a few weeks, I noticed a remarkable development. Both my sons and my daughter-in-law began utilising the equipment, incorporating regular training sessions into their daily routines. Witnessing their dedication and the positive impact it had on their well-being, I felt inspired to transform our temporary setup into a full-fledged home gym.

Soon enough, not only were my children benefiting from this new fitness space, but my parents and even my energetic 3-year-old granddaughter also became regular attendees. It was truly a delight to see my granddaughter enthusiastically engaging in gymnastics exercises and rapidly picking up the skills associated with it. When my sons were young, we had a table tennis board at home because my Dad had a great passion for the game and was a skilled player. Little did we know that this simple addition to our home would have a profound impact on our children's lives.

As they watched us play and enjoyed the spirited matches, it sparked their interest in table tennis. They eagerly picked up the sport and began practising regularly. Over time, their dedication and determination paid off, and they started excelling in the game, consistently winning matches wherever they played.

These examples underscore the power of a conducive environment in shaping our experiences and influencing our well-being. When the surroundings support and encourage our interests, passions and goals, they become catalysts for growth, learning and fulfilment. By providing the necessary tools, resources and opportunities, a conducive environment propels us to reach our full potential.

We can "shape the path" by making small environmental adjustments to help boost deep health.

Let's Consider The Concept Of "Environment" In A Broad Sense…

When we think about our environment, it encompasses various aspects that influence our daily lives and well-being. These can include the following –

- **Physical environment:** This refers to the tangible and perceptible surroundings we inhabit. It includes our homes, neighbourhoods, cities, gyms, running paths and workplaces. The physical environment comprises objects, smells, noise levels, infrastructure, climate, weather, air quality, lighting, safety and security. All of these factors have a direct impact on our experiences and can shape our behaviour and overall well-being.

- **Social environment:** Our social environment consists of the people we interact with, including family, friends, colleagues and acquaintances. It encompasses the dynamics, relationships, conversations and social interactions that shape our daily lives. The social environment plays a significant role in influencing our attitudes, behaviour and emotions, as well as our sense of belonging and social support.

- **Cultural environment:** The cultural environment encompasses the shared norms, values, traditions and customs that exist within a particular community or society. It includes the cultural rules, expectations and codes that influence our behaviour and shape our identities. Our cultural environment influences how we perceive the world, how we communicate and the beliefs and practices we uphold.

- **Intellectual and cognitive environment:** This aspect of our environment involves ideas, beliefs, knowledge and the intellectual stimulation we encounter. It includes our access to education, learning opportunities and exposure to diverse perspectives and information. Our intellectual and cognitive environment also encompasses our inner mental space, including our thoughts, feelings, beliefs, self-perception, coping strategies and overall mental health.

While the physical environment is tangible and directly observable, our social, cultural, and cognitive environments can involve abstract elements, such as ideas, expectations, and the thoughts and behaviour of people who are not physically present. Our interactions with technology, such as watching TV or engaging with social media, can also shape our perceptions, expectations and behaviour within our environment. Our environment contains both stressors and support system. Your surroundings affect your well-being and resilience.

This is why "environmental health" is one of the main components of deep health.

Pause & Reflect

Do An Audit Of Your Environment –

Layer 1: Your body. What's on your body? What "environment" is created by the things you have on or close to you? The clothes you wear. The high heel of your shoes.

Layer 2: **What's near you?** Consider what you can easily reach within your immediate surroundings. Reflect on the environment created by the objects within your grasp. Take a moment to observe the items around you. Perhaps you have a steaming cup of coffee, a pair of headphones, eyeglasses, a laptop or your favourite book. Some of these objects may serve as distractions and potential sources of stress. For example, a television blaring alarming news stories or a phone constantly buzzing with work emails.

On the other hand, certain items can be replenishing and uplifting. It could be a nutritious smoothie brimming with fruits and vegetables, or the comforting presence of your beloved pet cuddling up next to you.

Layer 3: Your home. Have you ever experienced a shift in mood or perspective after re-arranging your bedroom, living room, or office, or giving it a fresh coat of paint? The visual and sensory cues we receive from our environment can have a profound impact on how we feel. Factors such as lighting, windows, airflow, room size, wall colour (or lack thereof), flooring, architecture and decor all contribute to the ambience of a space and influence our emotional state. What are the things that give you peace in your room? What stresses you? Having a soothing, restful environment to sleep in can also help us feel mentally "clear", and ready to tackle the next day.

Layer 4: Your colony/apartment complex. Where we live also plays a significant role. Residing in a secluded rural area or spacious suburban neighbourhood provides a vastly different experience from living in a small apartment with thin walls. While we do have some influence over our environment, there are aspects beyond our complete control. Consider the example of an elderly person who has difficulty with mobility. Although they may have lived in their home comfortably for decades, certain areas of their living space may become inaccessible due to the presence of stairs.

Safety is another critical consideration. In extreme cases, individuals living in an abusive or violent environment may fear those they share their homes with. Alternatively, safety concerns may manifest in more mundane ways, such as having undrinkable tap water, the constant presence of street dogs barking the whole night, or an unfinished basement filled with years' worth of dust and potentially harmful debris.

Our neighbourhood can meaningfully affect our stress and recovery. If you have parks and convenience nearer to you, it keeps you relaxed and happy as compared to living in a honking neighbourhood in the downtown area.

Layer 5: Your community. Our social environment includes our family members (who might live in the same house) and even extended family (who might be farther away). But it also includes the people in our community who we see regularly, and who have a large influence on our behaviour within that community.

Think about how you interact with the people in your own community. For example –
- Do people on the street say hello, or ignore you?
- Do you feel like you 'fit in' or are 'seen' in the ways that matter to you?
- Can kids play outside with everyone keeping an eye out for them?

Layer 6: Your state and country. Each state/country has laws, regulations, institutions, systems and ways of doing things. These all affect our deep health resources and individual capacity. How's the sewage system? Do you get regular drinking water from your tap or you have to wait for a water tanker? How's law and order? How are laws against pollution? Is the infrastructure stable and reliable?

As a pioneering researcher Robert Bullard says: *"You tell me your zip code, and I can tell you how healthy you are."*

Layer 7: The World. The COVID-19 pandemic has taught us a valuable lesson: events occurring across the globe can spread rapidly and affect everyone, regardless of age, location or occupation. The advancement of technology and digital communication networks has further amplified our interconnectedness, allowing us to share in both the joys and pains of being human in real time or shortly thereafter.

This interconnectedness means that we are all impacted by major stressors like pandemics, the consequences of global warming and instances of armed conflict or violence. However, it also means that each of us possesses the power to contribute something positive (or negative, if that's our preference) to the world. For instance, you can choose to support global causes that align with your values by making donations, volunteering or mentoring others.

You can also make environmentally conscious decisions like recycling or reducing your carbon footprint. Simply lending your voice to advocate for others can have a profound impact. Sure, most of us can't do much about world politics, or the full scale of global warming, or about our neighbour who runs his noisy lawn mower early Sunday morning. But we can do at least some things to adjust our immediate or local environment to improve our rest, recovery, resilience and overall deep health.

Consider Using A Simple Two-Part Framework To Facilitate Positive Changes In Your Life: Where Can You Have Less Of What Makes Things Harder?

Identify and minimise environmental barriers, triggers and obstacles that make it difficult to engage in desired behaviour or maintain healthy habits. This may involve reducing exposure to negative influences, unhealthy peer pressure or distractions. For example, you could limit your time on social media, create boundaries against toxic relationships or avoid environments that tempt you to engage in unwanted behaviour.

Where Can You Have More Of What Makes Things Easier?

Enhance the environmental support and convenience that facilitate desired behaviour. Seek ways to amplify positive triggers and surround yourself with helpful people or resources.

For instance, you can set up reminders or cues to prompt desired actions, create a supportive social network that encourages and motivates you, or design your environment in a way that fosters the desired behaviour. For example, you could keep healthy snacks readily available, create a designated space for focused work or exercise, or establish a regular routine that supports your goals.

Consider exploring a wide range of environmental changes, ranging from significant life transformations to subtle adjustments that can have an impact. Here are two examples to illustrate this concept –

Think Big

Consider making major changes that can significantly impact your environment and well-being. This could involve relocating to a new apartment or neighbourhood that better aligns with your values and preferences. Redecorating your bedroom can create a fresh and inspiring space. Opting for alternative modes of transportation, such as selling your car and using a bike, can have a positive impact on your health and the environment. Volunteering for your local community centre allows you to contribute to the society and creates a sense of purpose.

Think Small

Pay attention to the subtle adjustments that can make a difference in your daily life. Placing your alarm clock across the room forces you to physically get out of bed, helping you start the day on a more energetic note. Installing blackout curtains in your bedroom can improve your sleep quality by creating a dark and peaceful environment. Wearing a shirt that makes you feel good can boost your confidence and overall mood. Donating to a local cause supports initiatives that you care about and creates a positive impact in your community.

Remember, both big and small changes can contribute to your well-being and personal growth. Consider your unique circumstances and goals when exploring environmental modifications and be open to experimenting with different strategies to find what works best for you.

We all are now addicted to our phones. Have you heard of the term **Nomophobia?** Nomophobia is a fear of losing touch with one's smartphone. The name is short for "no mobile phone phobia". It encompasses several key factors: anxiety related to the inability to communicate with others, fear of being disconnected from the outside world, concern about immediate access to information, and the dread of losing the comfort provided by smartphones. Similar to chronic stress responses, nomophobia triggers the cortisol-driven HPA (hypothalamic-pituitary-adrenal) axis, leading to increased stress levels.

Smartphones have become deeply intertwined with our lives to the point where they feel like an extension of ourselves. Some individuals, particularly teenagers, may experience intense anxiety if they do not have access to their phones, resembling the attachment and fear of separation experienced by a mother with a new born child. This attachment and fear are remarkably potent.

Consider the following statistics[49] –
- One-third of the population would prefer to give up sex rather than part with their smartphones.
- Approximately 20 per cent of adults would rather forgo seeing their spouse for a week than give up using smartphone apps.

Before criticising younger generations for their phone dependency, take a moment to ponder on how you feel when you are in a situation where you cannot use your phone, such as on a metro or in an airport with a dead battery. Remember waiting in line or at airport check-in without a phone, or going on a long car trip without electronic devices? If you were born after the 1990s, you might not recall these experiences.

Our constant connection to smartphones means we have grown accustomed to not having to calm, comfort or entertain ourselves without a device readily available. When our phones are taken away, we often feel disoriented and even panicky.

Apart from the anxiety caused by our attachment to phones and our inability or unwillingness to function without them, there is a direct issue at hand: screen use disrupts our circadian rhythms.

What Happens When We Stare At Our Phones At Night?

Whether we are scrolling through social media in bed or binge-watching our favourite series on Netflix, the light emitted from digital screens interferes with our sleep patterns.

As mentioned in the section on Sleep, light plays a crucial role in regulating our circadian rhythms. Our biological processes are designed to experience bright light during wakefulness (daytime) and dim light or darkness in the evening to promote sleep.

When exposed to evening darkness, our eyes send a signal to the suprachiasmatic nucleus (SCN) in the brain, which controls our circadian rhythms. One of the critical signals transmitted by the SCN is relayed to the pineal gland, triggering the synthesis and release of melatonin, the hormone that promotes sleep.

However, the light emitted from screens inhibits this signal, suppressing melatonin production and impairing our ability to fall asleep or experience restful sleep. And that's not all!

A study comparing reading on an iPad screen to reading a paper book found that even after getting eight hours of sleep following screen use, sleep quality was still compromised.[50] The reduced melatonin production caused by screens makes it harder to fall asleep, and the sleep itself is less restful, with less time spent in REM stages.

Our screen habits significantly impact the quality of our sleep, recovery and physical and mental performance during the day.

The Power Of Unplugging

What if we put our phones down? By turning off our screens one to two hours before bedtime and allowing our brains to settle into darkness, we initiate a cycle of small but positive changes. This leads to deeper, more consistent sleep and improved focus and energy levels throughout the day.

Enhanced energy levels enable better concentration and coping with daily challenges, resulting in increased productivity. Moreover, it becomes easier to relax mentally at the end of the day.

In line with our "little bit better" deep health approach, making this change can be as simple as placing your phone a few feet away or in another room instead of keeping it constantly attached to your body. You can still access it, but you create some physical and mental distance.

Understanding the multifaceted nature of our environment is crucial. It highlights that we do not simply respond to what is physically present, but we are also influenced by social dynamics, cultural norms, our intellectual and cognitive experiences. By recognising the impact of these different environments, we can intentionally shape and create environments that support our well-being and promote positive behaviour.

Gathering Grounds – Understanding Environment, Connections and Family

Pause & Reflect

- How does your current environment support or hinder your personal growth and stress levels?
- Do the elements of your surroundings encourage you to learn, grow and stay calm, or do they create obstacles and stress?
- What aspects of your environment would you like to change to foster a more positive impact on your well-being?
- Can you identify any specific environmental triggers for stress in your life?
- How can your environment support the goals or habits you want to cultivate?
- Can you identify any changes in your behaviour, mood or stress levels after modifying aspects of your environment?
- In what ways do you feel connected to the spaces you inhabit most frequently?
- How can you create a balance between your needs for social interaction and solitude in your environment?
- How does your phone usage affect your daily routine and productivity?
- Do you find that the use of your phone increases or decreases your stress levels?
- What measures have you taken to ensure that your phone usage does not negatively impact your sleep?
- How do you feel when you are without your phone for an extended period of time?
- Have you set any boundaries or limitations for yourself regarding phone usage to balance its impact on your life?

✎ PAUSE & REFLECT INSIGHTS

6.2 NETWORK OF STRENGTH

"Your network is your net worth."
— **Porter Gale**

I reached the Delhi airport gate and, as requested by security, reached into my laptop bag to retrieve my passport. To my shock, I discovered that I had mistakenly brought my Dad's passport instead of mine. I securely store the passports of all my family members together in my cupboard, but in the rush and juggling of tasks, I must have inadvertently grabbed my Dad's passport.

I was scheduled to embark on a week-long trip to Yala in Sri Lanka, where I intended to capture magnificent moments of leopards and elephants. With only 90 minutes left before my flight departure, my passport stowed away in my cupboard at home, a distance of 46 kilometres and given the heavily congested roads of Delhi, particularly during peak evening traffic, the situation seemed utterly bleak.

In a moment of desperation, I reached out to a dear friend who held a high position of authority and was privileged to use a car equipped with a red beacon. Understanding the urgency of the situation, he promptly offered to help. Making use of the special privileges associated with the red beacon, his car was granted clearance to navigate through the chaotic traffic and swiftly reach my home. Miraculously, my friend retrieved my passport and raced back to the airport.

The staff at Jet Airways, displaying exceptional understanding and compassion, extended their support in light of the unforeseen circumstances. With their assistance and the last-minute check-in approval, I managed to board the flight on time, clutching my passport tightly in hand. It was a testament to the power of connections.

Finding the Oasis

Early on in my life, I came to recognise the significance of connections. After completing my engineering studies in Nagpur, I returned to Purulia with ample time on my hands, still exploring various career paths. It was during this period that a friend and I decided to take up tennis at the local club.

The tennis court in our small township had fallen into a state of neglect, as nobody seemed to be interested in playing. Every day, we would diligently set up the nets ourselves; due to financial constraints, we were unable to hire ball boys. Consequently, our time on the court was spent more on retrieving balls than actually playing tennis.

Then, one day, a police escort vehicle followed by a red beacon-adorned Ambassador car arrived in the parking lot of the tennis court. To my surprise, the district magistrate of our district stepped out and requested to join us for tennis on a regular basis. He was an enthusiastic player who, in this small town, had been unable to find anyone to share his passion with. In those days, our impoverished district lacked a sports culture, and a majority of the population struggled to make ends meet.

With the district magistrate's arrival, everything changed. Alongside him came ball boys to assist us and the tennis court underwent a complete transformation. The neglected court was repaired, and eventually, an AstroTurf surface was installed. Furthermore, the nets were always set up prior to our arrival, ensuring that our time on the court was spent playing tennis rather than managing logistics.

In our fast-paced and interconnected world, making meaningful connections has become more important than ever. Whether in personal or professional settings, forging genuine relationships can have a profound impact on our well-being, success and overall happiness.

Your Social Health Is A Very Important Part Of Achieving Deep Health.

The Rewards Of Making Connections

The effort put into building authentic connections yields significant rewards –

Emotional support: Genuine connections provide a support system during both joyous and difficult period. Having someone to lean on, share your thoughts and feelings with, and seek advice from can significantly enhance your well-being.

Oprah Winfrey faced numerous challenges and hurdles in her journey to success. During her childhood, she experienced poverty, abuse and various personal struggles. However, she attributes much of her resilience and triumphs to the emotional support she received from important individuals in her life.

By surrounding yourself with a strong network of emotional support, you will be able to weather storms, maintain your mental and emotional well-being and achieve remarkable success. Her story serves as a reminder that, regardless of fame or fortune, genuine connections and emotional support play a vital role in our overall happiness and resilience.

Personal growth: Meaningful connections expose us to new ideas, perspectives and experiences, fostering personal growth and expanding our horizons. Through connections, we learn from others, challenge our assumptions and gain valuable insights that shape our journey.

Mark Zuckerberg, the co-founder and CEO of Facebook, reached out to Steve Jobs for advice and guidance. The two entrepreneurs engaged in deep conversations about technology, product design and the future of the digital landscape. Through this connection, Mark gained valuable insights into the industry, learnt from Steve's experiences and broadened his perspective on building successful companies.

By leveraging your connections for personal growth, you will be able to continuously learn, adapt and evolve as both an individual and a leader.

Collaboration and opportunities: Building connections in professional settings opens doors to collaboration, career opportunities and mentorship. Networking can lead to partnerships, new job prospects and access to valuable resources or knowledge.

Elon Musk's success can be attributed, in part, to his adeptness at building strategic connections in various industries. One prominent example is his collaboration with NASA. In 2008, SpaceX, under Elon's leadership, became the first privately funded company to successfully launch a spacecraft, the Falcon 1, into orbit. This achievement was made possible through a series of strategic connections and partnerships established by the businessman.

SpaceX secured contracts and collaborations with NASA, allowing them to deliver cargo to the International Space Station and eventually to participate in the commercial crew programme, where SpaceX's Crew Dragon spacecraft now transport astronauts to and from the space station.

In the early stages of my career, I encountered a few unsuccessful ventures, but thanks to my father's valuable connections and his close friend Raman Daga, I received guidance, mentorship and assistance to embark on a new entrepreneurial journey. It was through his support that the foundation of my company was laid.

Not only did Raman Daga offer his mentorship, but he went above and beyond by leveraging his connections to help me secure my first customer from the United States. This initial breakthrough was instrumental in establishing the credibility and potential of my enterprise.

Happiness and fulfilment: Meaningful connections contribute to our overall happiness and sense of fulfilment. Sharing experiences, creating memories and celebrating successes together enriches our lives and brings a sense of belonging and purpose.

The renowned poet, author and civil rights activist, late Maya Angelou emphasised the power of human connection and the impact it has on personal growth, happiness and fulfilment. In her autobiography *I Know Why the Caged Bird Sings*,[51] she explores her own journey and the profound influence of the relationships she formed along the way.

Her writings often touch upon themes of love, empathy and understanding. She believed that by embracing our shared humanity and connecting with others on a deep level, we can find solace, support and joy. Her life itself exemplified the transformative power of connections.

In November 2022, I organised a gathering at Rishikesh where my mentees and some friends came together for a transformative three-day experience aimed at fostering authentic connections. The event was named **Communion**. It was an extraordinary assembly of exceptional individuals from across the country, united under one roof for an immersive period. It was during this event that I personally witnessed the remarkable power of vulnerability in cultivating genuine connections.

As each participant took turns to share their stories and thoughts, a profound realisation began to unfold — the embracing of vulnerability is key to establishing deeper, more authentic relationships that bring about true fulfilment and happiness. This revelation echoed the insights shared by renowned author

Brené Brown in her ground-breaking book, *Daring Greatly: How the Courage to Be Vulnerable Transforms the Way We Live, Love, Parent, and Lead.*[52] During our gathering at Rishikesh, as the participants shared their vulnerabilities and authentic selves, a powerful sense of unity and understanding emerged. The walls broke down, allowing for genuine connections to form and flourish. It became evident that when we shed our protective facades and open ourselves up to others, we create an environment conducive to transformative connection and shared growth.

During our three-day stay at Communion, we had the privilege of engaging in discussions on a wide range of topics, including the remarkable life experiences shared by Vijay Sekhar Sharma, the founder of India's highly successful brand and new-age company, PayTm. Vijay captivated our attention as he recounted his early life and the challenges he faced due to his limited proficiency in spoken and written English during his college days.

He humbly revealed how he had to sell a significant portion of his PayTM shares to finance his sister's wedding. It was truly awe-inspiring to witness a person of his stature and accomplishment, yet vulnerable, connecting effortlessly with each and every person in the audience. This mutual vulnerability becomes the foundation upon which deep connections are built — a shared understanding that we are all human, imperfect and capable of supporting one another on our respective journeys.

Tools To Build Authentic Connections

In today's fast-paced and digitally driven world, authentic connections have become increasingly vital for our well-being and happiness. Building genuine relationships requires deliberate effort and the use of specific tools and strategies.

Gathering Grounds – Understanding Environment, Connections and Family

This essay explores various tools that can help people foster authentic connections in their personal and professional lives. From active listening and empathy to vulnerability and mindful communication, these tools offer a roadmap for nurturing meaningful relationships in an era dominated by technology and superficial interactions.

1. **Active listening:** Active listening is a fundamental tool for building authentic connections. It involves fully engaging with others by giving them our undivided attention, understanding their perspective and responding thoughtfully. By practising active listening, we demonstrate genuine interest and respect, fostering a deeper understanding of the other person's thoughts, emotions and experiences. This tool requires setting aside distractions, maintaining eye contact and using verbal and non-verbal cues to show attentiveness.

   The common feature of any talk show that we like on TV is the host's skills of active listening. With this tool, they immediately connect with the guest or other speakers. In her long-running talk show, *The Oprah Winfrey Show*, Oprah became known for her empathetic and attentive listening skills. She would often lean forward, maintain eye contact and nod to show her genuine interest in the stories and experiences shared by her guests.

   Oprah would actively listen to their words, allowing them to fully express themselves without interruption or judgement. Her active listening was also evident in her skilful questioning and follow-up. She would often delve deeper into the topic, seeking to understand the underlying emotions, motivations and perspectives of her guests.

2. **Be fully present:** Are you truly listening or preparing your response? In our fast-paced and conversation-driven

world, it's common to find ourselves eagerly formulating our response even before the other person has finished speaking. In these moments, we may miss out on the opportunity to truly listen and understand what the other person is saying. Instead of being an active listener, we become focused on our own thoughts and ideas. It's important to introspect on our listening habits to ensure we are fully present and engaged in conversation.

3. **Vulnerability and authenticity:** Authentic connections require vulnerability and openness. By sharing our experiences, emotions and aspirations, we create a safe space for others to do the same. Embrace vulnerability by being real and genuine in your interactions, allowing deeper connections to flourish. Throughout history, many famous individuals who have connected with the masses have shared their vulnerable side. By opening up about their own struggles, fears and imperfections, they have created deeper connections with people and gained their trust and admiration.

Mahatma Gandhi, Nelson Mandela, Oprah Winfrey, Mother Teresa and Princess Diana have all demonstrated that sharing vulnerability can be a powerful tool in building connections and inspiring change. By opening up about their own struggles and challenges, these famous personalities created spaces for empathy, understanding and collective action. Taking a moment to ponder and grasping our vulnerabilities can indeed help build authentic connections with others. Remember that vulnerability is a personal choice, and it's important to gauge the level of comfort and trust in any given situation. It's also crucial to be mindful of reciprocating vulnerability and providing a safe space for others to share their own experiences. By embracing vulnerability in our lives, we can cultivate authentic connections that are based on understanding, empathy and mutual growth.

4. **Align with your interests:** Networking is not limited to professional endeavours alone; it extends to various aspects of life, offering opportunities to forge valuable connections. One effective way to expand your network is by actively participating in events, conferences or joining online communities that align with your interests or professional field.

By immersing yourself in these environments, you create avenues for meaningful conversations, idea exchange and the establishment of relationships with like-minded people who can significantly contribute to your personal and professional growth.

During the restrictive days of the COVID-19 pandemic, a tweet discussing the art of baking sourdough bread piqued my interest. This initial spark led me to start baking. Surprisingly, this exploration connected me to Dipesh Sharma, a master baker, who offered his baking wisdom to an enthusiastic group. Our mutual love for baking united us, creating a close community embarking on a culinary quest under Dipesh's mentorship.

As days passed, our circle expanded, drawing more baking aficionados globally. This initial group morphed into a large collective of over a hundred, all unified by baking passion. Our relationship evolved past baking, as we began to uplift and aid each other during the pandemic's trying times. This community soon became a global circle of friends, with shared moments and an earnest wish to assist each other. Amidst the pandemic's challenges, our ties gained more significance, extending assistance from providing oxygen cylinders to aiding in blood donations.

What began as a bond over a hobby led to friendships that bridged global distances and cultural gaps. Our connection, stemming from shared passion, offered a sense of purpose and unity during uncertain times. This experience showcased the profound effect of connections, even virtual ones, as a shared interest and group support left an indelible mark. Our baking community's story highlights how genuine ties can foster empathy, teamwork and kindness.

5. **Maintaining relationships:** Building connections is just the first step; maintaining them requires effort and investment. This year, my wife and I set a beautiful goal to strengthen connections and nurture relationships. Every Sunday, we dedicate time to reach out to two old friends or relatives we have not been in regular touch with. It's amazing how a simple phone call can bring joy, laughter and rekindle bonds.

Making meaningful connections is an investment in love and support that lasts a lifetime. Stay connected with friends, family and professional contacts through regular communication, whether in person, through phone calls, or via digital platforms. Show interest in their lives, offer support and celebrate their successes. Small gestures of care and appreciation can go a long way in nurturing long-lasting connections.

In a world often characterised by rapid changes and fleeting interactions, the power of making meaningful connections stands out as a beacon of hope and fulfilment. These connections, be they with friends, family, or even strangers turned friends, have the remarkable ability to enrich our lives. They provide us with support during challenging times, share in our joys and triumphs, and remind us that we are not alone on this journey. Meaningful connections transcend distance and time, weaving a tapestry of love, understanding and shared experiences. As we continue to nurture these connections, we discover that the true essence of life lies in the deep bonds we forge with one another.

Pause & Reflect
- How do you approach networking and building professional relationships?
- Who are the people in your network that have been most influential to you and why?
- What do you bring to the relationships in your network?
- What strategies do you employ to maintain and strengthen your existing connections?
- How do you handle networking challenges or setbacks, such as a missed connection or a relationship that does not provide the anticipated benefits?
- How have your networking tactics evolved over the course of your career or life?
- In what ways has networking influenced your personal or professional growth?
- How do you balance the need to network and make new connections with maintaining your existing relationships?
- What networking goals do you have for the future and how do you plan to achieve them?

🖎 PAUSE & REFLECT INSIGHTS

6.3 TOGETHER IN JOY

"Family is not an important thing, it's everything."
— **Michael J. Fox**

If you have travelled to Northern California in the USA, chances are you have encountered the awe-inspiring redwood trees. These colossal beings claim the title of the most massive individual trees on earth, captivating visitors with their sheer magnitude. Rising high above the forest floor, some redwood species soar to heights exceeding 300 feet, firmly securing their place among the tallest arboreal giants.

Not only do these majestic beings stand tall, but they also possess incredible longevity, with lifespans stretching beyond 2,000 years. Yet, perhaps the most intriguing aspect lies hidden beneath the surface — their remarkably shallow roots, typically no more than 5-6 feet deep. At first glance, it appears to defy the laws of physics for these giants to remain upright for centuries and millennia. However, an essential revelation unveils their secret: Redwoods grow in dense groves, and their shallow roots intertwine and fuse together over time. As individuals, on maturing, they converge into a singular entity and flourish.

It is in this remarkable interplay of shallow roots that the essence of a thriving and contented family finds resonance. Just as the redwood trees grace the earth with their majestic presence, the creation of a happy family requires tending to the roots of love and connection. Like the redwood's towering heights, the aspiration for a joyous family can be realised by nurturing the very foundation from which it thrives.

Family is central to happiness in every culture, but in some countries like India and Mexico, this is more keenly felt. Family ties often have a stronger weight in collectivist cultures, those where the well-being of society is above the individual. Numerous studies have explored the connection between family happiness and individual health.[53] Research consistently suggests that a happy family environment can have a positive impact on an individual's physical and mental well-being.[54]

The term family is derived from the Latin word 'familia' denoting a household establishment and refers to a *"group of individuals living together during important phases of their lifetime and bound to each other by biological and/or social and psychological relationship."*

Indian families are considered classically as large, patriarchal, collectivistic, joint families, harbouring three or more generations vertically and kith and kin horizontally. Such traditional families form the oldest social institution that have survived through ages and functions as a dominant influence in the life of its individual members. Indian joint families are considered to be strong, stable, close, resilient and enduring with a focus on family integrity, family loyalty, and family unity at the expense of individuality, freedom of choice, privacy and personal space.

However, our society is changing with one of the most significant alterations, the disintegration of the joint family and the rise of nuclear and extended family systems. Social and cultural changes have altered entire lifestyles, interpersonal relationship patterns, power structures and familial relationship arrangements in current times. These changes, which include a shift from a joint/extended to a nuclear family, along with problems of urbanisation, changes of role, status and power with increased employment of women, migratory movements among the younger generation and loss of advantage of experienced elderly members in the family, have increased the stress and pressure. This, in turn, has led to an increased vulnerability to emotional problems and disorders.

The Indian family, which often feels bewildered in these times of changed values, changed roles, changed morality and changed expectations, needs to reinvent itself.

Every study shows the biggest reason for long-term happiness is a strong family. In 1938, a group of pioneering researchers from Harvard Medical School embarked on a bold and visionary endeavour — a study that would span the entire adult lives of a cohort of Harvard students, with the aim of unravelling the secrets of human development and happiness. Little did they know that this audacious undertaking, known as the Harvard Study of Adult Development,[55] would become a timeless source of wisdom and insight.

Over the years, these researchers diligently tracked the lives of 268 men, capturing their lifestyles, habits, relationships, work and overall well-being through regular questionnaires. As the original researchers passed away, a new generation took up the mantle, ensuring the continuity of this ground-breaking study.

Recognising the need for diversity, the dataset was later merged with the Glueck Study, which followed 456 disadvantaged youths from Boston. Now, for more than 80 years, these intertwined data sets have offered an unparalleled glimpse into the dynamics of human existence.

While fewer than 60 of the original participants remain, the Harvard Study of Adult Development continues to evolve, extending its focus to encompass the children and grandchildren of the initial cohort. It is a living legacy, constantly updated and enriched by the lives it touches. The study's profound findings resemble a crystal ball of happiness, providing a unique window into how people's choices and experiences in their 20s and 30s shape the trajectory of their lives in the following decades.

One key finding is that the quality of our relationships has a direct impact on our well-being. The study has shown that individuals who have close and supportive relationships tend to be happier, both emotionally and physically. Having someone you can rely on in times of need and sharing life's joys and challenges with loved ones has been linked to greater life satisfaction and a reduced risk of health problems.

The study emphasises the importance of nurturing deep and intimate relationships. It is not simply the number of connections that matters, but the depth and emotional closeness of those relationships. Those who have close, enduring friendships and loving, committed partnerships tend to have better overall health outcomes and a higher sense of fulfilment.

The quality of our family relationships, particularly with our parents and siblings, has a lasting impact on our well-being. A warm and supportive family environment during childhood has been associated with better physical health and emotional resilience in adulthood. Positive family dynamics contribute to a sense of belonging, security and overall life satisfaction.

One of the most interesting things that the researchers have done over the years is categorise the participants when old, with respect to happiness and health. The best off were called "Happy-Well," who enjoyed six dimensions of good physical health, as well as good mental health and high life satisfaction. On the other extreme end of the spectrum were the "Sad-Sick," who were below average in physical health, mental health and life satisfaction.

According to George Vaillant, there is a singular trait that stands out as the most crucial factor in the lives of Happy-Well elders: healthy relationships. **"The people who were the most satisfied in their relationships at age 50 were the healthiest at age 80."**

Residing in our multi-generational household brings together five generations, encompassing my beloved grandmother, parents, spouse, both my sons and daughters-in-law, and our precious granddaughter. However, maintaining the cohesiveness of five generations under one roof requires conscious effort and intentional actions. The existence of a joyful and harmonious family across generations does not simply occur by chance.

Here are some of the practices that have proven successful for us in fostering unity and happiness. They hold true whether it's a nuclear family or an extended joint family.

Shared values and common goals serve as the foundation for a happy family. When family members have a shared understanding of their core values and work towards common aspirations, it strengthens the family bond and fosters a sense of unity and purpose. As a united family, we made a heartfelt decision to prioritise staying together under one roof, recognising the immense value it brings to our lives.

Early on in my career, circumstances compelled me to relocate from Purulia to Faridabad in search of better professional opportunities. Those initial five to six years spent away from my parents and son were filled with immense pain and hardship. Witnessing first-hand the challenges of living without the whole family, I became acutely aware of the importance of the values and wisdom that my parents and grandparents could impart to my children.

Motivated by this realisation, I decided to bring everyone together in one place. This meant uprooting ourselves from our ancestral home in Purulia, a place we had called home for 150 years. As a cohesive unit, we collectively believed that living together would bring us more happiness and fulfilment than residing in separate cities. This philosophy has remained steadfast throughout the years. Though my elder child moved to Pune and the younger one to Gurgaon in pursuit of their careers, we continually made efforts to create a conducive environment for staying together as a joint unit.

These efforts involved significant adjustments, such as building a larger home that could accommodate everyone comfortably. We ensured that each family member had their own space and privacy while also establishing common ground rules that promoted harmony and mutual respect. **Family First is the number one motto in everything we do.**

As a traditional and conservative Marwari family, we held firm to certain dietary practices, even going so far as to refrain from bringing onions into our home. However, when our younger son returned from Pune after completing his studies, his palate had developed a taste for dishes prepared with onions and garlic. Our daughter-in-law faced similar challenges as well. In light of these circumstances, we collectively made a family decision to accommodate their preferences while upholding our values.

To address this, we created a separate cooking space within our kitchen, specifically dedicated to preparing dishes that included onions. This allowed our son and daughter-in-law to enjoy the flavours they had grown accustomed to while respecting the traditional practices that held significance for our family. We may not always eat the exact same food during our dinners, but the overarching priority remains the act of eating together as a family, cherishing the shared experience and fostering unity.

Engage in open discussions with your family to identify the values that are most important to all members. These values can include honesty, respect, integrity, kindness, empathy, or any other principles that you collectively deem essential.

Discuss why these values matter and how they can guide your family's actions and decisions. Craft a family mission statement that encapsulates your shared values and aspirations.

This statement acts as a guiding light for the family, providing a clear direction and purpose. It can include objectives such as fostering love and support, promoting personal growth, giving back to the community, or maintaining strong bonds across generations. Regularly revisit and reinforce this mission statement to ensure it remains relevant and aligned with your family's evolving needs. Creating a mission statement for your family needs some dedicated uninterrupted time but can be accomplished in three steps.

First, brainstorm the purpose, values and dreams of your family together. Accept all ideas at this stage without judgement, no matter how wacky they may seem! Think possibilities, not limitations.

Second step. Combine the ideas into a single set of expressions that capture everything about your family. Perfection is not necessary, but it is important to write things down. You can always revisit the statements later.

The third step is to use your mission statement to keep your family on track. Put it where you can all see it. You might even want to frame it. Use it to guide your family in all that you do. When you stray from it, come back to it to correct your course. And do not forget to revise and update your statement as your family's needs and desires evolve, and the issues it faces change.

Our family's mission statement proudly hangs on one of the walls, serving as a constant reminder for all of us. This mission statement inspires us to support and uplift one another, nurture our relationships and foster an environment of love, respect and growth.

In our house,
We never give up.
We say I am sorry.
We like to have fun.
We say please & thank you.
We give big hugs.
We are crazy.
We forgive.
We make mistakes.
We give second chances.
We chase dreams.
We say I love you.
We are family.

Encourage family members to embody the shared values in their daily lives. This involves aligning actions, behaviour and decisions with the identified core values. Lead by example as parents or older family members, demonstrating the values in your own conduct.

Encourage open discussions about how family members can apply these values in different situations, reinforcing their importance in shaping a harmonious and fulfilling family life.

Resolve conflicts with empathy and understanding: Hedgehogs hate the cold. Yet they must endure winter. To do so, they often huddle close together to share body heat. But as they come close to each other, they prick each other with their spikes. They separate but because of the cold, they again slowly try to adjust by minimising the pain, forced back together out of necessity. We humans go through the same process.

Just like hedgehogs enduring the cold, our journey as a family often involves moments of hurt and discomfort. However, the benefits of a happy and united family far outweigh these temporary pains. It's not that we do not have our conflicts. You can imagine with five different generations and women in the house coming from four different backgrounds and families, conflicts are inevitable. However, our approach to conflict resolution is rooted in empathy and understanding. We prioritise resolving disagreements through calm discussions, active listening and seeking mutually beneficial solutions. This approach strengthens our relationships, promotes harmony and teaches valuable skills to younger generations.

Look at the bigger picture: One of the most valuable lessons I learnt about creating a joint family came from our family friend living in the USA. In a country where it is common for children to start living separately as soon as they go to college, this friend has managed to live harmoniously with his wife, son, daughter-in-law and grandkids under one roof. Curious about this aspect, I asked him for insights, and he shared a simple yet powerful example from their home.

He explained that his daughter-in-law enjoys drinking coffee every morning. However, she has a habit of carrying her coffee mug to her room, where it remains until she cleans her room once every week or ten days. On one particular day, his wife was in need of a coffee mug but could not find any in the kitchen. She became upset with her daughter-in-law and voiced her frustration to her husband.

In response, his wise suggestion was to order a dozen more coffee cups from Amazon for a mere six dollars instead of engaging in unnecessary and potentially contentious conversation about trivial issue. His approach was rooted in the bigger picture, emphasising the importance of harmony and peace within their joint family.

This simple example highlights a crucial aspect of building a happy joint family — choosing battles wisely. It's essential to recognise that conflicts may arise over small matters, but it's often more beneficial to prioritise peace and understanding over engaging in unnecessary confrontations. In this case, ordering additional coffee cups not only resolved the immediate issue but also prevented potential discord and maintained a positive atmosphere within the family.

By choosing peace over unnecessary arguments, we can nurture strong bonds and build a happy joint family that thrives on mutual respect and harmony.

Be proactive: I vividly recall an evening, nearly 25 years ago, that remains etched in my memory. It was a particularly challenging day at work, filled with immense stress. Our company had faced a setback as one of our consignments was rejected by a valued customer, resulting in a significant financial loss. To add to the burden, one of our engineers had also resigned, increasing the pressure on me.

When I finally arrived home, carrying the weight of the day's difficulties, I was greeted with a scene that heightened my emotional turmoil. My younger son was crying over something, while my elder son approached me from behind, seeking solace through a hug. Lost in my thoughts while I was drinking water, the glass slipped from my hand and shattered on the floor. Caught up in the heat of the moment, I reacted impulsively and struck my elder son, unaware of the consequences that would follow.

The once harmonious atmosphere in our home instantly transformed into a tense and unpleasant environment. The incident led to a period of strained communication between my wife and I, resulting in several days of silence. Furthermore, my actions had a lasting impact on my elder son, as he grappled with fear and apprehension towards me.

In a reactive mindset, one might immediately feel frustrated, blame others, or dwell on the inconvenience of the situation. However, adopting a proactive approach can lead to a more positive outcome.

Between anything that happens to us and our response, there's a 'space'. In that time, we are free to choose how we respond. What we choose ultimately affects how we grow and our happiness. First, focus on things you can do something about rather than on things outside of your control. Then, make sure you always use proactive language. Remember to pause, think and choose.

Press the "pause button" between anything that happens to you and how you respond. Think about the possible proactive responses. And choose the response with the best consequences. This incident served as a pivotal moment of self-reflection, teaching me the importance of managing my emotions and choosing compassion over impulsivity. It deepened my understanding of the profound impact our actions have on our family's well-being and happiness.

And do not forget the gift of humour. Laugh, smile and have fun when you can. You can even laugh at your own mistakes and clumsiness. Start by being proactive yourself and then inspire your family to be proactive too.

Quality time and shared experiences: Make your family and your relationships your top priority. Opt for regular family mealtimes to help you eat more healthily. It also aids in better family communication. Set aside at least one hour on a mutually convenient, consistent day for weekly family time. Nothing will provide your family with more opportunities to build relationships. Use it to review your schedules, and solve family problems. And finally, do not forget that everyone in the family is an individual. Use one-on-one time to be completely present with the other person. Use the time to understand the other person completely and build trust between you.

Every evening, at 9 pm, our family gathers in my grandmother's room for a special ritual, reciting the Hanuman Chalisa. While the practice holds spiritual significance, its purpose extends beyond religious devotion. It serves as a cherished opportunity for us to come together and reconnect at the end of each day.

During this family time, conversations naturally flow, and we create a space for open sharing. We take turns discussing our day and sharing any important family announcements or updates. The atmosphere is one of warmth, laughter and genuine connection. Even our guests who happen to be visiting us at that time eagerly join in, enriching the experience with their presence and perspectives.

This dedicated hour brings us closer as a family, fostering a sense of unity and togetherness. It's a time when all family members, present in the house at that moment, make a conscious effort to allocate this precious hour to be together. Regardless of the individual activities or commitments that occupied our day, we set them aside during this time to prioritise our family bond.

The Hanuman Chalisa becomes the backdrop for this shared experience, adding a touch of tradition and spirituality to our gathering. As we recite the verses, there is an air of reverence and gratitude, instilling a sense of peace and tranquillity within our hearts. More than just a religious practice, this hour of family time becomes a joyful and playful interlude before everyone retires to their respective rooms for the night. We engage in light-hearted conversations, share anecdotes and create memories that further strengthen our familial bonds.

Collaborative decision-making: Involve all family members in decision-making processes, particularly those that impact the family as a whole. Encourage each person to contribute their thoughts, opinions and perspectives based on the shared values and goals. This inclusive approach fosters a sense of ownership and shared responsibility, strengthening the commitment to achieve common objectives.

For the last six generations, our family has been blessed with the presence of a single boy in each generation. However, with two sons, I encountered a challenging decision that would shape the direction of our approach to life. The prospect of embracing meant breaking the pattern that had persisted for generations and navigating uncharted territory.

I realised that this decision held the power to redefine our family's values, traditions and aspirations. One evening, recognising the growth of our business and the potential need to expand manufacturing operations beyond Faridabad, I called for a family meeting. It was a crucial gathering where we collectively decided on our approach moving forward.

With unanimous agreement, we made a profound declaration: our enterprise would be defined as a family business rather than a business family. This meant that regardless of how far our business ventures took us, our unwavering commitment would be to stay together under the same roof. We understood that this decision would require dedication, sacrifice and ongoing evaluation.

By prioritising the value of unity and togetherness, we established a clear direction for our family's future. We recognised that staying connected and maintaining a strong familial bond was paramount, even in the face of expansion and geographic separation. This commitment served as a guiding principle that would guide our decisions and actions as we navigated the growth of our business.

Give your family the importance it deserves: By placing your family first, you acknowledge the significance of their presence in your life. Your spouse and children deserve your attention, care and quality time. They rely on you for support, guidance, and emotional connection. By actively prioritising them, you create a foundation of love and stability within the family.

While it's important to maintain a healthy balance between work, personal interests and social interactions, it's crucial not to neglect your family in the process. Your spouse and children should never be overlooked or overshadowed by other commitments. In building strong and loving family relationships, it is essential to understand that they are not hierarchical but reciprocal in nature. Simply giving our families the opportunity to spend time with us at our convenience or engaging in activities that solely interest us does not foster the deep connection and mutual fulfilment that love relationships require.

While we may have achievements and authority in our professional lives, it is crucial to recognise that this dynamic does not translate to our roles within the family. Love relationships thrive on empathy, understanding and selflessness. They require us to prioritise the needs and wants of our family members, rather than solely focusing on what is convenient for us as individuals.

Each family is unique. It has its characteristics, particularities and personalities. But in the end, they are composed of human beings. The advice that I have shared with you in this chapter is not all-encompassing or comprehensive. However, it can be useful for everyone, regardless of the culture and place where they live to strive to have a happy family.

Pause & Reflect

- Is family unity a challenge for you? In what ways have you tried to bring the members together?
- How do you prioritise quality time with your family amidst your daily commitments and responsibilities?
- What are some activities or traditions that you engage in to foster connection and create lasting memories?
- How do you ensure effective communication within your family, allowing each member to express their thoughts, concerns and aspirations?
- What steps do you take to cultivate an atmosphere of trust, understanding and emotional support within your family unit?
- How do you navigate conflicts and challenges within your family, promoting resolution, empathy and growth?
- In what ways do you actively listen to and validate the needs and wants of each family member?

🪶 PAUSE & REFLECT INSIGHTS

Unveiling my Inner Oasis

August 12, 2023, Umling La, Ladakh

Standing at an elevation of 19,025 feet above sea level, I find myself treading carefully and deliberately, ascending the final 500 metres. The air around me is noticeably thinner, each breath more laboured than the last, and gusts of wind challenge every step. Despite the heightened breathing, there is no sense of discomfort.

Surrounding me is the marvel that is Umling La, recognised as the highest motorable road in the world. It stands as a testament to the prowess and determination of the Border Road Organisation, which is responsible for its construction. As I take in the panoramic views, the majestic hills that once seemed like colossal giants from the ground now appear quaint and minuscule from this towering vantage point.

To the west, the setting sun casts a golden hue on the snow-capped peaks, making them shimmer like a sea of diamonds. The valleys below are cradled by these mountains, verdant and lush from the melting snow that feeds the rivers and streams snaking through them. This vast and varied tableau of nature's beauty is a testament to the resilience and adaptability of life, even in the harshest of environments. It's a humbling experience, one that underscores the majestic splendour of our planet.

As I settle down on a rock, my thoughts drift back nearly 11 years to a certain August evening spent at a neighbourhood Jagrata. Predominantly a North Indian ritual, a Jagrata involves communities or families coming together to spend an entire night singing bhajans, devotional songs and offering prayers to the Divine. Preparing for the event, I slipped into a Kurta Pyjama. However, the reflection that stared back at me from the mirror was disheartening.

A weary, overweight Sandeep gazed back, appearing years older than his actual age. Despite all the accomplishments I had gathered over the years, in that moment, everything felt like a shortfall. The vibrant, spirited and charming Sandeep seemed to have been buried beneath the weight of professional ambitions. There was disbelief. I found it hard to reconcile the man in the reflection with the vivacious, spirited young man I was. The lines on my face, the fatigue in my eyes, and the slouched posture were not just signs of physical changes; they were testimonies of the burdens I carried and the battles I faced, many of which went unseen.

A tinge of sadness crept in and intertwined with the sadness was regret. The regret was for the choices I made, the priorities I set and the moments I missed. I wondered about all the 'what ifs' — what if I had taken more breaks, what if I had made more time for friends and family, what if I had gone on holidays with my sons, what if I had paused to enjoy life's simple pleasures? I knew something had to be done and done now. While the journey back might be arduous, it was not impossible.

During that Jagrata, I happened to meet Rajiv, the son of our next-door neighbours. Being the same age as my son, Rajiv had carved a name for himself as a national-level boxer, proudly representing India in numerous Asian and Commonwealth Games. His athletic physique radiated vitality and his demeanour exuded the confidence typical of seasoned athletes. He shared a good camaraderie with my elder son. Feeling motivated by his presence, I approached him, seeking advice on reshaping my appearance and shedding the excess weight, especially the unwelcome accumulation around my waist.

Generously, Rajiv took it upon himself to become my mentor. Over the subsequent eight weeks, our mornings became ritualistic: he would arrive at my doorstep, and together we would head to a nearby park or sometimes a gym, depending on the day's regimen.

His unwavering belief in me was palpable. Even on days when my legs threatened to buckle under fatigue or my breath came short and ragged, he would push me forward with words of encouragement and steadfast support. I remember those early days, when a mere 100-metre walk would leave me winded, gasping for breath; squatting seemed like a challenge, and even lifting a modest 10 kg for a chest press felt like I was battling a tempest. Yet, Rajiv was undeterred. He was less focused on the immediate results and more on instilling in me a consistent exercise routine.

Eight weeks may seem short on a calendar, but for me, it felt like a lifetime of transformation. When I stood before the mirror again, the reflection that gazed back was almost unrecognisable. The visible changes in my physique were remarkable. Not only did I appear much fitter, but my clothes now hung loosely on my frame, with my previous size feeling noticeably roomier. Rajiv's dedication, combined with my own commitment, culminated in a transformation that was both physical and mental.

This was the beginning of my transformation journey. Since then I have never stopped exercising. Over the years I got some of the best mentors and coaches as I learnt running, pilates, yoga, cycling and rowing apart from strength training. The biggest game changer has been strength training. In just a year, the physical change was clear: I looked as though I had turned back the clock by nearly a decade.

However, despite the palpable physical changes, an intangible emptiness lingered within me. My heart felt heavy, aching from the chasm that time and circumstances had created. The house, once filled with the raucous laughter and playful banter of my two sons, now echoed with silence. Their departure for college left more than just their rooms empty; it left a void in my heart. Each passing moment was tinged with a deep-seated regret for the missed opportunities, the lost chances to witness their milestones and be an integral part of their growing-up years.

Alongside this, my relationship with my wife had evolved in a way neither of us had anticipated. Over the years, we had unknowingly drifted into separate lanes of existence. Though we shared a home, our lives felt increasingly parallel, rarely intersecting in meaningful ways.

To compound the emotional strain, the cruel hand of fate dealt a blow with both my parents being diagnosed with cancer. Witnessing their strength wane and seeing them grapple with the debilitating side effects of treatments, was a heart-wrenching experience. The ordeal not only left them physically weakened but also imposed a mental toll on the entire family, creating a lingering atmosphere of fear and uncertainty.

In the midst of all this, despite my accomplishments and possessions, I grappled with a deep sense of emptiness. A haunting feeling of aimlessness clung to me, making me question my purpose and direction in life. The outer facade of success and transformation belied the turmoil and longing within.

During that tumultuous period, a beacon of solace and wisdom emerged from three unexpected corners of my life: cherished moments with my grandparents, enlightening literature and spiritual discourses.

My grandparents, with their reservoirs of life experiences and endless fables, became my sanctuary. Their stories, rich in lessons of resilience, love and acceptance, offered a perspective that was both grounding and enlightening. Their aged eyes, filled with the wisdom of decades, saw the world with a clarity and simplicity that was both refreshing and instructive. Each tale, each shared memory was a testament to the enduring human spirit and the cyclical nature of life's highs and lows.

Alongside their wisdom, I found solace in books. They transported me to realms beyond my immediate reality, offering insights into the depths of human emotions, the intricacies of relationships and the quest for purpose. Through literature, I began to grasp the universal nature of my struggles and the transformative power of introspection and knowledge.

The spiritual discourses of Swami Ramsukh Dasji and Osho Rajneesh were the turning points. Their teachings, a blend of age-old wisdom and contemporary insights, resonated deeply with me. Swami Ramsukh Dasji's words, steeped in devotion and clarity, emphasised the significance of inner peace and the harmonious balance of mind, body and soul. Osho Rajneesh, with his revolutionary ideas and candid discourses, pushed me to challenge my own beliefs, urging me towards self-discovery and spiritual liberation. Through them, I began my journey from existential emptiness towards a life imbued with purpose and profound understanding.

Inspired by the wisdom and teachings I had been exposed to, I embarked on a transformative exercise in envisioning my future: I created a "mental destination postcard" of where I wanted to be during the final decade of my life, whenever that might unfold. This postcard was not just a mere picture; it was a vivid tapestry woven with intricate details. I imagined the environment I would be in, the emotions I would feel, the relationships that would surround me and the legacy I would want to leave behind. Would I be amidst nature, perhaps in a quiet cottage by the mountains or the serene shores of a beach? Would I be engrossed in intellectual pursuits, maybe writing a memoir or imparting wisdom to younger generations? Would I be surrounded by family, cherishing the moments with grandchildren, recounting tales of yore?

With this vibrant image of my desired future crystallised in my mind, I began the process of reverse engineering. If this was the destination I aimed for, what steps did I need to take today, and in the subsequent years, to ensure I arrived there?

This perspective shifted my approach to life dramatically. Decisions began to be made not on the spur of the moment but in alignment with that envisioned future. If I wanted to be healthy and active in that idyllic future, it meant adopting a holistic and sustained approach to health now. If I hoped for strong family bonds, it translated to investing time and love into those relationships in the present.

This "end-in-mind" approach became a compass, guiding my daily choices and actions. Every decision, big or small, was now a step towards that visualised postcard destination. It was no longer just about immediate gratification; it was about long-term fulfilment and ensuring that the twilight years of my life were imbued with purpose, contentment and joy.

The path I have walked has been far from smooth, and I recognise it's still unfolding. Life has thrown its fair share of challenges my way, and I remain cognisant of the fact that more hurdles await in the future. However, amid the tumult and trials, one pivotal lesson has emerged as the guiding light: the importance of having a clearly defined goal bolstered by a compelling 'Why'. With that foundation in place, the key is to take incremental steps, however small, each day, consistently moving towards that envisioned destination.

Aligned with the vision of my "destination postcard," I now find myself in a state where, metabolically, I'm a rejuvenated version of myself, clocking in at 15 years younger than my chronological age. Every medical marker indicates optimal health, painting a picture of vitality. Our home resonates with the harmony of five generations.

From my beloved grandmother, my doting parents, my supportive wife to my devoted sons and their wonderful spouses, and the joyous presence of my granddaughter — we are a weave of ages and experiences. Yet, we are bound together by shared beliefs and a common ethos: family comes first. Each member contributes uniquely, ensuring self-care and extending that care to every individual in our close-knit household.

We pray together, we eat together. We often take holidays together. We live in Now. We believe in giving our best efforts and not worrying much about the result. As my Grandfather taught me, "करने में सावधान, होने में प्रसन्न। **(Be cautious while doing, be content with the outcome.)**"

References

From Mirage To Oasis - Embracing The Concept Of Deep Health

(1) **Deep Health:** The term "deep health" had been popularised by Precision Nutrition (https://www.precisionnutrition.com), a company specialising in nutrition coaching and education. Dr. John Berardi, co-founder of Precision Nutrition, and his team have written extensively on the concept.

Section 1: The Shortcomings Of Conventional Health Practices

(2) **Outlive:** The Science and Art of Longevity by Peter Attia & Bill Gifford(Contributor). Published by Harmony, March 2023

2.1: Demystifying Nutrition For Health

(3) **The human gut is teeming with microorganisms..:** (PDF) Ten Times More Microbial Cells than Body Cells in Humans? https://www.researchgate.net/publication/270690292_Ten_Times_More_Microbial_Cells_than_Body_Cells_in_Humans

(4) **Our ancestors consumed between 50 and 150 grams of complex fibre:** Good gut advice: eat more fiber | PCC Community Markets https://www.pccmarkets.com/sound-consumer/2016-10/good-gut-advice/

(5) **The current recommended dietary allowance for protein:** Dietary protein intake and human health https://pubmed.ncbi.nlm.nih.gov/26797090/

(6) **Studies now suggest that excessive screen time:** Association Between Screen Time and Children's Performance on a Developmental Screening Test by Sheri Madigan; Dillon Browne; Nicole Racine https://jamanetwork.com/journals/jamapediatrics/fullarticle/2722666

(7) **Studies indicate that the minutiae of diets:** The macronutrients, appetite and energy intake by Alicia L Carreiro, Jaapna Dhillon, Susannah Gordon, Ashley G Jacobs, Kelly A Higgins, Breanna

M McArthur, Benjamin W Redan, Rebecca L Rivera, Leigh R Schmidt, and Richard D Mattes https://www.ncbi.nlm.nih.gov/pmc/articles/PMC4960974/

2.2: Unlocking Health Through Exercise

(8) **Physical inactivity is a significant contributor to premature death..:** *Physical inactivity* https://www.who.int/data/gho/indicator-metadata-registry/imr-details/3416

(9) **Modern research supports this notion, showing that walking provides numerous health benefits:** *Walking for Exercise* https://www.hsph.harvard.edu/nutritionsource/walking/

(10) **Strength training, a potent tool for health maintenance, has been consistently validated in numerous studies…:** *Strength training in elderly: An useful tool against sarcopenia* by Roberto Cannataro, Erika Cione, Diego A. Bonilla, Giuseppe Cerullo, Fabrizio Angelini, and Giuseppe D'Antona https://www.ncbi.nlm.nih.gov/pmc/articles/PMC9339797/

(11) **The prevailing guidelines for physical activity:** *Physical activity guidelines for adults aged 19 to 64* https://www.nhs.uk/live-well/exercise/exercise-guidelines/physical-activity-guidelines-for-adults-aged-19-to-64/#:~:text=Adults%20should%20aim%20to%3A,vigorous%20intensity%20activity%20a%20week

2.3: Sleep, The Silent Healer

(12) **Reports suggest that he devotes long hours to…:** *India TV. His interview with film actor Akshay Kumar* https://www.youtube.com/watch?v=Gvprbqrfaq4

3.1: The Positive Power of Stress

(13) **Perceived Stress Scale:** *The Perceived Stress Scale (PSS) was developed by Sheldon Cohen, Tom Kamarck, and Robin Mermelstein*

(14) **The Comfort Crisis:** *Embrace Discomfort To Reclaim Your Wild, Happy, Healthy Self by Michael Easter Publisher - Rodale Books*

(15) **Research has shed light on a fascinating concept known as "toughening,":** *Psychological Stress and the Human Immune System: A Meta-Analytic Study of 30 Years of Inquiry by Suzanne C. Segerstrom and Gregory E. Miller https://www.ncbi.nlm.nih.gov/pmc/articles/PMC1361287/*

3.2: From Isolation To Illumination

(16) **Survey conducted by the UK's Office for National Statistics revealed that young adults were the age group most likely to report experiencing feelings of loneliness:** *Children's and young people's experiences of loneliness: 2018 https://www.ons.gov.uk/peoplepopulationandcommunity/wellbeing/articles/childrensandyoungpeoplesexperiencesofloneliness/2018*

(17) **Nearly three out of four young adults experienced FOMO:** *Social Media and the Fear of Missing Out: Scale Development and Assessment Jessica P. Abel, Cheryl L. Buff, Sarah A. Burr https://core.ac.uk/download/pdf/268112726.pdf*

(18) **Social media can significantly impact our emotions:** *Social Media Use and Its Connection to Mental Health: A Systematic Review. Monitoring Editor: Alexander Muacevic and John R Adler*

Fazida Karim, corresponding author, Azeezat A Oyewande, Lamis F Abdalla, Reem Chaudhry Ehsanullah,and Safeera Khan https://www.ncbi.nlm.nih.gov/pmc/articles/PMC7364393/

(19) **Facebook itself conducted an experiment in 2014:** *Forbes June 28, 2014 : Facebook Manipulated 689,003 Users' Emotions For Science by Kashmir Hill https://www.forbes.com/sites/kashmirhill/2014/06/28/facebook-manipulated-689003-users-emotions-for-science/?sh=6fb2f094197c*

(20) **Social media use can indeed amplify feelings of loneliness, but only when it supplants offline activities:** *Associations between social media use and loneliness in a cross-national population: do motives for social media use matter?*

Tore Bonsaksen, Mary Ruffolo,Daicia Price, Janni Leung, Hilde Thygesen,Gary Lamph,Isaac Kabelenga, and Amy stertun Geirdal https://www.ncbi.nlm.nih.gov/pmc/articles/PMC7364393/

References

(21) **Lonely individuals are 32 per cent more likely to experience a stroke, 29 per cent more prone to heart disease and 64 per cent more at risk of developing clinical dementia:** *Loneliness, Social Isolation, and Cardiovascular Health by Ning Xia1 and Huige Li https://www.ncbi.nlm.nih.gov/pmc/articles/PMC5831910/*

(22) **A biography of Frida Kahlo by by Hayden Herrera Publisher:** *Harper Perennia*

(23) **Becoming by Michelle Obama, Publisher:** *Crown*

(24) **Renowned social psychologists and even tech czars like Mark Zuckerberg or Steve Jobs:** *Bill Gates, Mark Zuckerberg ban technology for their children but want rest of the world addicted to it by Priya Pathak, India Today https://www.indiatoday.in/technology/features/story/bill-gates-mark-zuckerberg-ban-technology-for-their-children-but-want-rest-of-the-world-addicted-to-it-1328462-2018-08-31*

(25) **Brené Brown, a well-known research professor and author, has spoken extensively about the importance of stepping outside our comfort zones:** *Brené Brown - Break Out of Your Comfort Zone, Find Self-Worth & Embrace Criticism by By Kris Deichler, Associate Partner & Mentorship Coach, Lighthouse International https://www.legends.report/brene-brown-break-out-of-your-comfort-zone-find-self-worth-embrace-criticism/*

3.3: From Mid-life To My Life

(26) **Middle age often marked a transformative period in their lives:** *Death and the mid-life crisis by Jaques, Elliott. The International Journal of Psycho-Analysis https://www.proquest.com/openview/f7931fc061e53e99298006613e0a9bd5/1*

(27) **Happiness levels tend to follow a U-shaped curve throughout our lives:** *Is well-being U-shaped over the life cycle? By David G Blanchflower 1, Andrew J Oswald https://pubmed.ncbi.nlm.nih.gov/18316146/*

(28) **Philosopher Friedrich Nietzsche emphasised the importance of finding a sense of purpose and meaning in life:** *Internet Encyclopaedia of Philosophy* https://iep.utm.edu/nietzsch/

(29) **Yeh Jawaani Hai Deewani is a 2013:** *Indian Hindi-language coming-of-age romantic comedy-drama film directed by Ayan Mukerji, written by Mukerji and Hussain Dalal, edited by Akiv Ali and produced by Karan Johar under Dharma Productions.*

(30) **Epicurean philosophy:** *Encyclopaedia Britannica, Lucretius by Arthur Frederick Wells* https://www.britannica.com/biography/Lucretius

(31) **Arthur Schopenhauer's philosophy:** *Stanford Encyclopaedia of Philosophy* https://plato.stanford.edu/entries/schopenhauer/

3.6: Dialogue Over Discord

(32) **Research conducted by psychologist Howard Markman:** *We Can Work it out: How to Solve Conflicts, Save Your Marriage by Clifford Notarius , Howard Markman , Publisher :TarcherPerigee*

4.1: Inner Echoes

(33) **Frequency illusion:** *The Baader–Meinhof Phenomenon Explained by Kassiani Nikolopoulou* https://www.scribbr.com/research-bias/baader-meinhof-phenomenon/

(34) **Dispositional Optimism and Physical Health:** *A Long Look Back, A Quick Look Forward by Michael F. Scheier and Charles S. Carver* https://www.ncbi.nlm.nih.gov/pmc/articles/PMC6309621/

(35) **Optimists often enjoy longer lives in comparison to pessimists:** *Optimism and Its Impact on Mental and Physical Well-Being by Ciro Conversano, Alessandro Rotondo, Elena Lensi, Olivia Della Vista, Francesca Arpone, and Mario Antonio Reda* https://www.ncbi.nlm.nih.gov/pmc/articles/PMC2894461/

(36) **The Choice:** *Embrace the Possible by Dr. Edith Eva Eger , Publisher: Scribner*

4.2: Calm In Chaos

(37) **Freakonomics:** *A Rogue Economist Explores the Hidden Side of Everything by Steven D. Levitt & Steven J. Dubner, Publisher: William Morrow*

4.3: Joyful Journey

(38) **Feel Better, Live More with Dr Rangan Chatterjee:** *Episode # 275 How To Become Happier Today (it's easier than you think) with Mo Gawdat*

(39) **The Choice:** *Embrace the Possible by Dr. Edith Eva Eger, Publisher: Scribner*

(40) **Happiness Equation - Solve for Happy:** *Engineer Your Path to Joy by Mo Gawdat, Publisher :Gallery Books*

4.4: Beyond Work

(41) **Hobby can help in curing certain diseases:** *Having hobbies and the risk of cardiovascular disease incidence: A Japan public health center-based study by Xiaowen Wang, Jia-Yi Dong, Kokoro Shirai, Kazumasa Yamagishi, Yoshihiro Kokubo, Isao Saito, Hiroshi Yatsuya, Hiroyasu Iso, Shoichiro Tsugane, Norie Sawada, for the Japan Public Health Center-based Prospective Study Group https://www.sciencedirect.com/science/article/abs/pii/S0021915021013186*

(42) **Research has linked high levels of stress to a variety of ailments:** *Life Event, Stress and Illness*

By Mohd. Razali Salleh https://www.ncbi.nlm.nih.gov/pmc/articles/PMC3341916/

(43) **Indulging in hobbies can help distract the mind from pain:** *Creativity, brain, and art: biological and neurological considerations by Dahlia W. Zaidel https://www.ncbi.nlm.nih.gov/pmc/articles/PMC4041074/*

5.2: Resurgence

(44) **The Statesman:** *Alfred Nobel: From "Merchant of Death" to Pioneer of Nobel Prize* https://www.thestatesman.com/features/alfred-nobel-from-merchant-of-death-to-pioneer-of-nobel-prize-1503117773.html

(45) **From Strength to Strength:** *Finding Success, Happiness, and Deep Purpose in the Second Half of Life by Arthur C. Brooks: Publisher – Portfolio*

(46) **On the Origin of Species:** *https://www.britannica.com/biography/Charles-Darwin/On-the-Origin-of-Species*

(47) **Fluid intelligence and crystallised intelligence:** *Raymond Cattell* https://www.newworldencyclopedia.org/entry/Raymond_Cattell

(48) **First century** *BC Roman statesman, Marcus Tullius Cicero writes about vocation in the second half of life in an open letter he wrote to his son titled, 'De Officiis'- https://www.worldhistory.org/De_Officiis/*

6.1: Shaping Spaces, Shaping Self

(49) **NBC News:** *https://www.nbcnews.com/news/world/survey-one-third-would-rather-give-sex-phone-flna121757*

(50) **Comparing reading on an iPad screen to reading a paper book:** *Reading from an iPad or from a book in bed: the impact on human sleep. A randomized controlled crossover trial*

Janne Grønli, Ida Kristiansen Byrkjedal, Bjørn Bjorvatn, Øystein Nødtvedt, Børge Hamre, Ståle Pallesen https://pubmed.ncbi.nlm.nih.gov/27448477/

6.2: Network Of Strength

(51) **I Know Why the Caged Bird Sings by Maya Angelou, Publisher:** *Ballantine Books*

(52) **Daring Greatly:** *How the Courage to Be Vulnerable Transforms the Way We Live, Love, Parent, and Lead by Brene Brown, Publisher: Penguin Life*

6.3: Together In Joy

(53) **Connection between family happiness and individual health:** *Positive family relationships across 30 years: Predicting adult health and happiness by Michelle C Ramos, Chia-Hsin Emily Cheng, Kathleen S J Preston, Allen W Gottfried, Diana Wright Guerin, Adele Eskeles Gottfried, Ronald E Riggio, Pamella H Oliver https://pubmed.ncbi.nlm.nih.gov/35298186/#:~:text=Our%20 prospective%20findings%20revealed%20that,with%20 greater%20health%20and%20happiness.*

(54) **A happy family environment can have a positive impact on an individual's physical and mental well-being:** *Children's and Adolescents' Happiness and Family Functioning: A Systematic Literature Review by Flavia Izzo, Roberto Baiocco, and Jessica Pistella https://www.ncbi.nlm.nih.gov/pmc/articles/PMC9778774/*

(55) **Harvard Study of Adult Development:** *https://www.adultdevelopmentstudy.org/*

About the Author

Sandeep Mall is a Level 2 certified Deep Health coach, known for his profound expertise in guiding individuals towards holistic well-being. His impactful mentorship has left an indelible mark on numerous prominent CXOs, professionals and entrepreneurs, shaping their journeys towards healthier and more fulfilling lives.

Sandeep's passion for spreading awareness about health and wellness has led him to deliver compelling keynote speeches on various platforms. His insights have ignited positive changes in the lives of those who have had the privilege to hear him speak. *Finding the Oasis* marks his debut as an author, showcasing his deep understanding of the intricate connections between the mind, body and soul.

Beyond his coaching and speaking engagements, Sandeep enriches the lives of his readers through his weekly newsletter, aptly named "Good Vibes". Through this medium, he consistently shares nuggets of wisdom, practical tips, and empowering stories that inspire readers to embark on their own paths towards well-being.

Sandeep's personal transformation highlights his strong commitment. His transition from facing significant challenges to embodying health and positivity motivates many seeking change. His genuine nature and relatability position him as a guiding light for others on transformative journeys.

Twitter : https://twitter.com/SandeepMall
LinkedIn : www.linkedin.com/in/sandmall
Website : https://www.sandeepmall.com